CHINESE COMMUNISM

selected documents

"Theory and practice can be combined only if the men of the CCP take the standpoints, concepts and methods of Marxism-Leninism, apply them to China, and build a theory . . . based on the realities of the Chinese revolution and Chinese history"—

MAO TSE-TUNG, 1942

CHINESE

COMMUNISM

selected documents

edited by

Dan N. Jacobs and Hans H. Baerwald

HARPER TORCHBOOKS · The University Library

HARPER & ROW, PUBLISHERS

New York, Evanston, and London

To Jan and Diane—
and the good year

CONTENTS

° Excerpted

vii

* Excerpted

PREFACE

It is the intent of the authors of this collection to document and interpret the course of Sino-Soviet relations from 1957 through mid-1962 and, in particular, to indicate that the recent difficulties between the two have not sprung forth full blown, but have clearly discernible origins in the earlier history and the nature of the Russo-Chinese relationship.

The translations of Mao's works are those of the Foreign Language Press in Peking, as is Liu's Report to the Second Session of the Eighth National Congress of the CCP, "Unite Under Lenin's Revolutionary Banner," and "The Strength of the Masses Is Limitless." The translations of the Commune Resolution of December 10, 1958, "Glorious Albanian Party of Labor," and the Press Communiqué on the National People's Congress of April 16, 1962, originally appeared in *Peking Review*. *Survey of the Chinese Mainland Press* is the source for the English version of "To Be a Revolutionary, One Must Have the Revolutionary Will," "Be Realistic and Practical" and "One Must Concretely Analyze Views Which Differ from One's Own." The translations of "Under the Banner of Comrade Mao Tse-tung," "Answers to Readers' Queries on War and Peace," "Our Age and Edward Kardelj's 'Dialectics'" and "A Great Anti-Imperialist Call" are from *Extracts (Selections) from China Mainland Magazines*.

The editors wish to acknowledge their indebtedness to Professor Cecil V. Crabb, Jr., of Vassar College, who urged the publishers to have this collection prepared, and to Dr. Rollin B. Posey for his constant encouragement. They also wish to gratefully note the contributions of Mr. Lawrence J. Hynes, Miss Jean Kocsis and Miss Ellen Yamasaki.

For promotional purposes, Mr. Jacobs' name has been listed first, but both editors contributed equally in the preparation of this volume.

DAN N. JACOBS
HANS H. BAERWALD

INTRODUCTION

In the political perspective of the future, the era through which we are living will be noted for the acceleration of nationalist divergences within the international Communist movement. Surely one of the most significant developments in this regard is the tension that has waxed and waned between the two giants of international communism, the Soviet Union and the People's Republic of China.

This tension has a history that can be seen in two principal dimensions: first, in the antagonistic history between Russia and China which dates back many centuries, one example being the efforts by one or the other to achieve preponderant influence in their mutual borderlands: second, in more recent Communist history wherein the Kremlin has alternately directed, misdirected, washed its hands of the Chinese Communists, reembraced them, and then shoved them away again. The most recent chapter of this story has been written in the 1950s and early 1960s.

✿   ✿   ✿

When the XXII Congress of the Communist Party of the Soviet Union convened in Moscow in October, 1961, the outside world expected this to be another in the series of humdrum order-taking sessions that had characterized party congresses following Stalin's rise to power. Before many hours had passed, however, it was evident that this congress would be anything but humdrum. The XXII Congress of the CPSU would turn out to be one of the most significant and eventful in the more than six decades of party history.

The major event scheduled for the opening day of the Congress was the report of the Central Committee of the CPSU, to be read by the party's First Secretary, Nikita Sergeyevich Khrushchev. For over six hours Khrushchev alternately droned, grimaced, and gesticulated his way through the expectedly sterile report.

Then, the stage set, Nikita Sergeyevich started talking about the members of the antiparty group, those "stars on the public horizon" who "think they are continuing to radiate light although they have long since turned into dying embers." But suddenly into the narrative about domestic party affairs he violently interjected an alien consideration: the behavior of the Albanian Party of Labor. He charged the leadership of the Albanian Communists with failing to "understand" the policy of overcoming the "cult of the individual," indeed, with conducting a struggle against it. He accused the Albanians of departing from the

1

commonly agreed line of the whole world Communist movement on the "major questions of our times." They were, he said, repeating the errors of the "cult of the individual" in their own country and were trying to "pull our party back to ways that they like but that will never be repeated in our country."

The thousands in the newly opened Palace of Congresses were startled. A public attack under such circumstances by the head of one Communist party against the leadership of another party was unprecedented. They were even more agitated because many realized that Khrushchev was aiming his shots not at the impotent Albanians, but at their Chinese protectors. And they understood that when Khrushchev warned that "no one will succeed in diverting us from the Leninist path," the "no one" he had in mind was not Hoxha and Shehu of Albania, but Mao and Chou En-lai of China.

In such fashion the reality and intensity of the Sino-Soviet differences were brought home to the Soviet and international comrades—and to the world. Until October, 1961, it was still possible to doubt that there was substance to the oft-reported allegations of Russian-Chinese discord. After the October Party Congress it was no longer reasonably possible to do so.

On the day following his marathon address to Congress XXII, Nikita Sergeyevich returned to discourse on the long-awaited new party program, then before the assembled delegates. Western observers noted that the Chinese delegation paid less than diligent attention to the First Secretary's embellishment of the Communist future. They could understand Chinese refusal to applaud when Khrushchev admonished that any country exhibiting nationalistic tendencies would stand in the way of its own progress because "it would deprive itself of the possibility of using the opportunities offered by the world socialist system." But they were astounded when, at the end of his address, Khrushchev walked over to the Chinese delegation hand extended, only to have Chou En-lai, the leading Chinese representative, turn his back and walk away.

On the following day, Chou had his opportunity to address the Congress. From the Moscow rostrum he extended the friendship of the Chinese People's Republic to the Soviet Union and to "all other countries of the socialist camp which extends from North Korea to the German Democratic Republic and from Vietnam to *Albania*." [1] Chou was letting all within earshot know that China would not back down, would not jettison Albania or kowtow to Soviet demands. He further made it clear that he considered Khrushchev's open attack upon Albania to have flaunted party agreements and endangered party unity. "If there are quarrels in the Socialist camp," he stated, "we consider that they should be settled through bilateral contacts and that a public denunciation does not contribute to the cohesion of the Socialist camp."

[1] Italics ours.

The well-trained Soviet audience responded with polite applause, until it noted that Nikita Sergeyevich was not applauding. The statement was concluded in silence.

Chou En-lai has generally been thought of as being one of the more "conservative" members of the Chinese hierarchy. When he went to Moscow in October it was probably with the thought that the differences between his country and the Soviet Union could be once more papered over as had been done the preceding year. Even after Khrushchev's provocative statements, Chou still hoped for a reconciliation. But Khrushchev was in pursuit of capitulation, not compromise. He and his associates continued the attack. Chou was not prepared to surrender. On October 23, he abruptly left the Congress still in mid-session and returned to Peking.

At this point, in late October to early November, 1961, the attention of the world began to focus on the dispute of the red Chinese dragon and the equally red Russian bear. What had split the behemoths of the Communist world? How had it happened that they had so lost control that internal disputes were allowed to explode into public view?

There is often a tendency to concentrate on recent developments as the source of the Sino-Soviet difficulties. It is then asserted that everything was fine between the Soviet Union and the Chinese People's Republic until something occurred *rather recently* which set matters askew.

In truth, however, the differences between the U.S.S.R. and China cannot be traced back to a single source or even to a precise period of time. They have their origin in such diverse and persisting matters as national attitudes, varying stages of economic development, differing experience, and rival ambitions. To ascribe the rift to one or another of these, or to some other particular cause, is a mistake. It springs from a multitude of sources, and as such it is very difficult of being resolved.

China's is probably the most ancient surviving civilization in the world. This theme is continuously stressed in domestic as well as foreign propaganda efforts by her contemporary leaders in Peking. Regardless of political affiliation, all modern Chinese take pride in their nation's emergence from foreign domination and in the fact that once again the outside world respects—and fears—the Middle Kingdom.

For nearly a century the Chinese people chafed under a variety of real and imagined indignities perpetrated by foreign "barbarians"; one of the crucial tasks of the Chinese Communist Party (CCP) has been to prove that under its leadership China could reestablish herself in a position of dignity. Working toward this goal the leaders of the CCP garnered for themselves the leadership of the nationalist movement, threads of which ran back to the middle of the nineteenth century when China erupted in the Taiping Rebellion. Since that time, the revolutionary upheaval which has been chronic in China during the past century has been largely a reaction of resurgent Chinese nationalism against western encroachments and influences. Under these circumstances, the rulers of China can be expected to guard jealously their independence.

It is, however, not only Chinese nationalism—important as this factor may be—which has influenced the course of relations between China and Russia. The experiences of the present leaders of the CCP in the 1920s and 1930s provide them with ample evidence that the Russian comrades may well be misinformed about conditions in China. Even more crucial from China's viewpoint is that the Kremlin may well be more interested in furthering Russian interests within the international Communist movement and outside of it, than concerned with the interests of the CCP in China.

Considerable controversy has surrounded the question of who played the major role in the founding of the CCP. The Chinese assert that they themselves founded their party; the Russians point to the role played by such Comintern agents as Maring, Pavel Mif, and Borodin. Both sides of the argument have merit, but it should be pointed out that a Marxist study group had been founded at Peking University by Chinese intellectuals prior to the arrival of the Comintern agents. The Chinese founders of the CCP could not disregard their dependence on foreign ideology. Yet, repeated efforts are made to underline the genius of Mao and his colleagues in reinterpreting and adapting Marxism-Leninism to Chinese circumstances, in short, to establish Chinese independence from foreign ideology.

Stalin sought to direct this adaptive process in the 1920s, theorizing that China was not ready for a communist revolution but would have to pass through a bourgeois revolution first. Trotsky, Stalin's prime antagonist for the mantle of Lenin, argued that the bourgeois revolution could be telescoped into the communist revolution. It was the sense of the Kremlin that its agents should work with the Nationalist Party (Kuomintang) of Sun Yat-sen, the "father of modern China." (Sun Yat-sen led the republican revolution in 1911 which brought about the downfall of the Manchu Empire and ushered in modern China.) For a time in the early 1920s, the members of the CCP, in accordance with Kremlin directives, joined the Nationalist Party *as individuals*. Leadership within the Kuomintang was unwilling to permit their then Communist allies to join as a unit.

The alliance between the Nationalists and Communists in China in the period 1923–1926—an alliance dictated more by Moscow politics than by an analysis of the political realities in China—ended disastrously for the CCP. The question of who was using whom—were the Nationalists using the Communists or vice versa?—had been a topic of heated debate within the CCP. In the spring of 1927, at a critical juncture in the Northern Expedition, which ended in the reunification of China under the Nationalists, Chiang Kai-shek (Sun Yat-sen's successor as leader of the KMT) turned upon his Communist allies, massacring about ten thousand (usual estimate) of his erstwhile comrades.

It took years of patient rebuilding for the CCP to reconstitute itself from this disaster. Largely under the leadership of Mao Tse-tung,[2] the CCP undertook to rehabilitate itself in the countryside. It is really from 1927 that the Chinese Communists identified themselves primarily with the interests of the peasantry rather than with those of the urban proletariat. To be sure, there was continued work among the latter by the CCP, but the period of the late 1920s and 1930s is one during which the CCP retreated to the countryside.

Chiang Kai-shek, once in control of China, attempted to dislodge his rivals in a series of military campaigns. These did not succeed in their objective. They did, however, ultimately have the effect of forcing the CCP to shift the base of its operations from southern China to the northwest. This transfer, a heroic episode celebrated as the Long March, made it possible for the CCP to find a stable base from which to operate—a cardinal principle in the developing tactics of "Maoism." But the U.S.S.R. was deeply immersed in its own problems of collectivization and industrialization, and paid little, if any, attention to the trials and tribulations of its nominal allies in their struggle for world revolution under the banner of international communism.

As late as the end of World War II, when even American observers were concerned about the future of the Nationalist Party (KMT) under Chiang Kai-shek, the Russians persisted in giving scant support to the CCP. Instead, Stalin continued dealing with the Chinese Nationalists. In fact, Stalin (as contrasted with Trotsky, who had overestimated the power of the CCP in the 1920s), was consistent in his belief that Chinese Communists such as Mao, who had not been Moscow trained, could not possibly amount to very much. Yet Mao and his comrades, in a short four-year period (1945–1949), pursued policies that ultimately left Chiang Kai-shek and the Nationalists with the island of Taiwan (Formosa) as their only possession.

Over the years, the leadership of the CCP has thus seen the Kremlin guilty of many errors and double dealings. For this reason alone it would be unrealistic to expect the Chinese Communists to be docile followers of a party line laid down in Moscow.

* * *

If the first thing that must be kept in mind about the Sino-Soviet quarrel is that it has long-standing antecedents, the second is that it is strongly rooted in rival concepts of national self-interest.

Although Stalin had opposed the conquest of China by the Chinese

---

[2] Mao's role is still a matter of controversy. Some students of China maintain that Mao's contributions to the rebuilding of the CCP have been enhanced deliberately in support of the cult of Mao's personality.

Communists and lamented their refusal to accept his advice, his government nonetheless enthusiastically greeted the establishment of the Chinese People's Republic in Peking, October 1, 1949. And shortly thereafter when Mao Tse-tung traveled to the Russian capital to work out the final details of Sino-Soviet relations, he was well, though not particularly charitably, received.

The nine weeks of Mao's stay in Moscow were spent in stiff bargaining. Stalin was in no mood to give anything away to the leader of a nation of half-a-billion people under the control of a successful party, albeit Communist, with a long history of independent tendencies. The best that Stalin would do economically was to grant the Chinese a five-year $300 million loan, a pitifully inadequate amount considering Chinese needs. And in return for this, the Chinese had to submit to joint operation with the Soviets of Manchuria's railroads and of Port Arthur, and to the establishment of joint companies for the exploitation of some of China's borderland resources. Stalin insisted on Russia's "special rights" in China, even though China was now a Communist country. The treaties of February, 1950, certainly did nothing to endear Moscow and Stalin to the Chinese; subsequent agreements would not appreciably improve this situation.

Sino-Soviet bargaining sessions and agreements since have been characterized by their hard nature. It is apparent that the U.S.S.R. had under Stalin and has under Khrushchev no intention of strengthening a potential rival. The Soviets are first in the Communist world in terms of industrial and military position and they intend to maintain that position.

Russia under Khrushchev has achieved major industrial strength. For various reasons including his own predilections and the need to fulfill at least to a minimal degree the aspirations of the Russian people, Khrushchev has decided to direct some of the nation's manufacturing capacity to the production of consumer goods. Though the Russian standard of living remains low, even in comparison with that of such satellites as Czechoslovakia and Hungary, it is on the rise. Despite some recent setbacks, life is becoming better for the Russian people.

On the other hand, for the Chinese, the standard of living remains stagnant; if, indeed, it does not recede. While desperate Chinese efforts to increase production have had some successes, they have fallen far short of what was hoped for or even minimally required. Even at the height of the unrealistic "Great Leap Forward" of 1958, the most grandiose vision that the Chinese could conjure up was that of outstripping British production within 15 privation-laden years.

If the Soviet system is fat enough to build tens of thousands of new apartment houses, to be concerned with problems of style and quality in clothing and furniture, and to make loans to bourgeois countries that are outside the Communist camp, why should it not divert more of this "surplus" to the side of the struggling Chinese comrades? This the

Chinese ask, and it has not only galled but embittered them to see the "affluent" Soviet society forging speedily ahead, whereas their own spits and sputters along—and sometimes even slides backwards.

The relative affluence of the U.S.S.R. and its seemingly favorable prospects for the future as contrasted with the poverty of China and its rather unencouraging prospects for speedy improvement unquestionably are at or very near the foundation of the present impasse between the two countries. Soviet successes have made the Russians, if not content with the present, at least comparatively satisfied with the pace of improvement in their situation. The Russians, by and large, would not be unhappy with a continuation of the present developments.

The Russians today have a stake in the preservation of their sizable accomplishments. They are aware that nuclear war would mean unprecedented destruction. Even if the Soviet Union should suffer less damage than the United States, the extent of the cataclysm would still be such that neither communism nor capitalism would emerge as victor. Consequently, the Russians are opposed to general war or threat of war. The Russians already *have* and they are unwilling to risk what they possess. But the Chinese *do not have*. They lack in abundance and they are consequently willing to risk all or very nearly all. In recent years the Chinese leaders must have experienced a sense of desperation, as they found their own country falling farther and farther behind their ambitions for it. They have been driven to radical designs and actions. The semicontent status quo of the Soviets has seemed completely unrealistic to them. To have experienced the Russians advocating "peaceful coexistence" [3] and more of the same as their own situation became increasingly desperate must have been infuriatingly frustrating. This was especially so after October, 1957.

On October 4, 1957, the Soviet Union successfully launched the first orbital flight into space. Sputnik was an unquestioned scientific accomplishment of huge proportions. This one achievement impressed —perhaps overimpressed—the world, as nothing before had done, with the extent of Soviet scientific progress. But evidently, and this is a thesis strongly put forth by the researchers of the Rand Corporation, the members of the world community most impressed were the Chinese. To them, Sputnik signified that the world balance of military power had been shifted in favor of the Communist camp. They declared that the Sputnik-ICBM development had induced a radical change that brought the overall strength of the camp ahead of that of the West. In Mao's terminology, the East wind was now prevailing over the West.

Such being the case, the Chinese advocated a much more adventurous policy against the West. Repeatedly Mao and his associates em-

[3] The Chinese also assert their dedication to "peaceful coexistence," but the term, in the current controversy, has a different meaning for them than for the Soviets.

bellished the theme that the United States and the West were "paper tigers," who *looked* fierce, but who would quickly disintegrate in a showdown.

The Russians, though scarcely underestimating the psychological significance of the Sputnik-ICBM development, never made such widespread claims for its military implications as did their Chinese allies. They never have stated that overall Soviet military strength exceeded that of the West. As a matter of fact, after October, 1957, the Soviet leadership became more publicly cognizant than ever before of the tremendous damage that would be heaped upon the Soviet Union in the event of a nuclear war. It was subsequent to October, 1957, that the drive for "peaceful coexistence" was pushed the hardest by the Soviet.

The refusal of the Russians to exploit their new superiority, as the Chinese saw it, served to raise the level of Chinese frustration even higher. Here were the Chinese in desperate straits, with their allies supposedly in possession of the means to instantaneously set everything to rights—and refusing to do so. Since 1958, the Chinese have from time to time made it clear in terms that cannot be mistaken by any Communist that they consider the Russians to be weak, faint-hearted, and cowardly.

Contrary to what has often been stated, the Chinese do not believe in the inevitability of world war. They do, however, believe that local wars are likely. Such a position obviously is necessary in order to make it possible for China to reacquire Taiwan and to expand into Southeast Asia. The Russians fear that any such moves, though starting as local actions, would create the danger of a world war. They are apprehensive that a small war would soon become a big one and in that big war, Russia, being a chief focus of military power, would be horribly mutilated. Again, this is a risk the Russians are not willing to take.

* * *

The foundation of the Sino-Soviet differences requires no special knowledge of the convolutions of Communist theory in order to be grasped. These differences are not rooted in communism. But in the Communist world all disputes tend to be argued out in terms of theory. This dispute is no exception.

In theoretical matters, Lenin is the ultimate arbiter, but Lenin wrote so voluminously and was such an opportunist that substantiation for often diametrically opposed positions can be found in his writings. Both Russians and Chinese turn to Lenin to seek support for their stands on such matters as the circumstances and the duration of "peaceful coexistence," the inevitability of war, the correct attitude towards the national bourgeoisie, and so forth. While the Chinese and the Russians in accord with interparty ground rules have generally refrained from publicly attacking one another by name, standard Communist epithets have been flung at the "adherents" of both. The Chinese have bitterly excoriated the Yugoslavs as "revisionists" and "opportunists." And in return the Russians have attacked the Albanians as "dogmatists" and "sectarians." The Russians and their supporters have struck out against "modern left-wing Communism" which "has now become a disease of senility," though Lenin said it was the "children's disease of communism." And the Chinese have warned that "modern revisionists can't frighten us." Communists tend to see all new party disputes in terms of earlier ones, thus the use of dogmatist, leftist, and revisionist, terms that were used to label earlier factions within the party. Perhaps the ultimate in this was achieved when Janos Kadar, the First Secretary of the Hungarian Communists, compared the Albanians (read Chinese) to Trotskyites, who "shrinking from work for the construction of socialism, which required daily effort, also resorted to adventurism and rhetoric."

In the above, Kadar is referring not only to the adventurous military policies advocated by the Chinese, but also to what the Russians consider to be their adventurous domestic economic policies as well.

By the fall of 1957 China's economic development had reached a crisis. In spite of the use of all the methods suggested by Soviet experience the Chinese economy was only very slowly moving ahead. Population was increasing rapidly. The situation had grown desperate and evidently Mao and company decided that radical solutions were necessary.

The Chinese had only one commodity in abundance and that was manpower. They determined to exploit it to its fullest. More than sixty million farm laborers were assigned to jobs in industry and on mammoth construction projects. Veritable ant hills of humanity were set to work building dams, hydroelectric power stations, roads, and railways. Manpower was substituted for machinery and it became official dogma that men were more important than machines. The year 1958 was designated as the year of the "Great Leap Forward."

Every Chinese citizen was supposed to become involved in industrial production. Hundreds of thousands of small "backyard" smelting furnaces were set up across the country; and office workers, nurses, and teachers were told to spend their spare time manufacturing steel for the fatherland. Every loose piece of metal in China was pirated for the furnaces. Streetcar tracks, bannisters, fire escapes where they existed, were melted down. Urban China became one huge factory.

In the countryside, 1958 was the year in which the communes were established. The entire structure of Chinese life was altered by them. The peasants who had at first been given land by the regime and then had most of it taken away as they were forced into cooperatives, now found themselves in the midst of still another upheaval, characterized by the establishment of the commune. In the commune, all vestiges of family life were destroyed. Children were permitted to see their parents only briefly each week. Men and women were quartered in separate dormitories. All food preparation was handled in public catering facilities. Private homes were literally destroyed and private kitchen utensils scrapped to provide material for the "backyard" furnaces which operated in the countryside as well as in the city.

The aim was to organize the Chinese population into an instantaneously responsive and unquestioningly obedient force. The population was roused in the morning by the bugle call, summoned for callisthenics, marched off to breakfast and then out into the fields. The left-wing leaders of the CCP who prevailed in the establishment of the Great Leap Forward and the communes believed that what China lacked in material resources and know-how could be made up by her vast manpower reservoir and by enthusiasm. The Chinese propaganda spokesmen proclaimed China's food problem would be permanently solved within a year or two. Her industry not too long thereafter would challenge for world leadership. The Chinese population was bombarded with requests, imprecations, and demands to produce more, faster. There was nothing that could stand in their way, they were told. Fighting together, they were indomitable. They were embarked upon a gigantic crusade which would shape the future not only of China but of the world as well.

It was this final allegation that further added fuel to the smoldering Chinese-Russian fire. For in their enthusiasm the Chinese made no pretense that the institution of the Great Leap Forward and the communes was suitable only for China. They more than hinted that these were new techniques that could enable *all* countries to move speedily ahead. It was even suggested that using the new methods, China and perhaps anyone following her lead, might enter communism *even before the U.S.S.R.*

China clearly had unmasked her aspirations for leadership of the international Communist movement. Moscow, of course, could not permit these allegations of Chinese Communist doctrinal superiority to go unanswered. Khrushchev pointed out that the Russian Communists also had tried the communes shortly after the revolution, with disastrous results. The peasants had ceased producing; agricultural supply had disintegrated. And Moscow emphasized that Communism could not be achieved through miraculous short-cuts, but only through hard work spread out over a long period of time.

One particular aspect of the Chinese innovations that troubled the Kremlin was the Chinese venture in introducing the free-supply system. The final achievement of communism supposedly will be characterized by the free distribution of commodities to all citizens according to their need; but this, according to Soviet theory, will only be realized at a much higher stage of development, certainly not before the Soviet economy has become far more affluent than at present. Thus, Soviet leaders have insisted that for the time being socialism requires a highly developed system of incentives to extract the maximum effort from workers and peasants. Khrushchev, as Stalin and Lenin before him, is opposed to "premature" egalitarianism. But in 1958, it was exactly this path that the Chinese took, paying their peasantry primarily in kind and services rather than in cash. Distribution in the main was ordered according "to need" and not according "to work."

The Soviets were hostile to these developments not only because the Chinese were "displaying" that they were much closer to achieving communism than the Russians, but also because they were convinced that the Chinese Communists, in moving towards premature egalitarianism, would do harm to their economy. The Russians understood that Marx meant the free-supply system to take over only in an economy with tremendous production capacities capable of over-supplying the needs of the population. Such preconditions did not exist in the U.S.S.R. Certainly they had not been realized in China.

By 1960, the commune had largely passed into the background as a major issue between Moscow and Peking, but it still rankled enough so that Khrushchev, in 1962, was moved to remind the Central Committee of the CPSU that "Communism must not be regarded as a table set with empty plates around which sit high-minded and fully equal peoples. To ask people to join such communism would be like inviting them to eat milk with an awl. It would be a parody of communism."

Moscow attacked the Chinese for trying to introduce "ascetic" communism, for behaving like "Utopians," for believing in simple solutions, and for thinking that propaganda could replace hard work. In short, Moscow did not have much faith in the "Great Leap Forward" or the communes. By November, 1958, Moscow's judgment was vindicated. For the Chinese had evidently come to the conclusion that the desired goals were not being gained and indeed that the entire economic system was being threatened. On December 10 a plenum of the Central Committee of the CCP adopted a resolution signifying a retreat. In sadness, the Central Committee acknowledged that socialism will "take a fairly long time to realize . . . . This whole process will take 15, 20, or more years to complete, counting from now."

How much actual mischief was done by the CCP's radical approaches of 1958 has only gradually become known to the outside world. Evidently the pig iron produced in the "backyard" furnaces was not suitable for heavy construction purposes. It was too brittle, or the ingots were not of proper size for industrial purposes, or the country was not equipped to transport or use the items that were manufactured. The railroads broke down. Huge quantities of machinery and supplies rotted outside the factories where they were produced or, reaching their destination, at the site of factories that were never built. The leaders of communes and others, to satisfy the demands placed upon them, supplied greatly inflated figures on the amount of grain and other crops harvested. The lying statistic became the norm and all attempts at effective planning went by the boards.

Gradually, the worst stringencies of the communes were repealed. The peasant was given a very minimal allotment of land. He was again permitted to own household utensils. His workday was cut. Husbands and wives were permitted to live together and to prepare their own food. Finally, in April, 1962, at the time of the meeting of the National People's Congress, the party leadership implied that the Great Leap Forward and the communal system had been introduced in error. In the meantime, however, the issues they had raised generated some very high-temperature Sino-Soviet heat.

Beginning in 1960, the main theoretical focus of the Sino-Soviet debate was the differences over global strategy, Moscow favoring the peaceful expansion of Communism by making it so attractive that the non-Communist world could not resist its blandishments, Peking resolutely refusing to push the possibility of revolution and war into the background. In April, 1960, with Khrushchev firmly committed to a policy of "peaceful coexistence," still operating in the "spirit of Camp David," Peking took the occasion of the 90th anniversary of Lenin's birth to issue its harshest statement yet against the Russian positions. It sought to prove its superior orthodoxy by stating that it was Lenin "who waged a thoroughly uncompromising struggle against the opportunists and revisionists. . . ." He believed that "so long as capitalist imperialism exists in the world, the sources and possibility of war will remain. . . . The emancipation of the proletariat can only be arrived at by the road of revolution, and certainly not by the road of reformism. . . . War is an inevitable outcome of systems of exploitation. . . . Until the imperialist system and the exploiting classes come to an end, wars of one kind or another will always occur." The development of the new techniques of atomic and hydrogen and missile warfare has not made Lenin obsolete. If the imperialists are so unwise as to unleash a new war, "the result will be the very speedy destruction of these monsters encircled by the peoples of the world, and the result will certainly not be the annihilation of mankind. . . . On the debris of a dead imperialism, the victorious people would create very swiftly a civilization thousands of times higher than the capitalist system and a truly beautiful future for themselves."

One of the arguments used most consistently by Peking against "peaceful coexistence" was that it permitted the West to prepare for war at its leisure, with no fear of a prior Communist attack. Not even the fact that the socialist system "has obviously gained the upper hand in its struggle with the capitalist world system" will make the latter desist from waging war. The imperialists are inevitably warlike, incapable of not plotting war. Mere socialist superiority will not make the bellicose circles of the imperialists "lay down the butcher knife" and "sell their knives and buy oxen."

In the context of the already heated Sino-Soviet dispute, the U-2 incident of May, 1960, must have seemed to many behind the Iron Curtain to substantiate the Chinese position. Even at the height of an era of good feeling, on the eve of "sincere" peace negotiations the United States could not be trusted. See, said the Chinese, we told you so.

Undoubtedly some leading Soviet figures, including those in the military, were now more favorably attracted to the Chinese argument. While Khrushchev had to trim his sails, however, he did not abandon the policy of "peaceful coexistence." Nor was the breach between Russia and China in any significant way narrowed. In the following month, at the assemblage of the World Federation of Trade Unions in Peking, the Chinese used the meetings to launch an all-out attack upon the Soviet policies and upon Khrushchev in particular. Later in the same month, Khrushchev, for the express purpose of counterattacking, traveled to Bucharest where a Rumanian party congress was being held. Openly, he warned that nuclear war could only lead to horrendous destruction. All wars, local as well, must therefore be avoided, for the latter will ultimately spread. In private, Khrushchev inveighed against Mao, sharply lashing out at him and making the extremely serious charge for a Communist, that Mao was incapable of correctly interpreting the movement of world events.

From June through November, 1960, the battle of accusations continued at fever pitch. In June, two Chinese publications aimed at Russian audiences disappeared from Moscow newsstands. In July, Moscow released two documents, one aimed domestically and the other at foreign Cps (Communist parties), substantiating its own position and renewing the attack on the Chinese. In August, an international congress of orientalists assembled in Moscow, without Chinese participation. The Russians withdrew their technicians *and plans* from Chinese construction projects, with disastrous results to the Chinese economy, the full extent of which has not yet become known. At the same time, the Chinese were obliquely warned in the provincial Soviet press that if they did not alter their behavior they ran the risk of being isolated from the other countries of the socialist bloc.

In the midst of the accusations and counteraccusations, attempts were made by third parties to bring the two feuding allies together. These efforts resulted in the meeting of the 81 Communist parties which assembled in Moscow in early November. For the balance of the month international communism bitterly debated the issues at hand. How bitter the battle was is indicated by the accusation that Enver Hoxha reportedly threw at Khrushchev, calling him "a traitor to the

Communist idea, a weakling and a revisionist." To which Nikita Sergeyevich angrily replied: "You will pay for that."

Out of the month-long sessions, a document came forth that can scarcely be called a compromise, for it failed to reconcile differences, but rather placed the rival positions alongside one another. In any event, both sides soon made it quite clear that they had no intention of being bound by any implications of compromise that might be read into the "Declaration." The dispute smoldered during the first half of 1961, and then in the early summer it again began to flare up. This became particularly observable in the events which surrounded the 40th anniversary of the founding of the CCP on July 1. Moscow generally disregarded the occasion and in particular downgraded the role played by Mao in the early history of the Chinese party. On the other hand, Moscow paid pointed and elaborate attention to the 14th anniversary of the Mongolian party, which was being celebrated at the same time. Also during this period Moscow acted with particular determination to cement its relations with North Korea, North Vietnam, and Outer Mongolia, the three Communist countries that bordered on China, in order to prevent them from joining the Chinese in opposition. The new program of the CPSU,[4] the draft edition of which appeared in late July, also had its role to play in the split. Coming at a time when the extent of the failure of the Chinese industrial and agricultural campaigns was first becoming public knowledge, the new program emphasized the great achievements of the Soviet Union. The Chinese, whose discouraging industrial production figures had recently been released by the U.S.S.R., were stumbling along, with starvation a continuing menace, whereas the U.S.S.R. had become one of the two greatest industrial powers on the globe and was rapidly scaling new heights. Moreover, the program also served to further Khrushchev's personal cause as a theoretician in the running battle with Mao that had developed over the respective merits of each as the leading Marxist-Leninist of the present epoch.

The new party program undoubtedly did much to strengthen the image of the Soviets on both sides of the Iron Curtain. Khrushchev was aware of this. He was also aware of the economic doldrums in which China languished and he believed that he had successfully isolated her from all other Communist elements, with the exception of the Albanians.

When Chou came to Moscow in October for the XXII Congress of the CPSU, he anticipated that the meetings and the international party meetings scheduled to follow soon after would be the scene of renewed attempts at reconciliation. Once again, as had happened the preceding November, the outstanding differences would be papered over if not reconciled. However, if this was his expectation, he was,

[4] See D. N. Jacobs, Ed., *The New Communist Manifesto*, 2nd ed., Harper & Row, New York, 1962.

as we have seen, woefully mistaken. Khrushchev evidently felt that he had dealt himself all the trump cards and he displayed no reluctance to play them.

But if Khrushchev thought that his all-out attack on the Albanians would force Peking to knuckle under, he was also badly mistaken. Chou did not capitulate and when he abruptly left the party congress any still existing doubts as to the reality and depth of the Sino-Soviet breach were removed. It was real and it was deep.

In subsequent weeks *Jenmin Jihpao (People's Daily)*, the organ of the CCP, carried reprints of Albanian articles attacking Khrushchev openly and personally with little of the veneer of doubletalk usually utilized under such circumstances. In an editorial, the same source warned that "no force on earth can shake Chinese-Albanian unity." Moscow countered by publishing statements by Togliatti and Thorez, the chiefs respectively of the Italian and French Cps, attacking Chou for criticizing the Soviet Union in public.

The New Year brought further crises as the Communist parties of the world were themselves swept up in discussion of the Sino-Soviet arguments. Generally speaking, the Western parties supported Moscow, some more readily than others, and those in the underdeveloped nations tended to go along with Peking. Many of the parties were not entirely unhappy over the split, because it augmented their own importance, being courted by both sides, and gave them a good deal more freedom of action than they had enjoyed in almost four decades.

At the turn of the New Year also came reports of renewed attacks upon one another by both Moscow and Peking. The usually well-informed Yugoslavs reported that there would soon be *open* admission of the break by the Russians if the Chinese did not act before. At the end of February, a gratuitous insult was aimed at the Chinese when Lieutenant General Panyushkin, *a specialist on military intelligence*, was appointed Central Committee secretary for relations with China. In March came reports of an anti-Soviet word-of-mouth campaign being launched in China. But, in the meantime, events were also moving in another direction. Beginning in February, in various ways, it became apparent that a new, more moderate tone was being sounded in Peking, one that might increase the possibility of reconcilation with Moscow.

In early March, the Central Committee of the CPSU met. Foreign observers generally expected a major statement on Sino-Soviet relations to be issued. But as far as the outside world was able to discover, the matter was not even discussed, though this seemed scarcely credible. Two weeks later the Chinese People's Congress assembled in Peking. For the first time, its sessions were in secret. The meetings continued for three weeks and according to official accounts were highlighted by "frank" and "heated" exchanges of opinion, on both domestic and foreign themes. At the end of the meetings a communique was issued, which dealt with intrabloc relations in only the vaguest and most general terms. There was no reference to the inevitability of war; Albania was not mentioned at all. Even earlier, Peking, as we have seen, implied that the commune and the Great Leap Forward had been mistakes. Now, the CCP revealed that China had suffered three successive years of what were termed "natural calamities," ordered a sharp cutback in capital construction, and turned its attention to consumer needs.

Thus, Khrushchev, for the time being, apparently emerged victorious, China's critical internal position having forced her to retreat domestically and to muffle her disagreements with the Soviet Union.

But that state of affairs, as subsequent events were to prove, by no means indicated that the split between the two Communist goliaths had been healed. By late 1962 the possibility of an outright rupture appeared more likely than ever.

Issues dividing China and the U.S.S.R. exist in profusion. The "retreat" of the Spring of 1962 settled nothing. The major divisive issues we have discussed include rival national interests; differing traditions, experiences, and stages of industrial development; antithetical theoretical positions. There are still others: Mao's resentment because the Russians for so long interfered to keep him from what he considered his rightful position at the head of the Chinese movement; Chinese contempt for Moscow's handling of the Hungarian revolution; China's greater concern for the maintenance of discipline within the bloc.

As opposed to these divisive forces, upon which we have admittedly dwelt, it must be recognized that there are also strong factors at work to keep the two united: a common aim, a common ideology (though it is every year interpreted less in common), a common enemy, the belief that in unity there is strength, and the evident necessity of both to depend upon one another for economic and propaganda purposes.

Both sets of forces are extremely powerful. It is possible that the doctrinal dispute will be argued out to a complete break. Theoretical differences in Bolshevik history have usually been so concluded. There are deep, perhaps even unreconcilable, differences between the Chinese and the Russians. Though the fire dies down, it is not and will not be extinguished.

But the forces working for cooperation are also strong. Both sides share much in common. They have needed one another in the past and probably have much to gain by cooperating and presenting a common front in the future.

On balance, it would appear likely that for the near future the prospect is that there will not be a complete break between the Soviet Union and the Chinese People's Republic, but the chances of their continuing to make common cause over the long run probably will be less favorable with each passing year, unless external influences act in such a way as to make the Communist nations believe that unity is the prime value.

MAO IN HUNAN

Report of an Investigation into the Peasant Movement in Hunan to the Central Committee of the Chinese Communist Party, February, 1927 by Mao Tse-tung.

One of the contributing factors to the Russo-Chinese difficulties is the independent posture of the leader of Chinese communism. Mao was not Moscow trained. He was not placed in power by Moscow. In more cases than not he was not even supported by Moscow. Indeed, it must many times have seemed to him that both he and communism in China came to power, in spite of Moscow.

In May, 1925, an industrial outbreak occurred in Shanghai, which the Communists were able to turn to their own advantage with considerable initial successes. The news of the Communist triumphs in the north greatly excited the young Mao, who was then "in retirement" in his native Hunan. Until then he had worked among the working population, attempting to recruit them for the movement. But under the excitement of the Shanghai successes he went for the first time out into the countryside and sought to incite the peasantry.

To the young, dynamic Mao, it proved to be an easy task. The fervor of revolution caught on quickly in the Hunan tinderbox. Much of the area was aroused. Ultimately, the urban movement was suppressed; but throughout 1926 and into 1927, revolutionary excitement continued to run high in the countryside.

In January, 1927, Mao was sent back to Hunan to look into the activities of the peasant associations which he had helped to have formed there. He was greatly impressed by what had transpired. In his explosive "Report" to the Central Committee, he notes that under the peasant associations "the privileges which the feudal landlords have enjoyed for thousands of years are shattered to pieces." The members of the peasant associations "smash the sedan chairs" of the bad gentry and "crowds of people swarm into the homes of the local bullies and bad gentry. . . . They may even loll for a minute or two on the ivory beds" of the young daughters of the rich.

The traditional Marxist attitude towards the peasantry is that it is at heart conservative, lethargic, and undependable. Nevertheless, Lenin realized that in agricultural countries the support of the peasantry was indispensable for the success of the revolution. But always the peasants must be under the leadership of the urban proletariat. The initial successes of the urban proletariat in May, 1925, reinforced within the Comintern the certainty that the Chinese revolution would follow the doctrinally established pattern; it would be headed by the proletariat.

But in January and February, 1927, Mao, under the heady influence of what he had witnessed in Hunan, asserted that the leading role in the Chinese revolution is to be taken by the peasantry itself. In as explicitly an a-Marxist, if not anti-Marxist, statement as will ever be penned by him, Mao refers to the poor peasants as being the "vanguard of the revolution." Without them, says Mao, "there can be no revolution." At no time does Mao mention the proletariat specifically. And, to underline the revolutionary role which he ascribes to the peasantry, in a passage deleted from reprints of the Report published since the CCP came to power, probably in order not to incur the anger of the Russians, Mao writes: "To give credit where it is due, if we allot ten points to the accomplishments of the democratic revolution, then the achievements of the urban dwellers and the military units rate only three points while the remaining seven points should go to the peasants in their rural revolution."

Mao wrote the "Report" under the domination of the euphoria induced by the intensely revolutionary acts he had just observed. At the time it is likely, Marxist though he was, that he did not recognize the extent of the heresy he was advocating. In 1927, few Chinese Marxists agreed with his thesis. It was, however, to become one of the pillars of Maoism and ultimately to make it possible for communism to triumph in China.

The Importance of the Peasant Problem

During my recent visit to Hunan I conducted an investigation on the spot into the conditions in the five counties of Hsiangtan, Hsianghsiang, Hengshan, Liling, and Changsha. In the 32 days from January 4 to February 5, in villages and in county towns, I called together for fact-finding conferences experienced peasants and comrades working for the peasant movement, and listened attentively to their reports and collected a lot of material. Many of the hows and whys of the peasant movement were quite the reverse of what I had heard from the gentry in Hankow and Changsha. And many strange things there were that I had never seen or heard before. I think these conditions exist in many other places. All kinds of arguments against the peasant movement must be speedily set right. The erroneous measures taken by the revolutionary authorities concerning the peasant movement must be speedily changed. Only thus can any good be done for the future of the revolution. For the rise of the present peasant movement is a colossal event. In a very short time, in China's central, southern, and northern provinces several hundred million peasants will rise like a tornado or tempest, a force so extraordinarily swift and violent that no power, however great, will be able to suppress it. They will break through all shackles that now bind them and dash forward along the road to liberation. They will send all imperialists, warlords, corrupt officials, local bullies, and bad gentry to their graves. All revolutionary parties and all revolutionary comrades will stand before them to be tested, and to be accepted or rejected as they decide. To march at their head and lead them? Or to follow at their rear, gesticulating at them and criticizing them? Or to face them as opponents? Every Chinese is free to choose among the three, but circumstances demand that a quick choice be made.

Get Organized!

The peasant movement in Hunan, so far as it concerns the counties in central and southern sections of the province, where the movement is already developed, can be roughly divided into two periods. The first period was the period of organization, extending from January to September of last year [1926]. In this period, there were the stage from January to June—a stage of underground activities, and the stage from July to September when the revolutionary army expelled Chao Heng-ti[1]—a stage of open activities. In this period, the membership of the peasant association totaled only 300,000–400,000, and the masses it could directly lead numbered only little more than a million; as there was hardly any struggle in the rural areas, so very little criticism was made on the association. Since its members served as guides, scouts, and carriers, officers in the Northern Expedition Army even had a good word or two for the peasant association. The second period was the period of revolutionary action, extending from last October to this January. The membership of the peasant association jumped to two million and the masses over whom it could exercise direct leadership increased to ten million people. As the peasants mostly entered only one name for each family when joining the association, a membership of two million therefore means a mass following of about ten million. Of all the peasants in Hunan almost half are organized. In counties like Hsiangtan, Hsianghsiang, Liuyang, Changsha, Liling, Ninghsiang, Pingchiang, Hsiangyin, Hengshan, Hengyang, Leiyang, Chenhsien, and Anhua, nearly all the peasants have rallied organizationally in the association and followed its leadership. The peasants, with their extensive organization, went right into action and within four months brought about a great and unprecedented revolution in the countryside.

[1] The ruler of Hunan and agent of the warlords of the Northern clique.

Down with the Local Bullies and Bad Gentry!
All Power to the Peasant Association!

The peasants attack as their main targets the local bullies and bad gentry and the lawless landlords, hitting in passing against patriarchal ideologies and institutions, corrupt officials in the cities, and evil customs in the rural areas. In force and momentum, the attack is just like a tempest or hurricane; those who submit to it survive and those who resist it perish. As a result, the privileges which the feudal landlords have enjoyed for thousands of years are shattered to pieces. The dignity and prestige of the landlords are dashed to the ground. With the fall of the authority of the landlords, the peasant association becomes the sole organ of authority, and what people call "All power to the peasant association" has come to pass. Even such a trifle as a quarrel between man and wife has to be settled at the peasant association. Nothing can be settled in the absence of people from the association. The association is actually dictating in all matters in the countryside, and it is literally true that "whatever it says, goes." The public can only praise the association and must not condemn it. The local bullies and bad gentry and the lawless landlords have been totally deprived of the right to have their say, and no one dare mutter the word "No." To be safe from the power and pressure of the peasant association, the first-rank local bullies and bad gentry fled to Shanghai; the second-rank ones, to Hankow; the third-rank ones, to Changsha; and the fourth-rank ones, to the county towns; the fifth-rank ones and even lesser fry can only remain in the countryside and surrender to the peasant association.

"I'll donate ten dollars, please admit me to the peasant association," one of the smaller gentry would say.

"Pshaw! Who wants your filthy money!" the peasants would reply.

Many middle and small landlords, rich peasants, and middle peasants, formerly opposed to the peasant association, now seek admission in vain. Visiting various places, I often came across such people, who solicited my help; "I beg the committeeman from the provincial capital to be my guarantor!" they would say.

The census book compiled by the local authorities under the Manchu regime consisted of a regular register and a special register; in the former honest people were entered, and in the latter burglars, bandits, and other undesirables. The peasants in some places now use the same method to threaten people formerly opposed to the association: "Enter them in the special register!"

Such people, afraid of being entered in the special register, try various means to seek admission to the association and do not feel at ease until, as they eagerly desire, their names are entered in its register. But they are as a rule sternly turned down, and so spend their days in a constant state of suspense; barred from the doors of the association, they are like homeless people. In short, what was generally sneered at four months ago as the "peasants' gang" has now become something most honorable. Those who prostrated themselves before the power of the gentry now prostrate themselves before the power of the peasants. Everyone admits that the world has changed since last October.

"An Awful Mess!" and "Very Good Indeed!"

The revolt of the peasants in the countryside disturbed the sweet dreams of the gentry. When news about the countryside reached the cities, the gentry there immediately burst into an uproar. When I first arrived in Changsha, I met people from various circles and picked up a good deal of street gossip. From the middle strata upwards to the right-wingers of the Kuomintang, there was not a single person who did not summarize the whole thing in one phrase: "An awful mess!" Even quite revolutionary people, carried away by the opinion of the "awful mess" school which prevailed like a storm over the whole city, became downhearted at the very thought of the conditions in the countryside, and could not deny the word "mess." The very progressive people could only remark, "Indeed a mess but inevitable in the course of the revolution." In a word, nobody could categorically deny the word "mess." But the fact is, as stated above, that the broad peasant masses have risen to fulfill their historical mission, that the democratic forces in the rural areas have risen to overthrow the rural feudal power. The patriarchal-feudalistic class of local bullies, bad gentry, and lawless landlords has formed the basis of autocratic government for thousands of years, the cornerstone of imperialism, warlordism, and corrupt officialdom. To overthrow this feudal power is the real objective of the national revolution. What Dr. Sun Yat-sen wanted to do in the 40 years he devoted to the national revolution but failed to accomplish, the peasants have accomplished in a few months. This is a marvelous feat which has never been achieved in the last forty or even thousands of years. It is very good indeed. It is not "a mess" at all. It is anything but "an awful mess." To give credit where it is due, if we allot ten points to the accomplishments of the democratic revolution, then the achievements of the urban dwellers and the military units rate only three points, while the remaining seven points should go to the peasants in their rural revolution.[2] "An awful mess"—that is obviously a theory which, in line with the interests of the landlords, aims at combating the

[2] This sentence omitted from 1952 edition (Ed. note).

rise of the peasants, a theory of the landlord class for preserving the old order of feudalism and obstructing the establishment of a new order of democracy, and a counterrevolutionary theory. No revolutionary comrade should blindly repeat it. If you have firmly established the revolutionary viewpoint and have furthermore gone the round of the villages for a look, you will feel overjoyed as never before. There, great throngs of tens of thousands of slaves, i.e., the peasants, are overthrowing their cannibal enemies. Their actions are absolutely correct; their actions are very good indeed! "Very good indeed!" is the theory of the peasants and all other revolutionaries. Every revolutionary comrade should know that the national revolution requires a profound change in the countryside. The Revolution of 1911 did not bring about this change, hence its failure. Now the change takes place, which is an important factor necessary for completing the revolution. Every revolutionary comrade must support this change, or he will be taking the counterrevolutionary stand.

The Question of "Going Too Far"

There is another section of people who say, "Although the peasant association ought to be formed, it has gone rather too far in its present actions." This is the opinion of the middle-of-the-roaders. But how do matters stand in reality? True, the peasants do in some ways "act unreasonably" in the countryside. The peasant association, supreme in authority, does not allow the landlords to have their say and makes a clean sweep of all their prestige. This is tantamount to trampling the landlords underfoot after knocking them down. The peasants threaten: "Put you in the special register"; they impose fines on the local bullies and bad gentry and demand contributions; they smash their sedan chairs. Crowds of people swarm into the homes of the local bullies and bad gentry who oppose the peasant association, slaughtering their pigs and consuming their grain. They may even loll for a minute or two on the ivory beds of the young mesdames and mesdemoiselles in the families of the bullies and gentry. At the slightest provocation they make arrests, crown the arrested with tall paper hats, and parade them through the villages: "You bad gents, now you know who we are!" Doing whatever they like and turning everything upside down, they have even created a kind of terrorism in the countryside. This is what some people call "going too far," or "going beyond the proper limit to right a wrong," or "really too outrageous." The opinion of this group, reasonable on the surface, is erroneous at bottom. First, the things described above have all been the inevitable results of the doings of the local bullies and bad gentry and lawless landlords themselves. For ages these people, with power in their hands, tyrannized over the peasants and trampled them underfoot; that is why the peasants have now risen in such a great revolt. The most formidable revolts and the most serious troubles invariably occur at places where the local bullies and bad gentry and the lawless landlords are the most ruthless in their evil deeds. The peasants' eyes are perfectly discerning. As to who is bad and who is not, who is the most ruthless and who is less so, and who is to be severely punished and who is to be dealt with lightly, the peasants keep perfectly clear accounts and very seldom has there been any discrepancy between the punishment and the crime. So even Mr. Tang Meng-hsiao once said: "When the peasants attacked the bullies and bad gentry in the villages, in nine cases out of ten they were correct." [3] Secondly, a revolution is not the same as inviting people to dinner or writing an essay, or painting a picture, or doing fancy needlework; it cannot be anything so refined, so calm and gentle, or so mild, kind, courteous, restrained, and magnanimous. [4] A revolution is an uprising, an act of violence whereby one class overthrows another. A rural revolution is a revolution by which the peasantry overthrows the authority of the feudal landlord class. If the peasants do not use the maximum of their strength, they can never overthrow the authority of the landlords which has been deeply rooted for thousands of years. In the rural areas, there must be a great, fervent revolutionary upsurge, which alone can arouse hundreds and thousands of the people to form a great force. All the actions mentioned above, labeled as "going too far," are caused by the power of the peasants, generated by a great, fervent revolutionary upsurge in the countryside. Such actions were quite necessary in the second period of the peasant movement (the period of revolutionary action). In this period, it was necessary to establish the absolute authority of the peasants. It was necessary to prevent malicious criticisms against the peasant association. It was necessary to overthrow all the authority of the gentry, to knock them down, and even stamp them underfoot. All actions labeled as "going too far" had a revolutionary significance in the second period. To put it bluntly, it was necessary to bring about a brief reign of terror in every rural area; otherwise one can never suppress the activities of the counterrevolutionaries in the countryside or overthrow the authority of the gentry. To right a wrong it is necessary to exceed the proper limit, and the wrong cannot be righted without the proper limit being exceeded. The opinion of this school that the peasants are "going too far" is on the surface different from the opinion of the other school mentioned earlier that the peasant movement is "an awful mess," but in essence it adheres to the same viewpoint, and is likewise a theory of the landlords which supports the interests of the privileged classes. Since this theory hinders the rise of the peasant movement and consequently disrupts the revolution, we must oppose it resolutely.

[3] This sentence omitted from 1952 edition (Ed. note).
[4] These were the virtues of Confucius, as described by one of his disciples.

The So-Called "Movement of the Riffraff"

The right wing of the Kuomintang says, "The peasant movement is a movement of the riffraff, a movement of the lazy peasants." This opinion has gained much currency in Changsha. I went to the countryside and heard the gentry say, "It is all right to set up the peasant association, but the people now running it are incompetent; better put others on the job!" This opinion and the dictum of the right wing come to the same thing; both admit that the peasant movement may be carried on (as the peasant movement has already risen, no one dare say that it shouldn't), but regard people leading the movement as incompetent and hate particularly those in charge of the associations at the lower levels, labeling them "riffraff." In short, all those who were formerly despised or kicked into the gutter by the gentry, who had no social standing, and who were denied the right to have a say, have now, to one's surprise, raised their heads. They have not only raised their heads, but have also taken power into their hands. They are now running the *hsiang* peasant association (peasant association at the lowest level), which has been turned into a formidable force in their hands. They raise their rough, blackened hands and lay them on the heads of the gentry. They bind the bad gentry with ropes, put tall paper hats on them, and lead them in a parade through the villages. (This is called "parading through the *hsiang*" in Hsiangtan and Hsianghsiang, and "parading through the fields" in Liling.) Every day the coarse, harsh sound of their denunciation more or less pierces the ears of the gentry. They are giving orders and directions in all matters. They rank above everybody else, they who used to rank below everyone else—that is what people mean by "upside down."

Vanguard of the Revolution

When there are two opposite approaches to a thing or a kind of people, there will be two opposite opinions. "An awful mess" and "very good indeed," "riffraff" and "vanguard of the revolution," are both suitable examples.

We have seen the peasants' accomplishment of a revolutionary task for many years left unaccomplished and their important contributions to the national revolution. But have all the peasants taken part in accomplishing such a great revolutionary task and making important contributions? No. The peasantry consists of three sections—the rich peasants, the middle peasants, and the poor peasants. The circumstances of the three sections differ, and so do their reactions to the revolution. In the first period, what reached the ears of the rich peasants was that the Northern Expedition Army met with a crushing

defeat in Kiangsi, that Chiang Kai-shek had been wounded in the leg
and had flown back to Kwangtung, and that Wu Pei-fu had recaptured
Yochou. So they thought that the peasant association certainly could
not last long and the Three People's Principles[5] could never succeed,
because such things were never heard of before. The officials of a
hsiang peasant association (generally of the so-called "riffraff" type),
bringing the membership register and entering the house of a rich
peasant, said to him, "Please join the peasant association." How would
the rich peasant answer? "Peasant association? For decades I have
lived here and tilled the fields here; I have not seen anything like the
peasant association but I get along all the same. You had better give
it up!"—this from a moderate rich peasant. "What peasant association?
Association for having one's head chopped off—don't get people into
trouble!"—this from a violent rich peasant. Strangely enough, the peasant association has been established for several months, and has even
dared to oppose the gentry. Some gentry in the neighborhood were
arrested by the association and paraded through the villages because
they refused to surrender their opium-smoking kits. In the county
towns, moreover, prominent members of the gentry were put to death,
such as Yen Yung-chiu of Hsiangtan and Yang Chih-tse of Ninghsiang.
At the meeting celebrating the anniversary of the October Revolution,
the anti-British rallies, and the grand celebration of the victory of the
Northern Expedition, at least ten thousand peasants in every county,
carrying big and small banners, with poles and hoes thrown in, marched
in demonstrations in great columns like rolling waves. When all this
happened, the rich peasants began to feel perplexed. In the grand
celebration of the victory of the Northern Expedition, they learnt that
Kiukiang had been taken, that Chiang Kai-shek had not been wounded
in the leg, and that Wu Pei-fu had been finally defeated. Furthermore,
"Long live the Three People's Principles!" "Long live the peasant association!" and "Long live the peasants!" were clearly written on the
"decrees on red and green paper" (posters). " 'Long live the peasants!'
Are these people to be regarded as emperors." [6] The rich peasants were
greatly puzzled. So the peasant association put on grand airs. People
from the association said to the rich peasants, "We'll enter you in the
special register," or, "In another month, the admission fee will be ten
dollars!" It was only in these circumstances that the rich peasants
tardily joined the peasant association, some paying fifty cents or a dollar
(the regular fee being only ten cents), others securing admission only
after people have put in for them a good word or two at their request.
There are also quite a number of die-hards who, even up to the present,

⁵ The Three People's Principles—Nationalism, Democracy, and the People's Welfare—were proposed by Sun Yat-sen as guiding principles for
China.
⁶ The Chinese phrase for "long live" is *wansui*, i.e., "ten thousand years,"
the traditional salute to the emperor which has become a synonym for
"emperor."

have not joined the association. When the rich peasants join the association they generally enter the name of some old man of 60 or 70 of their
family, for they are always afraid of "the drafting of the adult males."
After joining the association they never work for it enthusiastically.
They remain inactive throughout.

How about the middle peasants? Their attitude is vacillating. They
think that the revolution will not do them much good. They have rice
in their pot and are not afraid of creditors knocking at their doors at
midnight. They too, judging a thing by whether it ever was there
before, knit their brows and think hard: "Can the peasant association
really stand on its own legs?" "Can the Three People's Principles succeed?" Their conclusion is, "Afraid not." They think that all these
things depend entirely on the will of Heaven: "To run a peasant association? Who knows if Heaven wills it or not?" In the first period,
people from the peasant association, registers in hand, entered the
house of a middle peasant and said to him, "Please join the peasant
association!" "No hurry!" replied the middle peasant. It was not until
the second period, when the peasant association enjoyed great power,
that the middle peasants joined up. In the association they behave better than the rich peasants, but are as yet not very active, and still want
to wait and see. It is entirely necessary for the peasant association to
explain a good deal more to the middle peasants in order to get them
to join.

The main force in the countryside which has always put up the bitterest fight is the poor peasants. Throughout both the period of underground organization and that of open organization the poor peasants
have fought militantly all along. They accept most willingly the leadership of the Communist Party. They are the deadliest enemies of the
local bullies and bad gentry and attack their strongholds without the
slightest hesitation. They alone are prepared to do the destructive
work.[7] They say to the rich peasants: "We joined the peasant association long ago. Why do you still hesitate?" The rich peasants answer in
a mocking tone, "You people have neither a tile over your head nor a
pinpoint of land beneath your feet. What should have kept you from
joining!" Indeed, the poor peasants are not afraid of losing anything.
Many of them really have "neither a tile over their head nor a pinpoint
of land beneath their feet"—what should have kept them from joining
the association? According to a survey of Changsha County, the poor
peasants comprise 70 percent of the rural population; the middle
peasants, 20 percent; and the rich peasants and landlords, 10 percent.
The poor peasants who comprise 70 percent can be subdivided into
two groups, the utterly impoverished and the less impoverished. The
completely dispossessed, i.e., those who have neither land nor money,
and who, without any means of livelihood, are forced to leave home
and become mercenary soldiers, or hired laborers, or tramp about as

[7] This sentence omitted from 1952 edition (Ed. note).

beggars—all belong to the "utterly impoverished" and comprise 20 percent. The partly dispossessed, i.e., those who have a little land or a little money but consume more than they receive and live in the midst of toil and worry all the year round, e.g., the handicraftsmen, tenant-peasants (except the rich tenant-peasants), and semitenant peasants—all belong to the "less impoverished" and comprise 50 percent. This enormous mass of poor peasants, altogether comprising 70 percent of the rural population, are the backbone of the peasant association, the vanguard in overthrowing the feudal forces, and the foremost heroes who have accomplished the great revolutionary undertaking left unaccomplished for many years. Without the poor peasants (the "riffraff" as the gentry call them), it would never have been possible to bring about in the countryside the present state of revolution, to overthrow the local bullies and bad gentry, or to complete the democratic revolution. Being the most revolutionary, the poor peasants have won the leadership in the peasant association. Almost all the posts of chairmen and committee members in the peasant associations at the lowest level were held by poor peasants in both the first and second periods (of the officials in the *hsiang* associations in Hengshan the utterly impoverished comprise 50 percent, the less impoverished comprise 40 percent, and the impoverished intellectuals comprise 10 percent). This leadership of the poor peasants is absolutely necessary. Without the poor peasants there can be no revolution. To reject them is to reject the revolution. To attack them is to attack the revolution. Their general direction of the revolution has never been wrong. They have hurt the dignity of the local bullies and bad gentry. They have knocked the big and small local bullies and bad gentry to the ground and trampled them underfoot. Many of their deeds in the period of revolutionary action, described as "gone too far," were in fact the very needs of the revolution. Some of the county governments, county headquarters of the party,[8] and county peasant associations in Hunan have committed a number of mistakes; there are even some which at the request of the landlords sent soldiers to arrest the lower officials of the peasant associations. Many chairmen and committeemen of the *hsiang* associations are imprisoned in the jails in Hengshen and Hsianghsiang. This is a serious mistake which greatly encourages the arrogance of the reactionaries. To judge whether or not it is a mistake, one needs only see how, as soon as the chairmen and committeemen of the peasant associations are arrested, the local lawless landlords are elated and reactionary sentiments mount. We must oppose such counterrevolutionary calumnies as "riffraff movement" and "movement of the lazy peasants" and must be especially careful not to commit the mistake of helping the local bullies and bad gentry to attack the poor peasants. As a matter of fact, although some of the poor-peasant leaders certainly had shortcomings in the past, most of them have reformed themselves by now. They are

[8] Of the Kuomintang.

themselves energetically prohibiting gambling and exterminating banditry. Where the peasant association is powerful, gambling and banditry have vanished. In some places it is literally true that people do not pocket articles dropped on the road and that doors are not bolted at night. According to a survey of Hengshan, 85 percent of the poor-peasant leaders have now turned out to be quite reformed, capable, and energetic. Only 15 percent of them retain some bad habits. They can only be regarded as "the few undesirables," and we must not echo the local bullies and bad gentry in condemning indiscriminately everybody as "riffraff." To tackle this problem of "the few undesirables," we can only, on the basis of the association's slogan of strengthening discipline, carry on propaganda among the masses and educate the undesirables themselves so that the discipline of the association may be strengthened, but we must not wantonly send soldiers to make arrests, lest we should undermine the prestige of the poor peasantry and fan up the arrogance of the local bullies and bad gentry. This is a point we must particularly attend to.

MAO ON REVOLUTION

The Chinese Revolution and the Chinese Communist Party by Mao
Tse-tung, Yenan, 1939.

The first half of this collection of documents contains four representative writings by Mao Tse-tung which serve to introduce the historical background out of which the CCP emerged and which will
help the reader to understand some of the underlying tensions that
have contributed to the ambivalent character of the Peking-Kremlin
relationship since 1949, the year the CCP achieved power.

It was at Yenan, in Northwest China, that the CCP established
a firm base of operations from which it either fought the Kuomintang
(Nationalist Party) in civil war, or cooperated with Chiang Kai-shek
in the common fight against Japan. It was also at Yenan that Mao
lectured and wrote most widely, with his audience consisting largely
of party comrades.

The Chinese Revolution and the Chinese Communist Party, published in December, 1939, very quickly, as did everything that came
from Mao's pen, became part of Chinese Communist holy writ. As
the Commission on Publication of the Selected Works of Mao Tse-tung
of the Central Committee of the CCP put it, "This is part of a text-
book written jointly by Comrade Mao Tse-tung and several other
comrades in Yenan. . . ." Nevertheless the CCP, in its attempts to
build the "cult of Mao," has generally ascribed sole authorship to
Mao. The joint authorship of the work helps to explain its uneven
quality, which has been noted by western students of China. At times
it reads as though it had been written by an inadequately trained
sociologist or historian, heavily interlarded with Marxist jargon; and
yet there are passsages of poetic prose (Mao is a poet of considerable
repute). The poetry abounds particularly in those passages in which
Mao recalls the glories of China during her earlier history. Felicity
of language is absent in those passages in which Mao attempts to
explain the history of China in terms of Marxist dogmatism.

The first part of this work provides the reader with a cursory survey
of the millennia of Chinese history. Mao devotes himself at some
length to an exposition of the nature of feudalism in China and
China's transition to a semifeudal and semicolonial society. He ends
with the analysis that China must resolve two principal contradictions.
First, there is the contradiction between foreign imperialism—being
represented at the time by Japan—and Chinese nationalism. Second,
there is the contradiction between feudalism and the great mass of
the Chinese people who desire to rid themselves of its yoke. In the

second part, Mao proceeds to analyze and to theorize about the role of the CCP in resolving these contradictions. He concludes with a brief statement concerning the present stage of the revolutionary process, emphasizing the dual nature of the revolution, the "bourgeois-democratic" or "new-democratic" stage and the "proletarian-socialist" stage. (Mao's views on these respective stages, particularly his views on the new-democratic stage are explained more fully by him in his On the New Democracy, which is also included in this collection.)

The main themes of this selection from Mao's work can be summarized as follows: first, China's long and glorious history, of which all Chinese can be proud (Mao stresses the inventive genius of the Chinese people); second, the peculiarities of China's historical development (especially if an attempt is made to fit them into a rigid Marxist pattern); third, the role that the CCP should play in resolving the "contradictions" within China; fourth, the claim to legitimacy on the part of the CCP to being the true heirs of Sun Yat-sen and the nationalist revolutionary movement.

Of equal importance are the omissions. Even in 1939, with Mao being little more than the chieftain of a local satrapy, there are few references to the Soviet Union in which Mao expresses, even casually, any feeling of obligation to or alliance with the then undisputed headquarters of international Communism. He quotes Stalin approvingly in one instance, but with no hint of deference. In short, Mao views the role of the CCP as facing the problems of the Chinese Revolution with the twin ideologies of nationalism and Maoistic-Marxism.

The Chinese Nation

China is one of the largest countries in the world, with a territory almost as large as the whole of Europe. In this vast territory there are large areas of fertile land which provide us with food and clothing, large and small mountain ranges traversing the length and breadth of the country which provide us with extensive forests and rich mineral deposits, many rivers and lakes which provide us with facilities for water transport and irrigation, and a long coastline which facilitates communication with other nations beyond the seas. From very ancient times our forefathers have labored, lived and multiplied on this vast expanse of land.

The present boundaries of China are as follows: It borders on the U.S.S.R. in the northeast, the northwest and part of the west; on the People's Republic of Mongolia in the north; on Afghanistan, India, Bhutan and Nepal in the southwest and part of the west; on Burma and Indo-China in the south; and it borders on Korea and is near Japan and the Philippines on the east. From the point of view of foreign relations, the geographical situation of China affords both advantages and disadvantages to the Chinese people's revolution. It is to her advantage that China is contiguous to the Soviet Union, relatively remote from the major European and American imperialist countries, and has as her neighbors many countries which are colonies or semicolonies. The disadvantage is that Japanese imperialism, making use of its geographical proximity, is constantly threatening the existence of the various nationalities in China and endangering the Chinese people's revolution.

China's population now totals 450 million, almost a quarter of the world population. Over nine-tenths of them are the Hans. There are scores of national minorities including the Mongols, the Huis, the Tibetans, the Uighurs, the Miaos, the Yis, the Chuangs, the Chungchias, and the Koreans, all of whom have long histories, though they are at different stages of cultural development. China is a country with a very large population composed of many different nationalities.

Like many other peoples in their development, the Chinese (I am here referring mainly to the Hans) first lived in classless primitive communes for tens of thousands of years. It is approximately four thousand years since the collapse of the primitive communes and the transition to class society, which was first slave society and then feudal society. In the history of Chinese civilization there have been highly developed agriculture and handicraft which have always been famous; there have been many great thinkers, scientists, inventors, statesmen, military experts, men of letters, and artists; and there is a vast treasury of classical art and literature. The compass was invented in China in very early times. The art of paper making was discovered 1800 years ago. Blockprinting was invented 1300 years ago, and movable types 800 years ago. Gunpowder was used in China earlier than in Europe. China, with a recorded history of almost four thousand years, is therefore one of the oldest civilized countries in the world.

The Chinese have always been famous throughout the world for their powers of endurance and industriousness, and also as a freedom-loving people with a rich revolutionary tradition. The history of the Hans, for instance, shows that the Chinese people never submitted to the tyranny of reaction and always succeeded in overthrowing or changing it by revolutionary means. In the thousands of years of Han history, there have been hundreds of peasant insurrections, great or small, against the reactionary rule imposed by the landlords and nobility. Most dynastic changes came about in consequence of peasant uprisings. China's various nationalities have always resisted and rebelled against a foreign yoke and struggled to shake it off. They accept a union of all nationalities on the basis of equality and oppose the oppression of one nationality by another. In thousands of years of history many national heroes and revolutionary leaders have emerged in

China. So the Chinese are also a nation with a glorious revolutionary tradition and a splendid historical heritage.

Ancient Feudal Society

Although China is a great nation with a vast territory, an immense population, a long history, a rich revolutionary tradition, and a splendid historical heritage, she has remained sluggish in her economic, political, and cultural development since her transition from slave society to feudalism. The feudal system, beginning with the Chou and Ch'in dynasties, has lasted about three thousand years.

*   *   *

Under this feudal system of economic exploitation and political oppression the Chinese peasants throughout the ages lived like slaves in dire poverty and suffering. Under the yoke of feudalism they had no freedom of person. They had no political rights whatever: the landlords could at will beat, insult, and even kill them. The extreme poverty and backwardness of the peasants as a result of the landlords' ruthless exploitation and oppression is the basic reason why China's economy and social life has remained stagnant for thousands of years.

In feudal society, the main contradiction is between the peasantry and the landlord class. In this society, the peasants and the handicraftsmen are the two principal classes which create wealth and culture.

This ruthless economic exploitation and political oppression forced the peasants to rise repeatedly in revolt against the rule of the landlord class.

*   *   *

There were hundreds of uprisings, great and small, all of which were peasant rebellions, or rather, peasant revolutionary wars. The gigantic scale of some of these peasant uprisings and peasant wars in Chinese history is without parallel in the world. It is these class struggles, the peasant uprisings and peasant wars, that were the real motivating force of historical development in China's feudal society. Each major peasant uprising or war dealt a blow to the then existing feudal regime and to some extent furthered the development of the social productive forces. However, since no new productive forces, new relations of production, new class forces, nor an advanced political party existed in those days, the peasants lacked the correct leadership such as is given by the proletariat and the Communist Party today, and every one of their revolutions failed, the peasants were utilized during or after each revolution by the landlords and the nobility as a tool to bring about a dynastic change. Thus, although there was some social progress after each great peasant revolutionary struggle, the feudal economic relations and feudal political system remained basically unchanged.

It was only in the last hundred years that other and different changes took place.

Present-Day Colonial, Semicolonial, and Semifeudal Society

As explained above, Chinese society remained feudal for three thousand years. But is it still completely feudal today? No, China has changed. Since the Opium War of 1840 China has changed gradually into a semicolonial and semifeudal society. Since the Incident of September 18, 1931 when the Japanese imperialists started their armed invasion of China, Chinese society has changed still further into a colonial, semicolonial, and semifeudal society. We shall now explain the course of this change.

As [already] mentioned, Chinese feudal society lasted for about three thousand years. It was not until the middle of the nineteenth century that great changes took place inside China as a result of the penetration of foreign capitalism.

As the development of commodity economy in China's feudal society carried within itself the seeds of capitalism, China would of herself have developed slowly into a capitalist society without the influence of foreign capitalism. The penetration of foreign capitalism speeded up this development. Foreign capitalism was instrumental in disintegrating China's social economy by destroying the foundation of her self-sufficing natural economy and wrecking her handicraft industries in both the cities and peasant homes, and also by hastening the development of commodity economy in town and country.

Thus, apart from the collapse of the foundations of feudal economy, certain objective conditions emerged which made the development of capitalist production possible in China. For the destruction of the natural economy has created for capitalism a commodity market, while the impoverishment of large numbers of peasants and handicraftsmen has created for it a labor market.

In fact, as early as 60 years ago, in the latter half of the nineteenth century, under the stimulus of foreign capitalism and certain breaches in the feudal economic structure, some merchants, landlords, and bureaucrats started investing in modern industries. About 40 years ago at the turn of the century, China's national capitalism emerged in a rudimentary form. Then about 20 years ago during the first imperialist world war, China's own industry, chiefly textiles and flour milling, developed further because, preoccupied with the war, the European and American imperialist countries temporarily relaxed their oppression of China.

The emergence and development of national capitalism in China implied the emergence and development of the bourgeoisie and the proletariat. Just as certain sections of the merchants, landlords, and bureaucrats were predecessors of the Chinese bourgeoisie, so certain sections of the peasants and handicraftsmen were the predecessors of the Chinese proletariat. The Chinese bourgeoisie and proletariat, as two distinct social classes, are new-born classes which never existed before in Chinese history. In embryo in feudal society, they have evolved into new social classes. They are interlinked but antagonistic classes, the twins born of China's old feudal society. Moreover, the Chinese proletariat has emerged and developed with the Chinese national bourgeoisie, and also with the enterprises directly operated in China by the imperialists. As a result, a very large section of the Chinese proletariat has a much longer existence and more experience than the Chinese bourgeoisie, and is thus a greater social force with a broader social basis.

The emergence and development of capitalism constitutes, however, only one aspect of the change that has taken place since imperialist penetration into China. Alongside with this there is also the aspect which hampers Chinese capitalism, namely, the attempt to check its development by foreign imperialism in league with China's feudal forces.

The imperialist powers certainly do not invade China with the purpose of transforming a feudal China into a capitalist China. Their aim is just the opposite—to transform China into their semicolony or colony.

* * *

Imperialist penetration has hastened the disintegration of China's feudal society and introduced elements of capitalism, thereby transforming a feudal into a semifeudal society, and at the same time imposed their ruthless rule and reduced an independent China into a semicolonial and colonial China.

Taking both aspects together, we notice the following characteristics of China's colonial, semicolonial, and semifeudal society:

1. The self-sufficing natural economy of feudal times has been undermined; but the basis of feudal exploitation, the exploitation of the peasantry by the landlord class, remains intact and is linked with the exploitation of comprador and usurer capital, and obviously plays a dominant role in China's social-economic life.

2. National capitalism has developed to a certain extent and played a considerable part in China's political and cultural life, but, being still quite weak and more or less associated with foreign imperialism and domestic feudalism, has not become the principal social-economic form in China.

3. The autocratic rule of the emperors and the nobility has been overthrown, and in its place have arisen first the rule of the warlords

and bureaucrats of landlord-class origin and then the joint dictatorship of the landlord class and the big.bourgeoisie. In the occupied
areas there is the rule of Japanese imperialism and its puppets.

4. Imperialism controls China's vital financial and economic arteries
and also her political and military power. In the occupied areas everything is in the hands of Japanese imperialism.

5. Economic, political, and cultural development is very uneven in
China, because the country is big and has been under the complete
or partial rule of several imperialist powers, and in fact in a state of
permanent disunity.

6. Under the twofold oppression of imperialism and feudalism,
and especially as a result of the all-out offensive of Japanese imperialism, the broad mass of the Chinese people, particularly the peasants,
have become more and more impoverished and large numbers have
neither food nor clothing and all are without any political rights.
Such extreme poverty and complete lack of freedom have few paral-
lels in the world.

These are the characteristics of China's colonial, semicolonial, and
semifeudal society.

This situation has been brought about mainly by Japanese and
other imperialist forces, and is the result of the combination of foreign
imperialism and domestic feudalism.

The contradiction between imperialism and the Chinese nation, and
the contradiction between feudalism and the great mass of the people,
are the principal contradictions in modern Chinese society. There
are, of course, other contradictions, such as those between the bourgeoisie and the proletariat and within the reactionary ruling classes
themselves. The contradiction between imperialism and the Chinese
nation, however, is the principal one. As struggles arise between these
contradictions and become more and more intense, revolutionary
movements will develop rapidly. The great revolutions of modern
and contemporary China have emerged and developed on the basis
of these fundamental contradictions.

The Revolutionary Movements
in the Last Hundred Years

The course of transforming China into a semicolony and colony by
foreign imperialism in league with Chinese feudalism, is at the same
time the course of the struggle of the Chinese people against imperialism and its lackeys. The Opium War, the Movement of the
T'aip'ing Heavenly Kingdom, the Sino-French War, the Sino-Japanese
War, the *coup d'état* of 1898, the Boxer Movement, the Revolution
of 1911, the May 4 Movement, the May 30 Movement, the Northern
Expedition, the Agrarian Revolutionary War, and the present Anti-

Japanese War—all bear witness to the stubborn resistance of the Chinese people, who will never submit to imperialism and its lackeys.

*   *   *

The national revolutionary struggle of the Chinese people has a history of exactly 100 years dating from the Opium War of 1840, and of 30 years dating from the Revolution of 1911. As this revolution has not yet run its full course and has not yet accomplished any significant part of its tasks, it is still necessary for all the Chinese people, especially the Chinese Communist Party, to assume the responsibility of carrying on a determined struggle.

What, then, are the targets of this revolution? What are its tasks? What are its motivating forces? What is its character? And what are its perspectives? These are the questions we shall answer in the following pages.

The Targets of the Chinese Revolution

From the [previous] analysis, we already know that present-day Chinese society is colonial, semicolonial, and semifeudal. A clear recognition of this fact alone can enable us to reach a clear understanding of the targets of the Chinese revolution, its tasks, its motivating forces, its character and its perspectives and transition. A clear understanding of the character of Chinese society and of the actual situation in China is the prerequisite for an understanding of all problems of the revolution.

Such being the character of present-day Chinese society, what are the chief targets or who are the chief enemies of the Chinese revolution at this stage?

They are imperialism and feudalism, or the bourgeoisie of foreign imperialist countries and the landlord class at home. These are the principal agents oppressing China and obstructing her progress. They conspire to oppress the Chinese people; and, since national oppression by imperialism is the heaviest oppression, imperialism is the foremost and most ruthless enemy of the Chinese people.

*   *   *

The Chinese revolution has to deal with powerful enemies. Among them are not only powerful imperialist forces, but also powerful feudal forces and, at certain times, the reactionaries among the bourgeoisie who oppose the people in collusion with imperialist and feudal forces. It is wrong to underestimate the strength of the enemies of the revolutionary Chinese people.

Confronted with such enemies, the Chinese revolution becomes protracted and ruthless. Since the enemies are extremely powerful, the revolutionaries, unless given sufficient time, cannot be massed and steeled into a power that will crush them once and for all. Since the enemies are exceedingly ruthless in their suppression of the Chinese revolution, the revolutionaries must steel themselves into stubborn fighters or they cannot hold their own positions and dislodge their enemies. It is therefore wrong to think that the forces of the Chinese revolution can be built up in the twinkling of an eye and the Chinese revolutionary struggle can triumph overnight.

Confronted with such enemies, the principal means or the principal form of the Chinese revolution must be armed rather than peaceful. By depriving the Chinese people of all political freedoms and rights our enemies have ruled out any possibility for us to resort to peaceful political actions. "In China," says Stalin, "the armed revolution is fighting the armed counterrevolution. That is one of the specific features and one of the advantages of the Chinese revolution." [1] Stalin's formulation is perfectly correct. It is therefore wrong to underrate armed struggle, revolutionary war, guerrilla war, and military work.

Confronted with such enemies, the Chinese revolution has also to tackle the question of revolutionary base areas. Since the powerful imperialists and their allies, the reactionary forces, have long occupied China's key cities, if the revolutionary forces do not wish to compromise with them, but are determined to fight on, and if they intend to build up their strength and steel themselves and avoid decisive battles until they have mustered enough strength, then they must turn the backward villages into advanced, consolidated base areas, into great military, political, economic, and cultural revolutionary bastions from which they can fight their ruthless enemy who utilizes the cities to attack the rural districts and gradually achieve through a protracted struggle the complete victory of the revolution. In these circumstances, owing to China's uneven economic development, that is, to the absence of a unified capitalist economy, to her enormous size which gives the revolutionary forces room to maneuver, to the disunity and numerous contradictions in the counterrevolutionary camp, and to the fact that the struggle of the peasants, the main force in the Chinese revolution, is led by the party of the proletariat, the Communist Party—in these circumstances, a situation arises in which the Chinese revolution can be victorious first in the rural districts, but has to proceed at varying paces in various parts of the country so that the achievement of complete victory becomes protracted and arduous. It is evident that the protracted revolutionary struggle conducted in such revolutionary base areas is mainly a peasant guerrilla war led by the Chinese Communist Party. It is therefore wrong to neglect building up revolutionary base areas in the

[1] Stalin, *Works,* Eng. ed., Moscow, 1954, Vol. VIII, p. 379.

rural districts, doing sustained political work among the peasants, or carrying on guerrilla war.

*   *   *

In carrying on propaganda and organizational work in the cities and the countryside long occupied by the enemy and dominated by the forces of reaction and darkness, the Communist Party must, instead of a rash adventurist policy, follow the line of covering up its forces, simplifying its structure, building up its strength, and biding its time. In leading the people's struggle against the enemy, we must adopt the tactics of advancing slowly but surely by making the fullest possible use of all forms of open and legal activities permitted by laws and decrees and social customs and adhering to the principles of justifiability, expediency, and restraint: noisy boastfulness and rash actions will never produce results.

The Tasks of the Chinese Revolution

Imperialism and feudalism being the chief enemies of the Chinese revolution at the present stage, what are the immediate tasks of the revolution?

Unquestionably, the major tasks are to strike at these two enemies, by carrying out a national revolution to overthrow foreign imperialist oppression and a democratic revolution to overthrow the oppression of the feudal landlords at home; of the two tasks the primary one is the national revolution for the overthrow of imperialism.

*   *   *

As the main task of China's national revolution today is to resist the Japanese imperialist invaders, and as the task of her democratic revolution must be carried out before the resistance can be successful, the two revolutionary tasks are already linked together. It is therefore wrong to regard the national revolution and the democratic revolution as two distinctly different stages.

The Motivating Forces of the Chinese Revolution

In the light of the foregoing analysis and definitions, what are the motivating forces of the Chinese revolution?

Since Chinese society is colonial, semicolonial, and semifeudal, since the targets of the Chinese revolution are mainly foreign imperialist oppression and domestic feudalism, and since its tasks are to overthrow both, then which of the various classes and strata in Chinese society constitute the forces capable of fighting them? This is a question of the motivating forces of the Chinese revolution at the present stage. The correct solution of the problem of the basic tactics of the Chinese revolution depends upon a clear understanding of this question.

What classes are there in present-day Chinese society? There are the landlord class and the bourgeoisie; the landlord class and the upper strata of the bourgeoisie are the ruling classes in Chinese society. There are also the proletariat, the peasantry, and all sections of the petty bourgeoisie other than the peasantry which, in most parts of China, are still the subject classes.

The attitude and stand taken by these classes towards the Chinese revolution entirely depend upon their social-economic status. Thus China's economy determines not only the targets and tasks of the revolution, but also its motivating forces.

* * *

Among the Chinese proletariat, the modern industrial workers number from two and a half to three million, the hired laborers in small-scale industries and handicrafts and the shop assistants total about twelve million in the cities, and the rural proletariat, that is, the farm laborers, and other urban and rural proletarians are also numerous.

In addition to the basic merits of the proletariat in general—that it is associated with the most advanced form of economy, that it has a strong sense of organization and discipline, and that it owns no private means of production—the Chinese proletariat has many other outstanding qualities.

What are these qualities?

First, the Chinese proletariat is the victim of the threefold oppression of imperialism, the bourgeoisie and the feudal forces, an oppression almost unparalleled in the world in its severity and ruthlessness; and consequently it is more resolute and more thoroughgoing in the revolutionary struggle than any other class. Since there is in colonial and semicolonial China no economic basis for social reformism as in Europe, the whole proletariat, with the exception of a few traitors, is very revolutionary.

Secondly, ever since its appearance on the revolutionary scene, the Chinese proletariat has been under the leadership of its own revolutionary political party—the Chinese Communist Party—and has become the most politically conscious class in Chinese society.

Thirdly, since the Chinese proletariat is largely made up of destitute peasants, it has ties with the vast peasantry which facilitate a close alliance between the two classes.

Therefore, in spite of certain unavoidable weaknesses, for instance, its small size as compared with the peasantry, its youth as compared with the proletariat in capitalist countries, and its low cultural level as compared with the bourgeoisie, the Chinese proletariat has become the basic motivating force of the Chinese revolution. Without its leadership, the Chinese revolution will certainly not succeed.

*   *   *

The Chinese proletariat must understand that, although it is the class with the highest political consciousness and sense of organization, it cannot win victory by its own strength alone. To win victory it must unite, under various conditions, with all possible revolutionary classes and strata and organize a revolutionary united front. Among all the classes in Chinese society, the peasantry is the firm ally of the working class, the urban petty bourgeoisie is a reliable ally, and the national bourgeoisie is an ally in certain periods and to a certain extent. This is one of the fundamental laws established by the history of modern Chinese revolution.

*   *   *

The Character of the Chinese Revolution

*   *   *

It is now clear that Chinese society is still a colonial, semicolonial, and semifeudal society; that the principal enemies of the Chinese revolution are still imperialism and feudalism; that the task of the Chinese revolution consists in a national revolution and a democratic revolution for overthrowing these two enemies; that the bourgeoisie sometimes also takes part in this revolution; and that even if the big bourgeoisie betrays the revolution and becomes its enemy, our targets will still be imperialism and feudalism rather than capitalism and capitalist private property in general. That being so, the character of the Chinese revolution at the present stage is not proletarian-socialist but bourgeois-democratic.

However, the bourgeois-democratic revolution in present-day China is no longer of the usual old type, which is now obsolete, but a special new type. This kind of revolution is developing in China and in all colonial and semicolonial countries, and is described by us as the new-democratic revolution. The new-democratic revolution is part of the world proletarian-socialist revolution, which resolutely opposes imperialism or international capitalism. Politically it means the joint dictatorship of several revolutionary classes over the imperialists, collaborators, and reactionaries and opposition to the transformation of Chinese society into a society under bourgeois dictatorship. Economically, it means nationalization of all big capital and big enterprises of the imperialists, collaborators, and reactionaries; distribution of the land of the landlords among the peasants; and at the same time the preservation in general of private capitalist enterprises without the elimination of rich-peasant economy. It clears the way for capitalism but also lays the foundation for socialism. The present stage of the Chinese revolution is a transitional stage between the end of colonial, semicolonial, and semifeudal society and the beginning of socialist society, a process of new-democratic revolution. This process, which began only after the First World War with the October Revolution in Russia, started in China with the May 4 Movement of 1919. A new-democratic revolution is a revolution of the mass of the people led by the proletariat and directed against imperialism and feudalism. China can only advance to a socialist society by going through this kind of revolution.

This kind of new-democratic revolution differs greatly from the democratic revolutions in the history of European and American countries, in that it results not in the dictatorship of the bourgeoisie, but in the dictatorship of the united front of all revolutionary classes under the leadership of the proletariat.

*   *   *

This kind of revolution differs also from a socialist revolution in that it aims only at overthrowing the rule of the imperialists, collaborators, and reactionaries in China, but not at inflicting damage on any section of the bourgeoisie which can still take part in the anti-imperialist, antifeudal struggles.

*   *   *

In the course of China's bourgeois-democratic revolution, the proletariat, the peasantry, and the other sections of the petty bourgeoisie must not be ignored, either in the alignment of forces during the struggle, that is, in the united front, or in the composition of the government. Whoever tries to leave them out of account certainly cannot shape China's destiny or solve any of her problems. The democratic republic which the Chinese revolution is striving to create at the present stage must be one in which the workers, peasants, and other sections of the petty bourgeoisie are assigned definite places and definite roles. In other words, it is to be a democratic republic with a revolutionary alliance of the workers, the peasants, the urban petty bourgeoisie, and all others who fight against imperialism and feudalism. Only under the leadership of the proletariat can such a republic be completely realized.

The Perspectives of the Chinese Revolution

*   *   *

It is conceivable, and not at all surprising that after the victory of the revolution, capitalist economy will develop to a certain extent in Chinese society because the obstacles to its development will have been swept away. It is an inevitable result of the victory of the democratic revolution in economically backward China that capitalism will develop to a certain extent. But this will be only one of the results, not the whole outcome. The whole outcome will be the development of the capitalist factors and of the socialist factors. What are the socialist factors? They are the increasing political influence of the proletariat and the Communist Party in the whole country, the leadership of the proletariat and the Communist Party that has been or may be accepted by the peasantry, the intelligentsia and the urban petty bourgeoisie, and the state enterprises of the people's republic, and the cooperatives of the working people. These are the socialist factors. Given a favorable international situation, there is a strong possibility that the bourgeois-democratic revolution will finally steer China away from a capitalist future and towards the realization of socialism.

The Twofold Task of the Chinese Revolution and the Chinese Communist Party

Summing up the foregoing sections, we can see that the Chinese revolution taken as a whole involves a twofold task. That is to say, it embraces a bourgeois-democratic or rather a new-democratic revolution and a proletarian-socialist revolution, in other words, the tasks of both the present and the future stages in the revolution. The leadership in this twofold revolutionary task devolves upon the party of the Chinese proletariat, the Chinese Communist Party, for without the party's leadership no revolution can succeed.

*   *   *

Except for the Communist Party, no political party, bourgeois or petty-bourgeois, is equal to the task of leading China's two great revolutions, democratic and socialist, to their successful conclusion. The Chinese Communist Party, from the very day of its birth, has shouldered this twofold task and for more than 18 years has fought strenuously for its accomplishment.

This is a task at once glorious and arduous. It cannot be accomplished without a bolshevized Chinese Communist Party on a nation-wide scale and of a broad mass character, fully consolidated ideologically, politically, and organizationally. It is therefore the duty of every Communist to take an active part in building such a party.

MAO ON MILITARY STRATEGY

Problems of War and Strategy by Mao Tse-tung, Yenan, 1939.

In addition to his roles as Marxist dialectician, political leader, and poet, Mao Tse-tung is a military theorist of considerable creativity. His accomplishments in this area have done much to build his reputation in the Communist world. However, in the realm of the strategic and tactical aspects of war he has much preferred to restrict himself to theory, leaving its practical application to such trusted military lieutenants as Chu Teh or Teng Hsiao-ping, or, in a later era, Lin Piao.

Mao has lectured widely on military problems, especially on the relationship between martial and political goals. Many of these lectures have been collected into small handbooks which are widely distributed among his followers. Today, these volumes are studied not only by the Chinese Army, but also by military tacticians all over the world—in both Communist and non-Communist countries—who are interested in mobile and guerilla (as opposed to stationary) warfare.

Mao has written three important works on military affairs, of which Strategic Problems of China's Revolutionary War is his major dissertation on the subject. On the Protracted War is primarily an analysis of the CCP's military role against the Japanese. Most of the salient points made in both of these are more succinctly stated in Problems of War and Strategy, which is reproduced here.

When giving this particular lecture, Mao was much concerned with his comrades' lack of appreciation of the closely held Maoist principle that the military component is of primary importance in the acquisition of power. Mao herein invokes his famous, oft-quoted, and still important dictum that "political power grows out of the barrel of a gun." The reader will also note Mao's quick and pointed addition that it is the party (the political) leaders who control the gun, not vice versa.

Unless carefully examined the tone of the work might give the impression that Mao believes military power to be more crucial to Communist ascendancy than even ideology or the proper Marxist analysis of history. As Mao himself states, "the theory of war and strategy is the key to everything." This emphasis on martial matters must be viewed against the backdrop of events in China in the fall of 1938, if it is to be properly understood.

China—Nationalist and Communist together—is fighting a lonely and losing war against Japan. In the interest of national unity, Mao even goes so far as to compliment Chiang Kai-shek for having "grasped the vital point that whoever has an army has power and that war decides everything." Yet, even at the height of this war effort, Mao delivers Problems of War and Strategy in which he contrasts the military history of the Kuomintang (Nationalist Party) with that of the CCP and thereby reminds his listeners and readers that there are other objectives besides victory in war. He also reiterates his conviction that the military must be subordinated to the political and that "Communists do not and should never contend for personal military power . . . ," especially if they do not agree with Mao's policies, as was the case with Chang Kuo-t'ao, the individual specifically cited as an example.*

For Mao and his comrades there are always two goals: military victory and the achievement of political objectives. And, of the two, the latter has precedence.

China's Characteristics and the Revolutionary War

The central task—and the highest form of a revolution—is to seize political power by armed force and decide issues by war. This Marxist-Leninist principle of revolution holds good universally, in China as well as in all other countries.

It may, however, be variously applied by the proletarian parties according to different circumstances. The capitalist countries, when there is neither fascism nor war, at home have bourgeois democracy and no longer feudalism, while in external relations they oppress other nations but do not themselves suffer from foreign oppression. Owing to these characteristics, the task of the proletarian parties in the capitalist countries is to prepare for the final overthrow of capitalism by educating the workers and building up strength through a long period of legal struggle. It is a question of long legal struggle, of utilizing the legislative bodies as a platform, of staging economic and political strikes, and of organizing the trade unions and educating the workers. The forms of organization are legal and the forms of struggle are bloodless, that is, nonmilitary. On the question of war, the Communist Parties in capitalist countries are opposed to the imperialist wars waged by their own countries; if such wars occur their policy is to bring about the defeat of their own reactionary governments. The only war they want is the civil war for which they

* See Chang Kuo-t'ao, "Mao. A New Portrait by an Old Colleague," New York Times Magazine, August 2, 1953.

are preparing.[1] But a struggle of this kind, whether in the form of regular war or of armed insurrection, should not be launched until the bourgeoisie becomes really helpless, until the majority of the proletariat are determined to take up arms and wage war, and until the peasant masses are willing to give assistance to the proletariat. Moreover, when the time comes for launching insurrection and war, the first step will be to seize the cities and then advance on the countryside, not the other way round. All this has been done by the Communist Parties of capitalist countries and has been proved correct by the October Revolution in Russia.

The case of China is different. What distinguishes her is that she is not an independent democratic state but a semicolonial and semifeudal country, deprived of democracy by feudal oppression at home and of national independence by imperialist oppression from the outside. Thus the Chinese people have no legislative body to make use of, nor have the workers any legal right to organize strikes. Basically, therefore, the task of the Chinese Communist Party is not to go through a long period of legal struggles before launching an insurrection or war, nor to seize the big cities first and then occupy the countryside, but the reverse.

When there are no armed attacks launched by imperialism, the Chinese Communist Party either wages, together with the bourgeoisie, a civil war against the warlords, the lackeys of imperialism, as it did in Kwangtung[2] and the Northern Expedition in 1924–1927, or unites the peasants and the urban petty bourgeoisie to wage a civil war against the landlord class and the comprador bourgeoisie, who are also the lackeys of imperialism, as it did in the War of Agrarian Revolution of 1927–1936. When armed attacks are launched by imperialism, the party then unites all the classes and strata in the country that are opposed to foreign aggressors to wage a national war against the foreign enemy, as in the present Anti-Japanese War.

[1] See Lenin, "The War and Russian Social Democracy," "Conference of the Sections of the R.S.D.L.P. Abroad," "Defeat of One's Own Government in the Imperialist War," "The Defeat of Russia and the Revolutionary Crisis" (*Selected Works*, Eng. ed., New York, 1943, Vol. V, pt. 2); *History of the Communist Party of the Soviet Union* (*Bolsheviks*), *Short Course*, ch. 6, sect. 3.

[2] In 1924, Dr. Sun Yat-sen, in alliance with the Communist Party and the revolutionary workers and peasants, suppressed the revolt of the "Merchants Corps" in Canton, an armed force of the compradors and landed gentry in league with the British imperialists. Early in 1925, the revolutionary army, formed on the basis of Kuomintang-Communist cooperation, set out from Canton on an eastward expedition and, with the support of the peasants, defeated the troops of the warlord Ch'en Chiung-ming. Then it returned to overthrow the Kwangsi and Yunnan warlords entrenched in Canton. In the autumn it again advanced eastward and wiped out all the remnants of Ch'en Chiung-ming's forces. These battles, in which the Communist Party and the Communist Youth League fought in the forefront, brought about political unity in Kwangtung and prepared the way for the Northern Expedition.

All this shows the difference between China and capitalist countries. In China the main form of struggle is war, and the main form of organization is the army. Such forms as mass organizations and mass struggles are also very important and necessary and must not be overlooked, but they are all employed to support war. All organizational work and struggles before the outbreak of hostilities are undertaken as preparations for the war, as in the period from the May 4 Movement (1919) to the May 30 Movement (1925). All organizational work and struggles after the outbreak of hostilities are coordinated with the war either directly or indirectly; for instance, in the period of the Northern Expedition all organizational work and struggles in the rear areas of the revolutionary army were directly coordinated with the war, while all those in areas under the rule of the clique of Northern warlords were indirectly coordinated with it. Again, in the period of the War of the Agrarian Revolution all organizational work and struggles inside the Red areas were directly coordinated with the war while all those outside them were indirectly coordinated with it. Furthermore, in the present period of the Anti-Japanese War all organizational work and struggles in the rear areas of the anti-Japanese forces and in the enemy-occupied areas are also either directly or indirectly coordinated with the war.

"In China, armed revolution is fighting against armed counter-revolution. This is one of the peculiarities and one of the advantages of the Chinese Revolution." [3] Comrade Stalin's statement is perfectly correct and holds good equally for the Northern Expedition, the War of Agrarian Revolution, and the present Anti-Japanese War. These are all revolutionary wars waged principally by the revolutionary people against counterrevolutionaries, and they differ only as a civil war differs from a national war, a war waged by the Communist Party alone from a war waged jointly by the Kuomintang and the Communist Party. Such differences are by no means unimportant. They indicate the difference in the alignment of the main forces in the war, that is, whether the war is waged by an alliance of the workers and peasants only or by the workers, the peasants, and the bourgeoisie; they indicate the difference in the target of the war, that is, whether the war is waged against a domestic or a foreign enemy, and in the former case, against the clique of the Northern warlords or against the Kuomintang; and they also indicate that the Chinese revolutionary war is different in content at the different stages of its history. But all these wars are cases of armed revolution against armed counterrevolution, all are revolutionary wars, and all are characterized by the peculiarities and advantages of the Chinese revolution. The statement that the revolutionary war "is one of the peculiarities and one of the advantages of the Chinese revolution" fits in per-

[3] Stalin, "On the Perspectives of the Revolution in China," Eng. trans. in *Political Affairs*, New York, December, 1950, p. 29.

fectly with the conditions in China. Almost from the very beginning, the main task of the party of the Chinese proletariat has been to unite the largest possible number of allies and to organize armed struggles according to circumstances against internal or external armed counterrevolutionary forces for national and social liberation. In China, without armed struggle the proletariat and the Communist Party could not win a place for themselves or accomplish any revolutionary task.

For five or six years from its foundation in 1921 to its participation in the Northern Expedition in 1926, our party did not fully grasp this point. At that time it did not understand the supreme importance of armed struggle in China, it failed to prepare for war or organize armed forces in earnest, and it neglected the study of military strategy and tactics. During the Northern Expedition, concentrating its attention exclusively on the mass movement, it neglected to win over the armed forces, with the result that the whole mass movement collapsed the moment the Kuomintang turned reactionary. For a long time after 1927 many comrades kept on believing that the party's central task was preparation for insurrections in the cities and work in the White area. It was only after our victory in repelling the enemy's third campaign of encirclement and annihilation in 1931 that some comrades fundamentally changed their attitude on this question. But the attitude of the party as a whole did not change, and there were still some comrades who did not think as we do today.

Experience has shown that China's problems cannot be settled without armed forces. An understanding of this point will facilitate victory in the Anti-Japanese War. The fact that in the Anti-Japanese War the whole nation rises in armed resistance should teach the whole party to understand better the importance of this point, and every member of the party must be prepared to take up arms and go to the front at any moment. Our present session has decided that the party's main fields of work are in the war zones and in the enemy's rear, thus further providing an unequivocal direction for our efforts. This prescribes an excellent antidote against such tendencies among certain members as preference for the party's organizational work or mass work over study of war or participation in fighting, and among certain school authorities as neglect to encourage the students to go to the front. In most parts of our country the party's organizational work or mass work is directly linked with armed struggle, and neither is it nor can it ever be independent of or separated from the war. In some parts of our country which constitute the rear areas far away from the war zones like Yunnan, Kweichow, and Szechuan or in other parts which are now occupied by the enemy like Peiping, Tientsin, Nanking, and Shanghai, the party's organizational work and mass work are also coordinated with the war, and they can and must be adapted only to the needs of the front. In a word, the whole party must pay attention to war, study military science, and be ready to fight.

The War History of the Kuomintang

It will be instructive to examine the history of the Kuomintang and see how much attention it pays to war.

Even at the early stage when he was organizing a small revolutionary group, Sun Yat-sen staged several armed insurrections against the Manchus.[4] The period of the Chinese Revolutionary League was especially full of armed insurrections,[5] which continued until the Manchus were finally overthrown by force in the Revolution of 1911. During the period of the Chinese Revolutionary Party he carried out an armed campaign against Yuan Shih-k'ai.[6] The southward transfer of the navy,[7] the northern expedition from Kweilin[8] and the founding

[4] In 1894, Dr. Sun Yat-sen formed in Honolulu a small revolutionary organization, called the Hsing Chung Society or Society for China's Regeneration. With the support of the secret societies, he staged two armed insurrections in Kwangtung province, one at Canton in 1895 and the other at Hweichow in 1900, against the Manchu regime which was tottering after its defeat in 1895 in the Sino-Japanese War.

[5] The Chinese Revolutionary League or the T'ung Meng Society was formed in 1905 through the merging of the Hsing Chung Society (see note above) and two other anti-Manchu groups—the Hua Hsing Society or Society for Building New China and the Kuang Fu Society or Society for Shaking Off the Foreign Yoke. Being a united front organization of the bourgeoisie, the petty bourgeoisie, and a section of the anti-Manchu landed gentry, it put forward a program of bourgeois revolution advocating "the expulsion of the Manchu barbarians, the recovery of China, the establishment of a republic, and the equalization of landownership." Dr. Sun Yat-sen, cooperating with the secret societies and a section of the armed forces of the Manchu government, staged a number of armed insurrections, notably those at Pinghsiang in Kiangsi, and Liuyang and Liling in Hunan in 1906; at Hwangkang in Hupeh, Chaochow and Chinchow in Kwangtung, and at Chennan Pass in Kwangsi in 1907; at Hokow in Yunnan in 1908; and at Canton in 1911. The last was followed in the same year by the Wuchang uprising which led to the overthrow of the Manchu dynasty.

[6] In 1912, the Chinese Revolutionary League was reorganized into the Kuomintang and compromised with the clique of the Northern warlords headed by Yuan Shih-k'ai. In 1913, Yuan's troops marched southward to suppress the revolutionary forces in the provinces of Kiangsi, Anhwei, and Kwangtung, and Dr. Sun's attempts at resistance were crushed. Realizing the mistake of the Kuomintang's policy of compromise, Dr. Sun formed in 1914 in Tokyo, Japan, the Chung Hua Ke Ming Party or the Chinese Revolutionary Party, an organization separate from the Kuomintang. This new party, an anti-Yuan Shih-k'ai alliance of the political representatives of certain sections of the petty bourgeoisie and bourgeoisie, staged a minor insurrection in Shanghai in 1914. In 1915, when Yuan Shih-k'ai proclaimed himself emperor and Ts'ai Ngo and others started an expedition against Yuan, Dr. Sun took an active part in it.

[7] In 1917, Dr. Sun Yat-sen went from Shanghai to Canton at the head of a naval force which had been influenced by his revolutionary propaganda.

of the Whampoa Military Academy[9] were among Sun Yat-sen's subsequent military undertakings.

Under Sun Yat-sen's successor Chiang Kai-shek, the Kuomintang's military power reached its highest point. During all the three periods, the Northern Expedition, the civil war and the Anti-Japanese War, he has looked upon the army as his very life. The Chiang Kai-shek of the last ten years has been a counterrevolutionary. He created a huge "Central Army" for counterrevolutionary purposes. He has firmly grasped the vital point that whoever has an army has power and that war decides everything. In this respect we ought to learn from him. And in this respect both Sun Yat-sen and Chiang Kai-shek are our teachers.

Since the Revolution of 1911, all the warlords have clung to their armies for dear life; they all subscribe to the principle: "Whoever has an army has power."

T'an Yen-k'ai,[10] a clever bureaucrat who came into power several times in Hunan, was never the civil governor pure and simple but always insisted on being both the civil and the military governor. Even when he served as the Chairman of the National Government in Canton and Wuhan, he was at the same time the commander of the Second Army. There are many such warlords who understand this peculiar situation in China.

Certain political parties in China do not want an army, most important among them being the Progressive Party;[11] yet even this party knows that it cannot get posts in the government unless it has the backing of some warlord. Thus Yuan Shih-k'ai,[12] Tuan Ch-i-jui[13]

Using Kwangtung as a base and making an alliance with the clique of the Southwestern warlords, he set up a military government in opposition to the government in Peking which was controlled by the clique of the Northern warlords.

[8] In 1921, Dr. Sun Yat-sen planned a northern expedition from Kweilin, Kwangsi. But his plan was frustrated by the mutiny of his subordinate, Ch'en Chiung-ming, who was in league with the clique of the Northern warlords.

[9] Established after the reorganization of the Kuomintang in 1924 at Whampoa, near Canton by Dr. Sun Yat-sen with the help of the Chinese Communist Party and the Soviet Union. Before Chiang Kai-shek's betrayal of the revolution in 1927, the Academy was run jointly by the Kuomintang and the Communist Party. Comrades Chou En-lai, Yeh Chien-ying, Yun Tai-ying, Hsiao Ch'u-nu, and others all held responsible posts in the Academy at one time or another. Many of the cadets were members of the Communist Party or the Communist Youth League, and formed the core of the Academy.

[10] An opportunist member of the landed gentry in Hunan, who successively advocated constitutional monarchy, participated in the Revolution of 1911, and joined the Kuomintang. His career reflected the contradiction between the landlords of Hunan and the clique of the Northern warlords.

[11] A political party under the aegis of Yuan Shih-k'ai during the early days of the Republic.

[12] Head of the clique of the Northern warlords formed during the last years of the Manchu dynasty. When the Manchu regime was overthrown

and Chiang Kai-shek have one after another become its patrons, and the Political Science Group,[14] formed out of a section of the Progressive Party, has attached itself to Chiang.

A few small political parties with a short history, for instance, the Youth Party,[15] have no army, and so count for nothing in spite of all their ballyhoo.

In foreign countries no bourgeois party needs to have armed forces under its direct control. But the situation is different in China, where owing to the feudal divisions in the country, the landlord or bourgeois blocs or parties which have guns, have power, and whichever has more guns has more power. In these circumstances the party of the proletariat should also understand clearly this essential point.

Communists do not and should never contend for personal military power like Chang Kuo-t'ao; they must contend for military power for the party and for the people. As a national war of resistance is going on, we must also contend for military power for the nation. If we fall victim to infantilism on the question of military power, we shall achieve nothing. It is very difficult for the working people, who have been for several thousand years deceived and intimidated by the reactionary ruling classes, to awaken to the importance of having guns in their own hands. Now that the oppression of Japanese imperialism and the nation-wide resistance have pushed the working people into the arena of war, Communists should prove themselves the most conscientious leaders in this war. Every Communist must grasp this truth: "Political power grows out of the barrel of a gun." Our principle is: the party controls the gun, the gun will never be

---

by the Revolution of 1911, Yuan took advantage of the tendency to compromise on the part of the bourgeoisie then leading the revolution and jockeyed for the position of the president of the Republic with the support of the imperialists and on the strength of a counterrevolutionary army under his command. He formed the first government of Northern warlords representing the big landlord and big comprador classes. In 1915, he restored the imperial regime with himself on the throne and accepted the Twenty-one Demands of Japanese imperialism. An uprising in Yunnan province in December touched off a nation-wide revolt. Yuan was forced to abolish the imperial government in March, 1916, and died shortly afterwards.

[13] A henchman of Yuan Shih-k'ai and head of the Anhwei group in the clique of the Northern warlords. After Yuan's death he held power several times in the Peking government.

[14] An extremely right-wing group formed in 1916 by members of the Progressive Party and the Kuomintang. After the Northern Expedition, its pro-Japanese members collaborated with Chiang Kai-shek and helped him to build up a counterrevolutionary regime.

[15] A group of fascist politicians formed the Chinese Etatiste Youth League, later renamed the Chinese Youth Party. Subsidized by the imperialists and the reactionary cliques in power, they were professional anti-Communist and anti-Soviet counterrevolutionaries. The word Etatistes is used to translate "Kuochia-ists" to distinguish them from the Kuomintang which is usually translated "the Nationalist Party." In theory the Chinese Etatistes also laid more emphasis on the state than on the people.

allowed to control the party. But it is also true that with guns in our hands we can build up the party organizations, as the Eighth Route Army has built up a powerful party organization in northern China. We can also train cadres, establish schools, develop culture, and promote mass movements. Everything in Yenan has been brought about by the gun. Anything can grow out of the barrel of a gun. According to the Marxist theory of the state, the army is the main component of the political power of the state. Whoever wants to seize state power and to keep it must have a strong army. Some people ridicule us as advocates of the omnipotence of war; yes, we are advocates of the omnipotence of revolutionary war, and this is good, not bad—indeed it is a Marxist concept. With the help of guns the Russian Communists brought about socialism. We shall bring about a democratic republic. Experience in the class struggle in the era of imperialism shows us that the working class and the laboring people cannot defeat the armed bourgeois and landlords unless they have guns, and in this sense we can even say that the whole world can be reshaped only with the gun. We are for the abolition of war, we do not want war; but war can only be abolished through war and, to get rid of the gun, we must first grasp it in our own hands.

The War History of the Chinese Communist Party

Although for a period of three or four years, from 1921 when the Chinese Communist Party was founded, to 1924 when the First National Congress of the Kuomintang took place, our party failed to grasp the importance of making immediate preparations for war and organizing an army, and although in the period of 1924–1927 or even later, it still lacked adequate understanding of this question, yet since 1924, after taking part in running the Whampoa Military Academy, it entered a new stage and began to see the importance of military affairs. Having helped the Kuomintang in the war of Kwangtung and the Northern Expedition, the party got hold of some armed forces.[16] Having learned a bitter lesson from the failure of the revolution, the party organized the Nanchang uprising,[17] the Autumn

[16] Comrade Yeh T'ing commanded an independent regiment during the Northern Expedition of 1926. With Communists as its nucleus the regiment became a famous fighting unit, and was first enlarged into the Twenty-fourth Division after the capture of Wuchang by the revolutionary army and then into the Eleventh Army after the Nanchang uprising.

[17] The Communist Party organized the famous uprising on August 1, 1927, in Nanchang, Kiangsi, to combat the counterrevolution of Chiang Kai-shek and Wang Ching-wei and to carry on the revolution of 1924–1927. With Comrades Chou En-lai, Chu Teh, Ho Lung and Yeh T'ing as the leaders, an armed force of more than 30,000 took part in the uprising. The armed forces

Harvest uprising,[18] and the Canton uprising,[19] and thus ushered in the new period of the founding of the Red Army. That was the crucial period in which our party came to understand thoroughly the importance of the army. If in this period there had been no Red Army or the battles fought by it, that is, if the Communist Party had adopted the liquidationism of Ch'en Tu-hsiu, the Anti-Japanese War would never have been started or, at any rate, kept up for any length of time.

The emergency meeting of the Party Central Committee on August 7, 1927, combated political Right opportunism and enabled the party to take a big stride forward. The Central Committee's plenary session of January, 1931 (the fourth since the Sixth National Congress), though nominally combating political "left" opportunism, in actual fact continued the same mistaken policy. Although the two meetings differed in their content and historical role, neither paid much attention to the problems of war and strategy, and this showed that the party did not yet center its work around war. After the Central Committee moved into the Red areas in 1933, a fundamental change was brought about in this respect, but mistakes in principle were committed in military as well as all other major problems with the result that we suffered serious losses in the revolutionary war. On the other hand, in response to the war situation, the Tsunyi meeting of 1935 gave first priority to the question of war and fought mainly against military opportunism. So far we can confidently claim that in the struggles of the past 17 years, the Chinese Communist Party has forged both a firm Marxist political line and a firm Marxist military line. We have been able to apply Marxism to solve both political and military problems; we have trained, as a powerful framework, large numbers of cadres capable of running the party and the state, and also large numbers of cadres capable of running the army. These

---

withdrew from Nanchang on August 5 as originally planned, but suffered a defeat when approaching Chaochow and Swatow in Kwangtung province. Led by Comrades Chu Teh, Ch'en Yi and Lin Piao, a part of the troops later fought their way to the Chingkang mountains and joined forces with the First Division of the First Army of the Workers' and Peasants' Revolutionary Army under Comrade Mao Tse-tung.

[18] In September, 1927, the people's armed forces of Siushui, Pinghsiang, Pingkiang, and Liuyang on the Hunan-Kiangsi border staged this famous uprising during the autumn harvest season under the leadership of Comrade Mao Tse-tung. These forces, organized as the First Division of the First Army of the Workers' and Peasants' Revolutionary Army, were led by Comrade Mao Tse-tung to the Chingkang mountains and established a revolutionary base there.

[19] Under the leadership of the Kwangtung Provincial Committee of the Chinese Communist Party, the workers and revolutionary soldiers in Canton jointly staged an uprising and set up a people's regime on December 11, 1927. They fought valiantly against the counterrevolutionary forces directly supported by imperialism, and failed only because the odds were overwhelming.

are the flowers of revolution watered by the blood of countless martyrs, a glory that belongs not only to the Chinese Communist Party and the Chinese people, but also to the Communist Parties and the peoples of the whole world. Since in the whole world there are only three armies which belong to the proletariat and the laboring people, led by the Communist Parties of the Soviet Union, of China, and of Spain, and since the Communist Parties in other countries have as yet no military experience, our army and our military experience are all the more to be treasured.

To carry through the present Anti-Japanese War to victory, it is extremely important to expand and consolidate the Eighth Route Army, the New Fourth Army, and all the guerrilla forces led by our party. On this principle the party should dispatch to the front a sufficient number of its best members and cadres. Everything must contribute to victory at the front: the organizational task must be subordinated to this political task.

Changes in the Party's Military Strategy in the Civil War and the National War

The changes in the party's military strategy are worth studying. I shall deal separately with the course of events in the civil war and in the national war.

As concerns startegy, the course of the civil war can be roughly divided into two periods. In the first period, the principal form was guerrilla warfare and in the second, regular warfare. But this regular warfare was of the Chinese type, regular only in the concentration of forces for a mobile war and a certain degree of centralization and planning in command and organization, while in other aspects it retained a guerrilla and primitive character; it cannot be classed with wars fought by foreign armies, or even with those fought by the Kuomintang forces. It was in a sense only guerrilla warfare on a higher level.

So far as our party's military tasks are concerned, the course of the Anti-Japanese War can also be roughly divided into two strategic periods. In the first period, which includes the stages of strategic defensive and strategic stalemate, the principal form is and will be guerrilla warfare and, in the second period, which is the stage of strategic counteroffensive, it will be regular warfare. However, this guerrilla warfare differs considerably in content from that in the first period of the civil war, because we now have what is to a certain degree a regular armed force, the Eighth Route Army, carrying out in dispersion the task of the guerrillas; and the regular warfare in the Anti-Japanese War will also be different from that in the second period of the civil war, because we can expect that, given up-to-date equipment, a great change will take place both in the army and in its operations. The army will attain a high degree of centralization and organization; the operations, losing much of their guerrilla character, will attain a high degree of regularity; what is now primitive will become more advanced, and the peculiar Chinese type of war will be changed into a type common to all countries. That will be our task in the stage of strategic counteroffensive.

Thus we see that in the two series of events, the civil war and the Anti-Japanese War, or in the four strategic periods, there will be altogether three changes of strategy. The first was the change from guerrilla warfare to regular warfare in the civil war. The second was the change from regular warfare in the civil war to guerrilla warfare in the Anti-Japanese War. The third will be the change from guerrilla warfare to regular warfare in the Anti-Japanese War.

In introducing the first of these three changes we encountered great difficulties. We had a twofold task. On the one hand we had to combat the rightist tendency of localism and guerrillaism, which clung to guerrilla habits and refused to advance towards regular warfare, a tendency arising out of a failure on the part of our cadres to appreciate fully the changes in the enemy situation and our own tasks. In the Central Red Area, this tendency was gradually corrected only after arduous ideological education. On the other hand, we had also to combat the leftist tendency of overcentralization and adventurism, of overemphasizing regularization, a tendency which arose because some of the leading cadres overestimated the enemy, set themselves too big a task, and mechanically applied the lessons derived from wars fought by foreign countries regardless of actual conditions. The tendency was corrected in the Central Red Area only at the cost of three long years (up to the Tsunyi meeting) of enormous suffering and heavy casualties. This was one of the achievements of the Tsunyi meeting.

The second change took place in the autumn of 1937 at the juncture of two different wars after the Lukouchiao Incident. At that time we faced a new enemy, Japanese imperialism, and had as our ally our former enemy, the Kuomintang, who still harbored hostile intentions, while the theater of war was the whole expanse of northern China which was temporarily the front of our army, but was soon to become for a long time the enemy's rear. Introduced in such unusual circumstances, our change of strategy was an extremely serious one. Under such unusual circumstances, we had to transform the regular army of the past into guerrilla units, that is, in respect to their operation in dispersed formations, not their organization or discipline, and the mobile warfare of the past into guerrilla warfare so that we could adapt ourselves to our new task and deal with the new enemy. But such a change, to all appearances a step backward, was necessarily very difficult to effect. Both underestimation and excessive fear of the enemy, tendencies likely to occur at such a juncture, did actually occur in the Kuomintang ranks. When the Kuomintang changed over from civil war to national war, it incurred many unnecessary losses mainly because it underestimated the enemy, and at the same time it felt an excessive fear of him, too; the conduct of Han Fu-ch'u or Liu Chih[20] is an example of the latter tendency. But we effected the change fairly smoothly, both avoiding losses and achieving great successes. These successes were gained because, in spite of a serious controversy between a section of the army cadres and the Central Committee, the great bulk of our cadres accepted in time the correct guidance of the Central Committee and skillfully sized up the actual situation. We can easily realize that the change has an extremely important bearing on keeping up, developing, and bringing to a victorious conclusion the Anti-Japanese War as a whole and also on the future of the Chinese Communist Party, if we call to mind the historical significance of the anti-Japanese guerrilla war for the future of China's national liberation. In its unusually extensive and protracted character China's anti-Japanese guerrilla war is without precedent, not only in the East, but perhaps in the whole history of mankind.

The third change, the change from guerrilla warfare to regular warfare against Japan, depends upon the war's future developments, which will most probably confront us with new conditions and new problems, and we need not discuss them now.

The Strategic Role of the Anti-Japanese Guerrilla War

As regards the Anti-Japanese War as a whole, regular warfare is the principal and guerrilla warfare the supplementary form, because regular warfare alone can decide the outcome of the war. As regards the country as a whole, of the three strategic stages, defensive, stalemate, and counteroffensive, in the entire process of the Anti-Japanese War, the first and the last are stages in which regular warfare is the principal and guerrilla warfare the supplementary form. Only in the intermediate stage, when the enemy seeks to hold on to the occupied areas and we, while making preparations for the counteroffenive, cannot yet actually launch it, will guerrilla warfare become the principal form and regular warfare the supplementary form; although this stage may be the longest, it is only one of the three stages in the whole war. Thus taking the war as a whole, regular warfare is the principal and

[20] Han Fu-ch'u, a Kuomintang warlord, was for many years the ruler of Shantung. When the Japanese invaders, after occupying Peking and Tientsin in 1937, advanced southward along the Tientsin-Pukow railway, Han took flight all the way from Shantung to Honan without fighting a single battle. Liu Chih, who commanded Chiang Kai-shek's personal troops in defence of the Paoting area in Hopei, also fled before the Japanese without firing a shot.

guerrilla warfare the supplementary form. If we do not understand this, if we do not see that regular warfare is decisive, if we neglect to build up a regular army or to study regular warfare and its direction, we shall not be able to defeat Japan. This is one aspect of the matter.

Guerrilla warfare, however, does play an important strategic role throughout the war. If we drop guerrilla warfare altogether, if we neglect to build up guerrilla units and guerrilla armies or to study guerrilla warfare and its direction, we shall not be able to defeat Japan. The reason is as follows: since the greater part of China's territory will have become the enemy's rear, unless guerrilla war is spread to the widest extent and kept up very stubbornly, the enemy, entrenched in the occupied area absolutely safe from attacks in the back, will launch increasingly fierce offensives and inflict heavy losses on our main forces on the main front, and we will find it very difficult to bring about a stalemate or even to keep up the armed resistance; even if things do not turn out as badly as that, there will be unfavorable results, such as inadequate strength built up for and lack of concerted action in our counteroffensive and the possibility of the enemy making good his losses. If there is no widespread and stubborn guerrilla war to remove these conditions when they arise, it will also be impossible for us to defeat Japan. Hence, though guerrilla warfare plays only a supplementary role in the war as a whole, it does play an extremely important role in strategy. To resist Japan and yet to neglect guerrilla warfare is undoubtedly a grave error. This is the other aspect of the matter.

Given one condition, a big territory, guerrilla warfare can be carried on anywhere; hence there was guerrilla warfare even in the past. But guerrilla warfare can be kept up only under the leadership of the Communist Party. That is why most guerrilla wars in the past ended in failure, and only in the big countries of modern times where Communist Parties have emerged, like the Soviet Union during its civil war and China at present, can they achieve victories. In the Anti-Japanese War, a division of labor between the Kuomintang and the Communist Party is necessary and proper under the present general conditions; and as a matter of mutual need, coordination and mutual assistance, the Kuomintang should carry on regular warfare on the main front while the Communist Party carries on guerrilla warfare in the enemy's rear.

From this it can be readily understood how important and necessary it is to change our party's strategic line from regular warfare in the second period of the civil war to guerrilla warfare in the first period of the Anti-Japanese War. The advantages of this change can be summed up in the following eighteen points: (1) reducing the areas occupied by the enemy; (2) expanding the base areas of our own forces; (3) in the stage of defense, pinning down the enemy by fighting in coordination with the operations on the main front; (4) in the stage of stalemate, facilitating the rehabilitation of the troops on the main front by firmly holding the base areas in the enemy's rear; (5) in the stage of the counteroffensive, taking coordinated actions with the main front to recover lost territory; (6) expanding our forces in the most speedy and effective manner; (7) expanding the Communist Party to the greatest possible extent so that a party branch can be organized in every village; (8) extending the mass movements as much as possible so that all the people behind the enemy lines, except those in his strongholds, can be organized; (9) creating organs of anti-Japanese democratic political power over the widest possible area; (10) developing extensively anti-Japanese cultural and educational work; (11) improving living conditions of the people over the widest possible area; (12) accelerating most effectively the disintegration of the enemy troops; (13) keeping up the spirit of the people and heightening the morale of our troops over the widest areas and with the most enduring effect; (14) giving the most extensive help possible to friendly armies and parties so that they become progressive; (15) adapting ourselves to the situation in which the enemy is strong and we are weak, so as to reduce our losses to a minimum and win all possible victories; (16) adapting ourselves to the fact that ours is a big country and the enemy's is small, so as to inflict the maximum losses on the enemy and reduce his victories to a minimum; (17) training large numbers of leading cadres in the most speedy and effective manner; and (18) solving the problem of provisioning in the most convenient way.

It is also beyond doubt that in the long course of struggle guerrilla units and guerrilla warfare should not remain as they are but develop towards an advanced stage, so that they will gradually change into a regular army and regular warfare. We shall, through guerrilla warfare, build up our strength and become a decisive factor in crushing Japanese imperialism.

Pay Attention to the Study of Military Problems

The conflict between two hostile armies can only be resolved by war, and China's survival or extinction depends on her victory or defeat. Hence there must not be a moment's delay in our study of military theory, of strategy and tactics, and of political work in the army. Although our study of tactics is inadequate, comrades engaged in military work have in the last ten years achieved much and have made a number of discoveries based on Chinese conditions; the only weakness is that a general summing-up is still lacking. So far only a few have taken up the study of the problem of strategy and the theory of war. Our study in political work has yielded first-rate results and, in the wealth of our experience and the number of our excellent innovations, we surpass any country except the Soviet Union; but here again the weakness is that there is no adequate synthesis or systematization. To meet the demands of the party and the whole country the popularization of military knowledge is an urgent task. We must now pay attention to all these things, but the theory of war and strategy is the key to everything. I think it is necessary to attract and direct the attention of the whole party to the study of military problems through the study of military theory.

MAO ON "MAOISM"

On the New Democracy by Mao Tse-tung, Yenan, 1939. Published in *Chinese Culture*, 1940.

Mao Tse-tung first fully—and rather redundantly—expounded his analysis of the theoretical foundations of Chinese Communism in a speech lasting eight hours, under the title, On the New Democracy. Then and since, this overly repetitive document has received wide circulation; upon it rests a good deal of the claim that Mao is an innovator of Communist doctrine.

The question of whether Mao is or is not a theoretician of the same stature as Lenin or even Stalin is, strange to say, a paradox. On the one hand, Mao is considered as such by his comrades, who, indeed, sometimes even place Maoism above Leninism and Stalinism as a specific subspecies of Marxism. Yet, in the current controversy between Peking and the Kremlin, one of the recurrent themes is the claim by both camps to being the true heirs of Marxism-Leninism—in short, to being the better or purer Communists. Thus, Mao is presented as being the truest, most faithful disciple of Marx and Lenin and as being superior to them. The choice of which element of the paradox is to be stressed by the Chinese propagandists in a specific situation seems to be determined more by the tactical advantages to be derived from one or the other than by philosophical commitment.

By the end of 1939, when On the New Democracy was written, the CCP had been firmly established for over three years in and around Yenan in the Northwest province of Shensi. Harassment by Chiang and his Nationalists had ceased to be a problem, thanks to the common enemy: Japan. In 1936, Chiang Kai-shek had been captured and held for about ten days by the Manchurian war lord Chang Hsueh-liang (the "Young Marshall"). For a time, it appeared that this was the end of Chiang, yet he lost neither his life nor his leadership of the nation, largely due to Chinese Communist intervention. Out of this episode came the catalytic agent necessary for the establishment of the united front against Japan. Meanwhile the Kremlin leaders, though having directed such a united front strategy from 1935 onwards, continued to play their own game—the Hitler-Stalin non-aggression pact being duplicated in Asia by a similar treaty between the Soviet Union and Japan.

Despite the USSR's seeming ambivalence toward Japan, Mao nonetheless appeared to carry out Moscow's orders, paying obeisance to the good Communist's responsibility of sacrificing all to come to the aid of "the one socialist country (the Soviet Union) and the international proletariat." In On the New Democracy the world outside China divides neatly into categories of friend and foe, with the Soviet Union occupying the place of honor as finest friend.

But, while singling out the Soviet Union as the principal ally of China's Communists, Mao continues his independence in analyzing the tactics to be pursued by the CCP in gaining power. Recurrent is the theme that it is the peasants upon whom the greatest reliance must be placed. Thus, there is a consistent thread in the development of Mao's strategy beginning with the Hunan "Report."

The picture that emerges from On the New Democracy is one of the CCP relying for counsel and guidance on the Kremlin in international affairs, but emphasizing the unique circumstances of the domestic situation in China. In retrospect it is apparent even at this date—late 1939, early 1940—that the Chinese Communists are determined that they—and they alone—will control the destiny of the CCP.

Whither China?

Since the War of Resistance began, people throughout the country have felt that at last they can see the way forward, and instead of knitting their brows and casting down their eyes in despair, are now cheerful and hopeful. Recently, however, the air has been once more filled with the dust and din of compromise and anticommunism and the people have again been thrown into confusion. Among the first to be affected are the cultural workers and young students, who are more susceptible than others. Again the questions are being asked: What is to be done? Whither China? On the occasion of the publication of *Chinese Culture*,[1] it may therefore be useful to explain the trends of Chinese politics and Chinese culture. Being a layman on the subject of culture, I hope to make a study of it and have just begun to do so. Fortunately many comrades in Yenan have written exhaustive articles on this subject, so my sketchy contribution can only serve as the beating of gongs and drums that precedes theatrical performances. Our observations, which may contain a useful hint or two in a host of suggestions, serve only as a brickbat thrown to induce the nation's advanced cultural workers to cast their precious stones, and I hope that they will join us in the discussion so as to reach correct conclusions and meet the needs of our nation. The scientific approach is to "seek truth from facts," and the presumptuous attitude summed up in

[1] A magazine founded in January, 1940, in Yenan, its first number featured this article.

sayings like "I'm always right" and "I'm telling you" can never be of any help. Our nation is in grave distress, and only a scientific approach and a sense of responsibility can lead it along the road to liberation. There is only one truth, and the criterion for settling the question as to who has really discovered it is to be settled not by any boastful claim, but by objective practice. The revolutionary practice of millions of people is the only yardstick for measuring truth. It is in this spirit, I think, that *Chinese Culture* is published.

To Build a New China

For many years we Communists have struggled for China's political and economic revolution and also for her cultural revolution; our aim is to build a new society and a new state for the Chinese nation. This new society and new state will have new politics, a new economy, and also a new culture. In other words, we want to change a politically oppressed and economically exploited China into a politically free and economically prosperous China, and also to change a China which has been kept ignorant and backward under the sway of the old culture into a China which will be enlightened and progressive under the sway of a new culture. In short, we want to build a new China. To build a new culture of the Chinese nation is our aim in the cultural sphere.

China's Historical Features

We want to build a new culture of the Chinese nation, but what kind of culture is it?

Any given culture as an ideological form reflects the politics and economy of a given society, and in turn has a tremendous influence and effect upon them; economy is the base of society and politics the concentrated expression of this economy.[2] This is our fundamental view on the relation of culture to politics and economy and on the relation between politics and economy. Hence, primarily given forms of politics and economy determine a given form of culture, and secondarily the latter in turn influences and affects the former. "It is not the consciousness of men that determines their being," says Marx, "but, on the contrary, their social being that determines their consciousness."[3] Again he says: "The philosophers have *interpreted* the

[2] See Lenin, "The Trade Unions, the Present Situation and the Mistakes of Comrade Trotsky; *Selected Works*, Eng. ed., New York, 1943, Vol. IX, pp. 17, 54.

[3] Marx, "Preface to a Contribution to the Critique of Political Economy," *Selected Works*, Eng. ed., New York, n.d., Vol. I, p. 356.

world in various ways; the point however is to *change* it." [4] These scientific formulations for the first time in human history gave the correct solution to the problem of the relation between consciousness and being, and constituted the fundamental viewpoint of the dynamic revolutionary theory of knowledge as the reflection of reality which was later profoundly expounded by Lenin. This fundamental viewpoint must be borne in mind in our discussion of China's cultural problems.

It is then quite clear that the reactionary elements of the old culture of the Chinese nation which we wish to eliminate cannot be separated from its old politics and old economy, while its new culture which we want to build cannot be separated from its new politics and new economy. The old politics and old economy of the Chinese nation form the basis of its old culture, and its new politics and new economy will form the basis of its new culture.

What are the old politics and old economy of the Chinese nation? And what is the old culture of the Chinese nation?

From the Chou and Ch'in dynasties onwards, China was a feudal society, with feudal politics and a feudal economy. The predominant culture which was a reflection of these politics and economy was feudal.

*　　*　　*

What, then, are the new politics and new economy of the Chinese nation? And what is the new culture of the Chinese nation?

In the historical course of the Chinese revolution there must be two steps, first, the democratic revolution, and second, the socialist revolution: these are two revolutionary stages different in character. The democracy in question belongs no longer to the old category, it is no longer the old democracy; it belongs to the new category, it is New Democracy.

Thus we can say that the new politics of the Chinese nation are the politics of New Democracy; the new economy of the Chinese nation, the economy of New Democracy; and the new culture of the Chinese nation, the culture of New Democracy.

*　　*　　*

The Chinese Revolution as Part of the World Revolution

The historical feature of the Chinese revolution consists of two steps, democracy and socialism; the first step is no longer democracy in a general sense, but democracy of the Chinese type, a new and

[4] Marx, "Theses on Feuerbach,' xi, *op. cit.*, p. 473.

special type—New Democracy. How, then, has this historical feature come into existence? Has it been in existence for the past hundred years, or is it of only recent birth?

If we make a study of the development of China and of the world we shall see that this historical feature did not emerge as a consequence of the Opium War, but began to take shape only after the first imperialist world war and the October Revolution in Russia. Let us now study the process of its formation.

Evidently, the colonial, semicolonial, and semifeudal character of present-day Chinese Society requires two steps in the Chinese revolution. The first step is to change a colonial, semicolonial, and semifeudal society into an independent, democratic society. The second is to push the revolution further and build a socialist society. The Chinese revolution at present is taking the first step.

The preparatory period for taking the first step began with the Opium War in 1840 when China began to change from a feudal into a semicolonial and semifeudal society.

*　　*　　*

A change, however, occurred in the Chinese bourgeois-democratic revolution after the outbreak of the first imperialist world war in 1914 and the founding of a socialist state on one-sixth of the globe in consequence of the October Revolution in Russia in 1917.

Before these events, the Chinese bourgeois-democratic revolution belonged to the category of the old bourgeois-democratic world revolution, and was part of it.

After these events, the Chinese bourgeois-democratic revolution changed its character and came within the category of the new bouregois-democratic revolution and, so far as the revolutionary front is concerned, formed part of the proletarian-socialist world revolution.

Why? Because the first imperialist world war and the first victorious socialist revolution, the October Revolution, have changed the course of world history and marked a new historical era.

This is an era in which the capitalist front has collapsed in one part —one-sixth—of the world and fully revealed its decadence in other parts; those parts still under capitalism cannot get along without depending more than ever on the colonies and semicolonies; a socialist state has come into being and has declared itself willing to help the liberation movement of all colonies and semicolonies; the proletariat of the capitalist countries is increasingly freeing itself from the social-imperialist influence of the Social-Democratic Parties and has also declared itself in support of the liberation movement of the colonies and semicolonies. In this era, any revolution that takes place in a colony or semicolony against imperialism, that is, against the international bourgeoisie and international capitalism, belongs no longer to the old category of bourgeois-democratic world revolution, but to a new category, and is no longer part of the old bourgeois or capitalist world revolution, but part of the new world revolution, the proletarian-socialist world revolution. Such revolutionary colonies and semicolonies should no longer be regarded as allies of the counter-revolutionary front of world capitalism: they have become allies of the revolutionary front of world socialism.

* * *

As early as 1918, Stalin wrote in an article commemorating the 1st anniversary of the October Revolution:

The great world-wide significance of the October Revolution chiefly consists in the fact that:
1. It has widened the scope of the national question and converted it from the particular question of combating national oppression in Europe into the general question of emancipating the oppressed peoples, colonies and semicolonies from imperialism.
2. It has opened up wide possibilities for their emancipation and the right paths towards it, has thereby greatly facilitated the cause of the emancipation of the oppressed peoples of the West and the East, and has drawn them into the common current of the victorious struggle against imperialism.
3. It has thereby erected a bridge between the socialist West and the enslaved East, having created a new front of revolutions against world imperialism, extending from the proletarians of the West, through the Russian revolution, to the oppressed peoples of the East.[5]
Since writing this article, Stalin has again and again expounded the theory that revolutions in colonies and semicolonies have departed from the old category and become part of the proletarian-socialist revolution.

* * *

Today the Chinese revolution assumes an even greater significance. This is a time when the world is being plunged more and more deeply into the Second World War by the economic and political crises of capitalism; when the Soviet Union has reached the period of transition from socialism to communism, and is now capable of leading and helping the proletariat and oppressed nations of the world in their fight against imperialist war and capitalist reaction; when the proletariat of the capitalist countries is preparing to overthrow capitalism and establish socialism; and when China's proletariat, peasantry, intelligentsia, and other sections of the petty bourgeoisie have become a mighty independent political force under the leadership of the Chinese Communist Party. At such a juncture, are we not right in claiming that the Chinese revolution has assumed a greater signifi-

[5] Stalin, *Works*, Eng. ed., Moscow, 1953, Vol. IV, pp. 169–170.

cance in the world? I think we are. The Chinese revolution has certainly become a very important part of the world revolution.

* * *

New-Democratic Politics

* * *

It is quite evident that whoever in China can lead the people to overthrow the imperialist and feudal forces will win the people's confidence, because these forces, especially imperialism, are the mortal enemies of the people. Today, whoever can lead the people to drive out Japanese imperialism and carry out democratic policies will be the saviour of the people. History has proved that the Chinese bourgeoisie is incapable of fulfilling this responsibility, which consequently falls upon the shoulders of the proletariat.

Therefore, in all circumstances, the proletariat, the peasantry, the intelligentsia, and other sections of the petty bourgeoisie in China are the basic forces which decide China's fate. These classes, some already awakened and others on the point of awakening, will necessarily become the basic components of the state structure and the structure of political power of the democratic republic of China, with the proletariat as the leading force. The democratic republic of China which we now want to establish can only be a democratic republic under the joint dictatorship of all antiimperialist and antifeudal people led by the proletariat, that is, a new democratic republic, or a republic of the genuinely revolutionary new Three People's Principles with the three cardinal policies.

While different from the old European-American form of capitalist republic under bourgeois dictatorship which is now out of date, this new-democratic republic is also different from the socialist republic of the type of the U.S.S.R., the republic of the dictatorship of the proletariat. The socialist republic is already flourishing in the Soviet Union, and will be established in all the capitalist countries and undoubtedly become the dominant form in the structure of state and political power in all industrially advanced countries but, during a given historical period, it is not yet suitable for the revolutions in colonial and semicolonial countries. Therefore a third form of state must be adopted by the revolutions in colonial and semicolonial countries during a given historical period, namely, the new-democratic republic. This is the form for a given historical period and therefore a transitional form, but it is the necessary form to which there is no alternative.

The multifarious types of state system in the world can be reduced to three basic kinds according to the class character of their political power: (1) republics under bourgeois dictatorship; (2) republics under the dictatorship of the proletariat; and (3) republics under the joint dictatorship of several revolutionary classes.

The first kind includes the old democratic states. Today, after the outbreak of the second imperialist war, there is no longer even a trace of democracy in many of the capitalist countries, which have come under or are coming under the bloody militarist dictatorship of the bourgeoisie. Certain countries under the joint dictatorship of the landlords and the bourgeoisie can be classed with this kind.

The second kind exists in the Soviet Union and conditions for its birth are ripening in all capitalist countries. In the future it will become the. dominant form throughout the world for a certain period.

The third kind is the transitional form of state to be adopted in revolutions ·in colonial and semicolonial countries. Of course, revolutions in different colonial and semicolonial countries necessarily have certain different characteristics, but these are only minor differences within a general framework of uniformity.

*　　*　　*

New-Democratic Economy

We must establish in China a republic politically and economically new-democratic.

In this republic big banks and big industrial and commercial enterprises shall be state-owned.

Enterprises such as banks, railways, and airlines, whether Chinese-owned or foreign-owned, which are monopolistic in character or too big for private management, shall be operated by the state so that private capital cannot control the livelihood of the people: this is the main principle of the restriction of capital.

This is another solemn statement in the Manifesto of the First National Congress of the Kuomintang during the period of the Kuomintang-Communist cooperation, and is the correct objective for the economic structure of the new-democratic republic. The state-owned enterprises in the new-democratic republic under the leadership of the proletariat will be socialist in character and constitute the leading force in the national economy as a whole, but the republic will neither confiscate other forms of capitalist private property nor forbid the development of capitalist production that "cannot control the livelihood of the people," for China's economy is still very backward.

The republic will by certain necessary measures confiscate the land of landlords and distribute it to those peasants having no land or only a little land, carry out Dr. Sun Yat-sen's slogan of "land to the tillers," abolish feudal relations in the rural areas, and turn the land into the private property of the peasants. In the rural areas, the economic activities of rich peasants will be tolerated. This is the line of equalization of landownership. The correct slogan for this line is land to the tillers. In this stage, socialist agriculture is in general not yet to be established, though various types of cooperatives developed on the basis of land to the tillers will contain elements of socialism.

China's economy must develop along the path of restriction of capital and equalization of landownership; it must not be "monopolized by a few"; we must never permit the few capitalists and landlords to control the livelihood of the people, or establish a capitalist society of the European-American type, or allow the old semifeudal society to remain. Whoever dares to go against this line will certainly not succeed, and will only be dashing his head against a wall.

Such are the internal economic relations which a revolutionary China, an anti-Japanese China, must and inevitably will establish.

This is new-democratic economy.

And new-democratic politics is the concentrated expression of such new-democratic economy.

Bourgeois Dictatorship Impossible

Such a republic, with its new-democratic politics and new-democratic economy, is approved by over 90 percent of our people; there is no alternative road.

Can we take the road leading to a capitalist society under bourgeois dictatorship? To be sure, that was the old road taken by the European-American bourgeoisie, but neither the international nor the domestic situation allows China to take it.

*   *   *

All the imperialist powers in the world are our enemies; so if China wants independence she can never attain it without the aid of the socialist state and the international proletariat. That is to say, she cannot attain it unless she gets assistance from the Soviet Union and support, in the form of anticapitalist struggles, from the proletariat of Japan, Britain, the United States, France, Germany, and Italy. Although the victory of the Chinese revolution does not necessarily depend upon the victory of all or some of the revolutions in Japan, Britain, the United States, France, Germany, and Italy, there is no doubt that we can win victory only with the added strength of the proletariat of these countries. In particular, aid from the Soviet Union is an absolutely indispensable condition for China's final victory in the War of Resistance. Refuse Soviet aid and the revolution will fail.

Are not the lessons of the anti-Soviet campaigns after 1927[6] particularly obvious? The world today is in a new era of revolutions and wars, an era when capitalism is definitely dying and socialism is definitely flourishing. Under such conditions, is it not utterly fantastic to want to set up a capitalist society under bourgeois dictatorship in China after having defeated imperialism and feudalism?

* * *

We hope that China's anti-Japanese united front will be maintained and that, with the cooperation of all the people, instead of the monopoly of a single clique, our cause against Japan will be victorious; this is the only good policy, any other policy is bad. This is the sincere advice of us Communists; do not blame us for not having warned you.

"If there is food, let all share it." This old Chinese saying contains much truth. Since all must fight when there is an enemy, then let all eat when there is food, let all be employed when there is work to do, and let all study when there are books to read. Such attitudes as expressed in "I alone must eat the whole cake" and "nobody can harm me" are merely old tricks of feudal lords and will never do in the 1940s.

We Communists will never exclude anyone who is revolutionary; we shall uphold the united front and persist in a long-term cooperation with all those classes, strata, political parties, and groups and individuals who are willing to fight Japan to the end. But if certain other people want to exclude the Communist Party, that will not do; if they want to split the united front, that will not do either. China must keep on fighting Japan, uniting and making progress: whoever tries to capitulate, to cause splits, or to move backward will not be tolerated by us.

"Left" Phrase-Mongering Refuted

If the road to capitalism under bourgeois dictatorship is not to be taken, is it possible then to take the road to socialism under proletarian dictatorship?

No, that is also impossible.

At present the revolution is undoubtedly taking the first step, and in the future it will advance to the second step, to socialism. It is true that only when China has entered the socialist era will her people

[6] On December 13, 1927, the Kuomintang government murdered the Soviet vice-consul in Canton and issued the next day the order to break off relations with Russia, closing down all the Soviet consulates and commercial establishments. In August 1929, Chiang Kai-shek, under the instigation of the imperialists, ordered the Kuomintang troops in the Northeast to commit acts of provocation against the Soviet Union, which resulted in armed clashes.

attain real happiness. But today is not yet the time to introduce socialism. The present task of the revolution in China is to fight imperialism and feudalism; and socialism is out of the question until this task is completed. Two steps have to be taken in the Chinese revolution: first, New Democracy, then socialism. Moreover, the first step will take quite a long time and cannot be accomplished overnight. We are not Utopians, and we cannot depart from the actual conditions confronting us.

* * *

[There are those who have] been taken in by the "theory of a single revolution" and by the purely fanciful notion of accomplishing both the political revolution and the social revolution at one stroke, not understanding that our revolution is divided into stages, that we can only proceed from one stage to another and that there is no such thing as accomplishing both at one stroke. Such a view is also very harmful, for it confuses the steps to be taken in the revolution and weakens the effort directed towards the present task. It is correct and fits in with the Marxist theory of development of the revolution to say that of the two revolutionary stages the first provides the conditions for the second and that the two must be consecutive without an intervening stage of bourgeois dictatorship. It is however a Utopian view, unacceptable to true revolutionaries, that the democratic revolution has not its specific task to be accomplished during a definite period of time, and that this task can be merged and carried out simultaneously with what is of necessity a future task, that is, the socialist task, thus accomplishing both at one stroke.

The Die-Hards Refuted

Next, the bourgeois die-hards come forward and say: "Well, since you Communists have postponed the socialist social system until a later stage, and since you have declared, 'The Three People's Principles being what China needs today, our Party pledges itself to fight for their complete realization,' then tuck away your communism for the time being." A frantic clamor has recently been made with this sort of argument, expressed in the slogan "one doctrine." Such clamor essentially represents the bourgeois despotism of the die-hards. However, we may, out of courtesy, merely call it a complete lack of common sense.

Communism is at once the complete proletarian ideological system and a new social system. Different from any other ideological system or social system, it is the most complete, the most progressive, the most revolutionary and the most rational system since human history began. The ideological system and social system of feudalism have a place only in the museum of history. The ideological system and social system of capitalism have also become museum pieces in one part of the world, in the Soviet Union, while in other countries they resemble "a person on the brink of death sinking fast like the sun setting beyond the western hills," [7] and they too will soon be relegated to the museum. On the other hand, only the communist ideological system and social system enjoy perpetual youth and are sweeping the world with the momentum of a landslide and the power of a thunderbolt. The introduction of scientific communism into China has broadened the people's outlook and transformed the features of the Chinese revolution. Without the guidance of communism, the democratic revolution in China cannot succeed, to say nothing of the later stage which follows it. This is the reason why the bourgeois die-hards are so noisily demanding that communism be tucked away. But it must not be tucked away; for once communism is tucked away, China will be doomed. Today the whole world depends on communism for its salvation, and China is no exception.

Everybody knows that, as regards the social system, the Communist Party has its immediate and its long-term programs, or a minimum program and a maximum program. For the present, New Democracy and for the future, socialism: these are two parts of an organic whole under the guidance of communist ideology. Is it not, therefore, utterly absurd to demand noisily that communism should be tucked away on the ground that the minimum program of the Communist Party is in basic agreement with the political tenets of the Three People's Principles?

*　　*　　*

The Old and the New Three People's Principles

*　　*　　*

The revolutionary Three People's Principles of the new period, the new or genuine Three People's Principles, contain the three cardinal policies of alliance with Russia, cooperation with the Communists, and assistance to the peasants and workers. Without these three cardinal policies or without any one of them, they become, in the new period, false Three People's Principles or incomplete Three People's Principles.

In the first place, the revolutionary new or genuine Three People's Principles must include alliance with Russia. The present situation makes it quite evident that without a policy of alliance with Russia, that is, with the socialist state, there will necessarily be a policy of

[7] A quotation from the famous memorial submitted by Li Mi (A.D. 3rd century) to the first emperor of the Western Chin dynasty. It is in these terms that he described his nonagenarian grandmother.

alliance with imperialism. Don't you see that this was exactly the situation after 1927? With the increasingly intensified conflict between the socialist Soviet Union and imperialism, it is inevitable that China should take her stand either on one side or on the other. Is it possible to be impartial? No, that is an illusion. All the countries in the world will be swept into one or the other of these two fronts, and in the world today "neutrality" is merely a deceptive word. Especially is this true of China: she is fighting an imperialist power which has penetrated deep into her territory; her final victory is inconceivable without aid from the Soviet Union. If alliance with Russia is replaced by alliance with imperialism, then the Three People's Principles will have to forfeit their claim to be revolutionary and become reactionary. In the final analysis, there can be no neutral Three People's Principles; they must be either revolutionary or counterrevolutionary.

❆ ❆ ❆

Stalin has said that "the national question is *virtually* a peasant question." [8] That is to say, the Chinese revolution is virtually the peasants' revolution, and the resistance to Japan now going on is virtually carried on by the peasants. New-democratic politics virtually consists in granting power to the peasants. The new or genuine Three People's Principles virtually mean the principles of the peasants' revolution. The problem of mass culture is virtually the raising of the cultural level of the peasants. The Anti-Japanese War is virtually a peasants' war. Now is the time for following the "principle of going into the hills," [9] where we hold meetings, conduct affairs, attend classes, publish newspapers, write books, put on theatrical performances, all virtually for the sake of the peasants. And everything that sustains the resistance to Japan and our own livelihood is virtually provided by the peasants. By "virtually" we mean in the main, and, as Stalin himself has explained, not neglecting other sections of the people. As every schoolboy knows, 80 percent of China's population are peasants. So the peasant problem is the main problem of the Chinese revolution, and the strength of the peasants constitutes the main force of the Chinese revolution. In the Chinese population the workers rank second to the peasants in number. There are in China several million industrial workers and several tens of millions of handicraftsmen and agricultural workers. China cannot get along without her workers in various industries, because they are the pro-

[8] Stalin said in "The National Question in Yugoslavia": "The peasantry represents the main army of the national movement. . . . Without the peasant army, there is not nor can there be a powerful national movement. This is what is meant by saying that the national question is *virtually* a peasant question." (*Marxism and the National and Colonial Question*, Eng. ed. London, 1947, p. 202).

[9] A gibe made by some doctrinaires in the party at Comrade Mao Tsetung's emphasis on rural revolutionary bases.

ducers in industrial economy. The revolution cannot succeed without the modern industrial working class, because it is the leader of the Chinese revolution and is the most revolutionary. Under such conditions, the revolutionary, new, or genuine Three People's Principles must be the Three People's Principles with a policy of assisting the peasants and workers. If any kind of Three People's Principles lacks this policy, gives no sincere and whole-hearted assistance to the peasants and workers, or fails to carry out the instruction to "arouse the people," it will certainly perish.

* * *

New-Democratic Culture

We have explained above the historical features of Chinese politics in the new period and the question of the new-democratic republic. We can now proceed to the question of culture.

A given culture is the ideological reflection of the politics and economy of a given society. There is in China an imperialist culture which is a reflection of the political and economic control or partial control of imperialism over China. This culture is promoted and fostered not only by the cultural organizations run directly by the imperialists over China, but also by their shameless Chinese toadies. All culture which breeds slave ideology belongs to this category. There is also in China a semifeudal culture which is a reflection of semifeudal politics and economy and has as its exponents all those who, while opposing the new culture and new ideologies, advocate the worship of Confucius, the study of the Confucian canon, the old ethical code, and the old ideologies. Imperialist culture and semifeudal culture are affectionate brothers, who have formed a reactionary alliance to oppose China's new culture. This reactionary culture serves imperialism and the feudal class, and must be swept away. Unless it is swept away, no new culture of any kind can be built up. The new culture and the reactionary culture are locked in a life-and-death struggle: there is no construction without destruction, no release without restraint and no movement without rest.

* * *

The Historical Features of China's Cultural Revolution

On China's cultural or ideological front, the period preceding the May 4 Movement and the period following it form two distinct historical periods.

Before the May 4 Movement, the struggle on China's cultural front was a struggle between the new culture of the bourgeoisie and the old culture of the feudal class.

*   *   *

But since the May 4 Movement things have gone differently. Since then a fresh and brand-new cultural force has appeared in China—the Communist cultural ideology guided by the Chinese Communists, that is, the Communist world outlook and theory of social revolution.

*   *   *

Before the May 4 Movement, the new culture of China was a culture of old democracy and a part of the capitalist cultural revolution of the world bourgeoisie. Since the May 4 Movement, it has become a culture of new democracy and a part of the socialist cultural revolution of the world proletariat.

Before the May 4 Movement, China's new cultural movement, her cultural revolution, was led by the bourgeoisie, which was still playing a leading role. After the May 4 Movement the ideology of bourgeois culture which lagged even behind bourgeois politics was totally incapable of playing the leading role, and during the revolution could at most merely join to a certain extent an alliance in which the leadership inevitably devolved upon the ideology of proletarian culture. This is a hard fact which no one can deny.

The new-democratic culture is the anti-imperialist and anti-feudal culture of the people; today it is the culture of the anti-Japanese united front. This culture can be led only by the proletarian cultural ideology, by Communist ideology, and not by the cultural ideology of any other class. New-democratic culture is, in a word, the popular anti-imperialist, antifeudal culture under the leadership of the proletariat.

The Four Periods

A cultural revolution is the ideological reflection of the political and economic revolutions which it serves. In China there is a united front in the cultural revolution just as in the political revolution.

The history of the united front in this cultural revolution during the last 20 years is divided into four periods: the first covering the two years from 1919 to 1921; the second, the six years from 1921 to 1927; the third, the ten years from 1927 to 1937; and the fourth, the three years from 1937 up to the present day.

*   *   *

Wrong Ideas About the Nature of Culture

*   *   *

A national culture with a socialist content must be the reflection of socialist politics and economy. As there is a socialist factor in our politics and economy, so it will be reflected in our national culture, but in our society as a whole, we have not yet reached the stage where politics and economy are wholly socialist, and therefore there cannot be a wholly socialist national culture.

*   *   *

A National, Scientific, and Mass Culture

The new-democratic culture is national. It opposes imperialist oppression and upholds the dignity and independence of the Chinese nation. It belongs to our own nation, and bears the stamp of our national characteristics. It unites with the socialist and new-democratic cultures of all other nations and establishes with them the relations whereby they can absorb something from each other and help each other to develop, and form together the new-world culture; but, being a revolutionary national culture, it can never unite with the reactionary imperialist culture of any nation. China should assimilate from foreign progressive cultures in large quantities what she needs for her own culture. We did not sufficiently do so in the past. We must assimilate whatever we find useful today, not only from contemporary foreign socialist or new-democratic cultures, but also from the older cultures of foreign countries, such as those of the capitalist countries in their age of enlightenment. However, we can benefit only if we treat these foreign materials as we do our food, which should be chewed in the mouth, submitted to the working of the stomach and intestines, mixed with saliva, gastric juices and intestinal secretions, and then separated into nutriment to be absorbed and waste matter to be discarded; we should never swallow anything whole or absorb it uncritically. So-called wholesale Westernization is wrong. China has suffered a great deal from the mechanical absorption of things foreign. Likewise, in applying Marxism to China, Chinese Communists must fully and properly unite its universal truth with the specific practice of the Chinese revolution, that is to say, the truth of Marxism must be integrated with the national characteristics and given a definite national form before it can be useful; it must not be applied subjectively as a mere formula. Formula-Marxists are only playing with Marxism and the Chinese revolution, and there is no place for them in the ranks of the Chinese revolution. China's culture should have its own form, which is national. National in form, new-democratic in content—such is our new culture today.

The new-democratic culture is scientific. Opposed to all feudal and superstitious ideas, it stands for seeking truth from facts, for objective truth, and for the unity between theory and practice. In this respect, the scientific thought of the Chinese proletariat can, to fight imperialism, feudalism, and superstition, form a united front with the still progressive bourgeois materialists and natural scientists, but it can never do so with any reactionary idealism. Communists may form an anti-imperialist and antifeudal united front for political action with certain idealists and even with religious people, but without implying any approval of their idealism or religious doctrines. A splendid old culture was created during the long period of China's feudal society. To chart the process of development of this old culture, to throw away its feudal dross and to assimilate its democratic essence is a necessary condition for the development of our new national culture and for the increase of our national self-confidence, but we must not swallow anything and everything uncritically. In the culture of the past we must separate all the dross of the feudal ruling class from the fine popular elements which are relatively democratic and revolutionary in character. As China's present new politics and new economy have developed out of her old politics and old economy, and China's new culture has also developed out of her old culture, we must respect our own history and not snap the thread of historical continuity. However, this respect for history means only giving history its proper place among the sciences, showing due regard for its dialectical development, but not praising the ancient at the expense of the modern, or recommending any harmful feudal element. As to the people and the student youth, the essential thing is to direct them not to look backward, but to look forward.

The new-democratic culture belongs to the people, hence it is democratic. It should serve the toiling masses of workers and peasants who make up over 90 percent of the nation's population, so that it may gradually become a culture of their own. There should be a difference in degree between the knowledge imparted to the revolutionary cadres and that imparted to the broad revolutionary masses, but they must also be linked; and similarly the raising of cultural standards must be distinguished from popularization but they too must be linked. Revolutionary culture is a powerful revolutionary weapon for the people. Ideologically it prepares the way for the revolution before its outbreak and becomes a necessary and important sector in the general front when the revolution breaks out. Revolutionary cultural workers are the commanders of various ranks on this sector. From the saying: "Without a revolutionary theory, there can be no revolutionary movement," [10] we can see how important the revolutionary cultural movement is to the revolution in practice. The cultural movement and revolutionary practice both have a mass character. Therefore all progressive cultural workers should have their own cultural army in the Anti-Japanese War, and this army is the broad mass of the people. A revolutionary cultural worker who keeps aloof from the people is merely a general without an army, and without enough fire-power to destroy the enemy. To attain such an aim, Chinese writing must be reformed under certain conditions, and our spoken language must be brought close to that of the people, for it must be borne in mind that revolutionary culture has its inexhaustible source in the people.

National, scientific, and mass culture is the anti-imperialist, anti-feudal culture of the people, the new-democratic and the new Chinese national culture.

When the new-democratic politics, new-democratic economy, and new-democratic culture are combined we shall have a republic of New Democracy, a republic of China in name and in fact, the new China we want to build.

New China is within sight of everyone of us; let us hail her!

New China is like a ship whose mast is appearing above the horizon; let us acclaim her!

Let us welcome with both hands the new China that is ours!

[10] Lenin, *What Is To Be Done?* Eng. ed., Moscow, 1947, p. 35.

THE CHINESE THAW

"Let a Hundred Flowers Blossom, Let a Hundred Schools of Thought Contend" * by Mao-Tse-tung, included in the speech "On the Correct Handling of Contradictions Among the People," delivered before a closed session of the Supreme State Conference, Peking, February 27, 1957. Subsequently revised for publication.

For decades Mao has been intrigued by the possibility of the existence of "contradictions" within a postrevolutionary society. The standard Marxist view is that contradictions exist in relations between classes. When classes cease to exist, contradictions disappear, as well. Mao's attitude, to the contrary, is that contradictions may and should develop—even within a classless society. Here they arise out of the different vantage points from which leadership and the masses view the same situation, leadership being primarily concerned with long-term objectives, whereas the masses tend to see only their immediate needs. Thus the conflict of contradictions.

Probably the most important statement of Mao's recurring concern with contradictions was made in February, 1957. For almost a year Mao had been trying to introduce a greater measure of diversity into the intellectual life of the Chinese People's Republic. Largely because of the unexpected ease with which collectivization and the nationalization of small industry and commerce had been realized in China, as contrasted with the Soviet Union's bloody experiences of the 1930s, Mao had come to the conclusion that the Chinese people were solidly behind him and the party. He verged on the mystical in his belief that in China there was an underlying sense of national unity that was capable of eliminating the brutality of the class struggle as experienced elsewhere. The ease and speed of the collectivization and nationalization campaigns reinforced this belief and gave him the confidence to pursue a policy of cautious "liberalization."

In May, 1956, a new party slogan was issued: "Let a hundred flowers blossom, let a hundred schools of thought contend." It was meant to be a signal to the intellectuals of China to begin to free their thoughts from the party straitjacket in which they had been bound. However, the intellectuals, having been subjected to years of "rectification" campaigns, were extremely wary.

The events of October and November, 1956, terminating in the Hungarian revolution further convinced Mao that it was necessary to have a freer—though still not free—expression of opinion in China.

* Complete text in D. N. Jacobs, Ed., *The New Communist Manifesto*, 2nd ed., Harper & Row, New York, 1962.

In Mao's eyes, the violent outburst of the Hungarian Revolution was to be attributed to the isolation of the Hungarian Communist bureaucracy from the masses. Mao was aware that such alienation was widespread in China, as well, and he determined to prevent it from developing into a counterrevolutionary situation.

Therefore, on February 27, 1957, he appeared before a closed session of the Supreme State Conference in Peking and delivered an address "On the Correct Handling of Contradictions Among the People," which includes the following "hundred flowers" statement.

Even after February 27, the intellectuals apparently remained skeptical. But the inauguration on April 30 of a campaign "to rectify the style of work" within the CCP evidently began to convince them that Mao was in earnest—as he undoubtedly was. Commencing gradually, criticism of local conditions and the local bureaucracy, some of it perhaps even planted by the party itself to stimulate activity, appeared. But then rapidly, the volume and scope of the criticism increased. More and more it was characterized by invective and vituperation. No situation, circumstance, or individual escaped its sting, not even Mao himself. Writers, professors, journalists complained of the unbearable restraints and brutality of life in China under the Communists. They wrote that the masses distrusted the party which had become a "privileged class" and hovered over China "like an evil spirit that possesses you." One student went so far as to declare that in the "campaign" then going on, ten of the twelve million members of the party should be executed. Thousands in the universities, and elsewhere called for an end to communism.

No party in power, certainly not a Communist one, is prepared to endure such provocation for long. In early June the "hundred flowers" experiment was brought to an end. It had lasted less than six weeks and it was followed by an antiright rectification campaign that effectively silenced those who had accepted the invitation to raise their voices, by removing them from circulation.

"Let a hundred flowers blossom," and "let a hundred schools of thought contend," [1] "long-term coexistence and mutual supervision"— how did these slogans come to be put forward?

They were put forward in the light of the specific conditions existing in China, on the basis of the recognition that various kinds of contradictions still exist in a socialist society, and in response to the country's urgent need to speed up its economic and cultural development.

The policy of letting a hundred flowers blossom and a hundred schools of thought contend is designed to promote the flourishing of

[1] "Let a hundred flowers blossom," and "let a hundred schools of thought contend" are two old Chinese sayings.

the arts and the progress of science; it is designed to enable a socialist culture to thrive in our land. Different forms and styles in art can develop freely and different schools in science can contend freely. We think that it is harmful to the growth of art and science if administrative measures are used to impose one particular style of art or school of thought and to ban another. Questions of right and wrong in the arts and sciences should be settled through free discussion in artistic and scientific circles and in the course of practical work in the arts and sciences. They should not be settled in summary fashion. A period of trial is often needed to determine whether something is right or wrong. In the past, new and correct things often failed at the outset to win recognition from the majority of people and had to develop by twists and turns in struggle. Correct and good things have often at first been looked upon not as fragrant flowers but as poisonous weeds. Copernicus' theory of the solar system and Darwin's theory of evolution were once dismissed as erroneous and had to win through over bitter opposition. Chinese history offers many similar examples. In socialist society, conditions for the growth of new things are radically different from and far superior to those in the old society. Nevertheless, it still often happens that new, rising forces are held back and reasonable suggestions smothered.

The growth of new things can also be hindered, not because of deliberate suppression, but because of lack of discernment. That is why we should take a cautious attitude in regard to questions of right and wrong in the arts and sciences, encourage free discussion, and avoid hasty conclusions. We believe that this attitude will facilitate the growth of the arts and sciences.

Marxism has also developed through struggle. At the beginning, Marxism was subjected to all kinds of attack and regarded as a poisonous weed. It is still being attacked and regarded as a poisonous weed in many parts of the world. However, it enjoys a different position in the socialist countries. But even in these countries, there are non-Marxist as well as anti-Marxist ideologies. It is true that in China, socialist transformation, insofar as a change in the system of ownership is concerned, has in the main been completed, and the turbulent, large-scale, mass class struggles characteristic of the revolutionary periods have in the main concluded. But remnants of the overthrown landlord and comprador classes still exist, the bourgeoisie still exists, and the petty bourgeoisie has only just begun to remold itself. Class struggle is not yet over. The class struggle between the proletariat and the bourgeoisie, the class struggle between various political forces, and the class struggle in the ideological field between the proletariat and the bourgeoisie will still be long and devious and at times may even become very acute. The proletariat seeks to transform the world according to its own world outlook, so does the bourgeoisie. In this respect, the question whether socialism or capitalism will win is still not really settled. Marxists are still a minority of the entire population as well as of the intellectuals. Marxism therefore must still develop through struggle. Marxism *can* only develop through struggle—this is true not only in the past and present, it is necessarily true in the future also. What is correct always develops in the course of struggle with what is wrong. The true, the good, and the beautiful always exist in comparison with the false, the evil, and the ugly, and grow in struggle with the latter. As mankind in general rejects an untruth and accepts a truth, a new truth will begin struggling with new erroneous ideas. Such struggles will never end. This is the law of development of truth and it is certainly also the law of development of Marxism.

It will take a considerable time to decide the issue in the ideological struggle between socialism and capitalism in our country. This is because the influence of the bourgeoisie and of the intellectuals who come from the old society will remain in our country as the ideology of a class for a long time to come. Failure to grasp this, or still worse, failure to understand it at all, can lead to the gravest mistakes—to ignoring the necessity of waging the struggle in the ideological field. Ideological struggle is not like other forms of struggle. Crude, coercive methods should not be used in this struggle, but only the method of painstaking reasoning. Today, socialism enjoys favorable conditions in the ideological struggle. The main power of the state is in the hands of the working people led by the proletariat. The Communist Party is strong and its prestige stands high. Although there are defects and mistakes in our work, every fairminded person can see that we are loyal to the people, that we are both determined and able to build up our country together with the people, and that we have achieved great successes and will achieve still greater ones. The vast majority of the bourgeoisie and intellectuals who come from the old society are patriotic; they are willing to serve their flourishing socialist motherland, and they know that if they turn away from the socialist cause and the working people led by the Communist Party, they will have no one to rely on and no bright future to look forward to.

People may ask: Since Marxism is accepted by the majority of the people in our country as the guiding ideology, can it be criticized? Certainly it can. As a scientific truth, Marxism fears no criticism. If it did, and could be defeated in argument, it would be worthless. In fact, aren't the idealists criticizing Marxism every day and in all sorts of ways? As for those who harbor bourgeois and petty bourgeois ideas and do not wish to change, aren't they also criticizing Marxism in all sorts of ways? Marxists should not be afraid of criticism from any quarter. Quite the contrary, they need to steel and improve themselves and win new positions in the teeth of criticism and the storm and stress of struggle. Fighting against wrong ideas is like being vaccinated—a man develops greater immunity from disease after the vaccine takes effect. Plants raised in hothouses are not likely to be robust. Carrying out the policy of letting a hundred flowers blossom and a hundred schools of thought contend will not weaken but strengthen the leading position of Marxism in the ideological field.

What should our policy be towards non-Marxist ideas? As far as unmistakable counterrevolutionaries and wreckers of the socialist cause are concerned, the matter is easy: we simply deprive them of their freedom of speech. But it is quite a different matter when we are faced with incorrect ideas among the people. Will it do to ban such ideas and give them no opportunity to express themselves? Certainly not. It is not only futile but very harmful to use crude and summary methods to deal with ideological questions among the people, with questions relating to the spiritual life of man. You may ban the expression of wrong ideas, but the ideas will still be there. On the other hand, correct ideas, if pampered in hothouses without being exposed to the elements or immunized from disease, will not win out against wrong ones. That is why it is only by employing methods of discussion, criticism, and reasoning that we can really foster correct ideas, overcome wrong ideas, and really settle issues.

The bourgeoisie and petty bourgeoisie are bound to give expression to their ideologies. It is inevitable that they should stubbornly persist in expressing themselves in every way possible on political and ideological questions. You can't expect them not to do so. We should not use methods of suppression to prevent them from expressing themselves, but should allow them to do so and at the same time argue with them and direct well-considered criticism at them.

There can be no doubt that we should criticize all kinds of wrong ideas. It certainly would not do to refrain from criticism and look on while wrong ideas spread unchecked and acquire an audience. Mistakes should be criticized and poisonous weeds rooted out wherever they crop up. But such criticism should not be doctrinaire. We should not use the metaphysical method, but strive to employ the dialectical method. What is needed is scientific analysis and fully convincing arguments. Doctrinaire criticism settles nothing. We don't want any kind of poisonous weed, but we should carefully distinguish between what is really a poisonous weed and what is really a fragrant flower. We must learn together with the masses of the people how to make this careful distinction, and use the correct methods to fight poisonous weeds.

While criticizing doctrinairism, we should at the same time direct our attention to criticizing revisionism. Revisionism, or rightist opportunism, is a bourgeois trend of thought which is even more dangerous than doctrinairism. The revisionists, or right opportunists, pay lip service to Marxism and also attack "doctrinairism." But the real target of their attack is actually the most fundamental elements of Marxism. They oppose or distort materialism and dialectics, oppose or try to weaken the people's democratic dictatorship and the leading role of the Communist Party, oppose or try to weaken socialist transformation and socialist construction. Even after the basic victory of the socialist revolution in our country, there are still a number of people who vainly hope for a restoration of the capitalist system. They wage a struggle against the working class on every front, including the ideological front. In this struggle, their right-hand men are the revisionists.

On the surface, these two slogans—let a hundred flowers blossom and a hundred schools of thought contend—have no class character: the proletariat can turn them to account, so can the bourgeoisie and other people. But different classes, strata, and social groups—each has its own view of what are fragrant flowers and what are poisonous weeds. So what, from the point of view of the broad masses of the people, should be the criteria today for distinguishing between fragrant flowers and poisonous weeds?

In the political life of our country, how are our people to determine what is right and what is wrong in our words and actions? On the basis of the principles of our Constitution, the will of the overwhelming majority of our people, and the political programs jointly proclaimed on various occasions by our political parties and groups, we believe that, broadly speaking, words and actions can be judged right if they:

1. Help to unite the people of our various nationalities, and do not divide them;
2. Are beneficial, not harmful, to socialist transformation and socialist construction;
3. Help to consolidate, not undermine or weaken, the people's democratic dictatorship;
4. Help to consolidate, not undermine or weaken, democratic centralism;
5. Tend to strengthen, not to cast off or weaken, the leadership of the Communist Party;
6. Are beneficial, not harmful, to international socialist solidarity and the solidarity of the peace-loving peoples of the world.

Of these six criteria, the most important are the socialist path and the leadership of the party. These criteria are put forward in order to foster, and not hinder, the free discussion of various questions among the people. Those who do not approve of these criteria can still put forward their own views and argue their case. When the majority of the people have clear-cut criteria to go by, criticism and self-criticism can be conducted along proper lines, and these criteria can be applied to people's words and actions to determine whether they are fragrant flowers or poisonous weeds. These are political criteria. Naturally, in judging the truthfulness of scientific theories or assessing the aesthetic value of works of art, other pertinent criteria are needed, but these six political criteria are also applicable to all activities in the arts or sciences. In a socialist country like ours, can there possibly be any useful scientific or artistic activity which runs counter to these political criteria?

All that is set out above stems from the specific historical conditions in our country. Since conditions vary in different socialist countries and with different Communist Parties, we do not think that other countries and parties must or need to follow the Chinese way.

The slogan "long-term coexistence and mutual supervision" is also a product of specific historical conditions in our country. It wasn't put forward all of a sudden, but had been in the making for several years. The idea of long-term coexistence had been in existence for a long time, but last year when the socialist system was basically established, the slogan was set out in clear terms.

Why should the democratic parties of the bourgeoisie and petty bourgeoisie be allowed to exist side by side with the party of the working class over a long period of time? Because we have no reason not to adopt the policy of long-term coexistence with all other democratic parties which are truly devoted to the task of uniting the people for the cause of socialism and which enjoy the trust of the people.

As early as at the Second Session of the National Committee of the People's Political Consultative Conference in June, 1950, I put the matter in this way:

"The people and the People's Government have no reason to reject or deny the opportunity to anyone to make a living and give their services to the country, so long as he is really willing to serve the people, really helped the people when they were still in difficulties, did good things, and continues to do them consistently without giving up halfway."

What I defined here was the political basis for the long-term coexistence of the various parties. It is the desire of the Communist Party, also its policy, to exist side by side with the other democratic parties for a long time to come. Whether these democratic parties can long exist depends not merely on what the Communist Party itself desires but also on the part played by these democratic parties themselves and on whether they enjoy the confidence of the people.

Mutual supervision among the various parties has also been a long-established fact, in the sense that they advise and criticize each other. Mutual supervision, which is obviously not a one-sided matter, means that the Communist Party should exercise supervision over the other democratic parties, and the other democratic parties should exercise supervision over the Communist Party. Why should the other democratic parties be allowed to exercise supervision over the Communist Party? This is correct because for a party as much as for an individual there is great need to hear opinions different from its own. We all know that supervision over the Communist Party is mainly exercised by the working people and party membership. But we will benefit even more if the other democratic parties do this as well. Of course, advice and criticism exchanged between the Communist Party and the other democratic parties will play a positive role in mutual supervision only when they conform to the six political criteria given above. That is why we hope that the other democratic parties will all pay attention to ideological remolding, and strive for long-term coexistence and mutual supervision with the Communist Party so as to meet the needs of the new society.

TURN TO THE LEFT

Report of the Central Committee to the Second Session of the Eighth
National Congress of the Chinese Communist Party by Liu Shao-ch'i,
Peking, May 5, 1958.

Not all of the leading lights of the CCP went along with Mao's
experiment in liberalization which had reached its peak in the "hundred flowers" episode. Opposition elements had argued that the
Chinese people were not nearly so enamored of the regime as Mao
contended and that what China needed was more of the whip, not
less.

The hand of the "leftists" was greatly strengthened by the belliger-
ence demonstrated by the masses during May and early June, 1957.
Perhaps an even more powerful boost to their position was provided
by the economic crisis which had spread over China during the first
half of the same year. Famine and unemployment stalked the land.
The faltering economy also was attributed to a policy of liberalization
which had instituted a relaxation of pressures and begun to demonstrate a bit more concern for consumer needs.

During the summer of 1957 the struggle between the attackers of
the left and the defending rightists within the upper echelon, was
fiercely waged. The latter contended that the situation called for
still more concessions to the populace, while the former insisted upon
the reimplementation of a determined and vigorous "revolutionary"
policy in which "ideological incentives" would have precedence over
"material" ones. The first concrete evidence that the left had won
emerged with the inauguration in the summer of 1957 of an antiright campaign, aimed at those inside and outside the party who had
participated in the antigovernment outbursts in the days of the "hundred flowers."

The intensity of the dispute between right and left, and the respective positions held by the two sides was clearly reflected in the
report which the ascetic-appearing Liu Shao-ch'i, himself the leader
of the left and usually thought of as the number two man in the
Chinese hierarchy, made to the party congress in May of the following year.

In this report, Liu accuses the rightists of having "developed individualism, sectarianism, localism, and nationalism to an extreme
degree within the party" and having participated in "revisionist and

other antisocialist and anti-Communist activities." He presents the "hundred flowers" situation as a trick—it almost certainly was not—to unmask the "poisoned weeds," who otherwise "would have appeared in disguise and poisoned the people in secret."

In industry the struggle was waged, says Liu, between those who would do the work "faster and better" and those who would do it "slowly and not so well." "Some people criticize us for 'craving greatness and success,' for seeking 'quick success and instant benefits.' What they say about us is right! And shouldn't we crave greatness for our 600 million people and the success of socialism? Should we rather crave smallness and court failure, reject success and benefits, and rest content with lagging behind and doing nothing?"

It is a rhetorical question. China must move ahead. "None of the criticisms directed against the policy of increasing the speed of construction and of achieving greater, faster, better, and more economical results can hold water."

In the same address, Liu becomes the first party leader to put forth the term "uninterrupted revolution" as a description of the leftist concept of domestic postrevolutionary advancement. Hitherto, "uninterrupted revolution" was used by Marx and his disciples to characterize the development of the revolution before the event had actually transpired. Now, Liu uses it to explain what should happen after the seizure of power has been effected. The revolution does not stop. It is not confined to a relatively brief span of time; it goes on and on. This is an extension of Marxism-Leninism which Moscow, for several reasons, has refused to accept.

It is the responsibility of the party, declares Liu, to put forth "new revolutionary tasks in good time, so that there is no halfway halt in the revolutionary advance of the people, the revolutionary fervor of the masses will not subside with interruptions of the revolution, and party and state functionaries will not rest content with the success won and grow arrogant or apathetic." The revolutionary enthusiasm of the masses, "the main thing we must rely on if we are to make all our undertakings advance rapidly," cannot be allowed to flag. It is the means to triumph.

Liu advances the argument, heatedly refuted by the Kremlin, that what China, or almost any country, lacks in material wealth and production know-how can more than be equalized by involving the enthusiasm of the multitude. Thus, the decades of Soviet patience, struggle, and privation are no match for the mass and enthusiasm of the Chinese. They have been in vain, for enthusiasm conquers all.

Comrades!

On behalf of the Central Committee I now report to the Second

Session of the Party's Eighth National Congress on its work. My report deals with the present situation, the Party's general line for socialist construction, and its future tasks.

I

Over a year has passed since the First Session of the Eighth National Congress. During this time, the party has correctly carried out and developed the policies laid down at the First Session, and achieved great successes in every field of work.

In the past year or so, many changes of great historic significance have taken place, internationally and at home.

Internationally, all of us know the now famous conclusion drawn by Comrade Mao Tse-tung that the world situation has recently reached a new turning point in its development. In extent of popular support, size of populations, and rate of development of production, the socialist camp headed by the Soviet Union has long since surpassed the imperialist camp. For a time in 1956, however, the sky, was overcast. The imperialist camp and reactionaries in various countries on more than one occasion launched violent campaigns against communism, against the people, and against national independence. The imperialists incited and aided the counterrevolutionary uprising in Hungary, and at the same time carried out armed aggression against Egypt. At that time we pointed out that the dark clouds would soon disperse. As it turned out, the revolutionary proletariat of Hungary, with the help of the Soviet Union and the support of the revolutionary forces of the world, quickly stamped out the uprising. The struggles of Egypt and Syria against aggression also triumphed with the support of the Soviet Union and the forces of peace throughout the world. In October and November last year, the Soviet Union launched two artificial earth satellites. This made the whole world acknowledge that in science and technology too the Soviet Union has surpassed the United States, the most developed of the capitalist countries. In November last year, a meeting of the Communist and workers' parties of the socialist countries was held in Moscow, followed by a meeting of 64 Communist parties. These meetings issued two declarations of historic significance, greatly strengthened the solidarity of the ranks of the international working class and the socialist camp, and promoted the development of the world peace movement. All this shows that the East wind has prevailed over the West wind, and will continue to do so in the future.

*   *   *

In China, as everyone can see, the rectification campaign led by the Chinese Communist Party and conducted in accordance with the guiding principles laid down by Comrade Mao Tse-tung for the correct handling of contradictions among the people, has achieved great results on the political, economic, ideological, and cultural fronts. It is the purpose of the rectification campaign, by means of criticism and self-criticism, to raise the level of communist consciousness of the masses and to adjust relationships among the people in a systematic way so that they may meet the needs of consolidating the socialist system and further expanding the productive forces of society. Serving as a lever, the rectification campaign has pushed forward the work of the party and the state in every field. The rectification campaign of the Communist Party and the struggle against the rightists have developed into a rectification campaign among every section of the people, and the upsurge in this nation-wide rectification campaign has in turn brought about a new upsurge in production and construction throughout the country.

* * *

The antirightist struggle has been of profound significance within our party. We expelled a number of rightists from the party. They were alien class elements who had sneaked into the party and renegades to the cause of socialism. They developed individualism, sectarianism, localism, and nationalism to an extreme degree within the party and carried out revisionist and other antisocialist and anti-Communist activities. In league with the rightists outside the party, they attacked the party and the socialist system. To rid the party of these alien class elements and renegades is a great victory for its cause.

The national bourgeoisie, the bourgeois intellectuals, and the members of the various democratic parties, who stand in the middle of the road and are half-hearted about socialism, have changed, or are changing, to a greater or lesser degree, their old political outlooks in the course of the struggle against the rightists, in the subsequent drive against waste and conservative ideas and practices, and in the great leaps forward in production and other fields of socialist construction. Most of these people, sensing "the compelling force of circumstances," now feel that they must make further progress and must not remain in their middle-of-the-road position as before. They have begun to admit their dual character in relation to the socialist revolution and the need to correct their many wrong views. They have expressed their determination to remold themselves, "give their hearts" to the Communist Party and strive to become left-wingers. Many intellectuals have taken an active part in the rectification campaign and indicated their resolve to become socialist-minded and professionally expert so as to turn themselves into thoroughly red specialists. Some of them have gone among the working people, taking part in manual labor, so as to build sincere contacts with the broad masses of the working people.

In many regions inhabited by national minorities, in the course of the rectification campaign and the struggle against the rightists, local nationalism has been seriously criticized, certain separatists and bourgeois rightists among the national minorities who impair the unity of the motherland have been exposed, and, at the same time, the tendency towards Han chauvinism among certain Han cadres has been further overcome. In this way, the socialist consciousness of the masses among the national minorities has been stimulated and there is a new sense of the brotherhood and unity of the various nationalities.

The experience of the rectification campaign and the antirightist struggle once again shows that throughout the transition period—that is, before completion of the building of a socialist society—the main contradiction inside our country is and remains that between the proletariat and the bourgeoisie, between the socialist road and the capitalist road. In certain fields this contradiction manifests itself as a fierce life-and-death struggle between the enemy and ourselves; that was the case in the attack launched by the bourgeois rightists in 1957. This attack was repelled, but in the future they will try again to make trouble whenever opportunity arises. We must, therefore, be prepared to wage prolonged and repeated struggles against the bourgeois rightists before this contradiction can be fully resolved. We must also continue to suppress other remnants of counterrevolutionaries and all sorts of criminals breaking law and order. In the actual conditions existing in our country, however, the contradictions between the two classes and the two roads in most cases manifest themselves as contradictions within the ranks of the people. As to the contradictions among the people—be they contradictions between the national bourgeoisie and petty bourgeoisie on the one hand and the proletariat on the other, or contradictions within the proletariat arising from bourgeois and petty bourgeois influences upon sections of the proletariat—they should, as a rule, be resolved through the rectification campaign. As to contradictions among the working people arising from differences in their conceptions of right and wrong, or between the advanced and the backward elements among them, since some are connected with bourgeois and petty bourgeois influences, and most of them do not fall into the category of contradictions between classes at all, it is all the more obvious that such contradictions should be resolved by means of the rectification campaign.

The political atmosphere among the working people has also undergone a deep change following the rectification campaign and the antirightist struggle. The political consciousness and the socialist initiative of the masses, whether workers or peasants, have been greatly enhanced, first, as a result of the socialist revolution on the ideological and political fronts and the great debates on the capitalist road and the socialist road, which have been carried out on the broadest scale among the masses, and, second, as a result of the development to the fullest extent of criticism and self-criticism in regard to mistakes and shortcomings in our work, by encouraging a full and frank airing of views, great debates and the posting of *tatsepao*.[1] Leading cadres in many units have made sincere self-criticisms and earnest efforts to improve their work and ways. This has moved the masses and strengthened their faith in the leading role of the party; at the same time it led them on their own initiative, to criticize their own shortcomings, rectify the wrong ideas and backward habits which they carried over from the old society, and to improve their own work. This, in all places where the rectification campaign has been carried out thoroughly, has put both the masses and the cadres at ease; any estrangement that existed between them in the past has been eliminated. Feeling that the party has given its heart to them, the masses too give their hearts to the party. As a result, all sorts of negative trends reflecting surviving bourgeois ideas in these places have been greatly reduced and the just spirit of communism is in the ascendant. Many who were formerly backward are now ideologically emancipated and, becoming communist-minded, they are rapidly catching up with the more advanced. This is an important sign of the great victory we have won in the socialist revolution on the ideological and political fronts.

* * *

Radical changes in human relations have taken place in our country with the development of criticism and self-criticism. Cadres in industrial and mining enterprises and agricultural cooperatives have begun to devote regularly part of their time to participation in manual labor alongside the rank and file of workers and peasants. Many leaders of rural work are working on "experimental plots" alongside the peasants. Large numbers of office workers and intellectuals have gone to the countryside and the mountain areas or to work in the basic units of enterprises. The example set by the masses has inspired the cadres and that set by the cadres has also inspired the masses. Managerial personnel now directly participate in some manual labor; and the workers in some managerial work. The relationship of mutual aid and cooperation, of learning from each other and of emulation, between those in the upper and the lower grades, between the managerial personnel and those who directly take part in production, between brain and manual workers, between city and countryside has greatly developed. Many who were prone to bossiness have changed a great deal in this rectification campaign. So long as we continue to make use of the *tatsepao* and the debates, and constantly practice criticism and self-criticism, we shall certainly be able to get rid of the bossy style of

[1] Opinions and criticisms written out in bold Chinese characters on large sheets of paper and posted freely for everybody to see.

work effectively and thoroughly, and gradually eliminate the evil bureaucratic habits carried over from thousands of years of history.

*   *   *

The broad masses of the working people have realized more fully that individual and immediate interests depend on and are bound up with collective and long-term interests and that the happiness of the individual lies in the realization of the lofty socialist ideals of all the people. That is why they have displayed an heroic Communist spirit of self-sacrifice in the work. Their slogan is "Hard work for a few years, happiness for a thousand." This mighty torrent of Communist ideas has swept away many stumbling blocks—individualism, departmentalism, localism, and nationalism. In city and countryside, people vie with each other in joining in all kinds of voluntary labor. In building irrigation works, the peasants in many places have thrown aside the age-old narrow-minded idea of only looking after their native places. In the nation-wide emulation drive, many advanced units and individuals have enthusiastically passed on their technical experience, inventions, and creations to the backward units and individuals so that the latter can catch up with them. Many enterprises, organizations, schools, army units, and individuals have taken the initiative in coordinating their activities with those of others so as to promote the progress of all concerned. All this is, as Lenin said, "the actual beginning of communism," "the beginning of a change which is of world historic significance."

All the factors mentioned above have combined to form the great revolutionary drive for socialist construction. Comrade Mao Tse-tung has put forward the slogans "catch up with and outstrip Britain in 15 years," "build socialism by exerting our utmost efforts and pressing ahead consistently to achieve greater, faster, better, and more economical results," "to be promoters of progress not of retrogression," "build our country and run our households industriously and with frugality," and "battle hard for three years to bring about a basic change in the features of most areas"—all these calls have quickly gripped the imagination of the huge army of hundreds of millions of working people and have been transformed into an immense material force. There has emerged in physical labor and other work a high degree of socialist initiative, a surging, militant spirit, a keenness in learning and studying that will not rest short of its aims, a fearless creative spirit. An emulation drive in which the backward learn from and catch up and compete with the advanced has been launched between individuals, production teams, enterprises, cooperatives, counties, and cities. Set norms are being constantly surpassed and new techniques invented. Time after time the masses outstrip the targets set by enterprises and administrative organs.

The spring of 1958 witnessed the beginning of a leap forward on every front in our socialist construction. Industry, agriculture, and all other fields of activity are registering greater and more rapid growth.

* * *

The revolutionary energy of the masses of workers has also found expression in the trial manufacture of new products, in technical renovation, in the improvement of quality, and lowering of production costs. In the first few months of the year, many kinds of small-sized tractors were successfully produced on a trial basis. Several of them can be used equally well for the cultivation of paddy fields, dry fields, mountain areas, and terraced fields or for transport, for operating irrigation machinery, or generating power for the processing of agricultural products and other purposes. In the first four months of the year, Shanghai successfully produced more than one thousand kinds of new products on a trial basis.

* * *

An upsurge is shaping up in capital construction in industry this year. Nearly one thousand above-norm projects will be under construction this year; this is more than the total number of such projects under construction in the First Five-Year Plan period. In addition, construction work has already started on thousands of medium and small-sized coal mines, power stations, oil refineries, iron and steel plants, nonferrous mines, chemical fertilizer plants, cement plants, engineering works, and agricultural and animal products processing plants.

The output of local industry this year will show a considerable increase as a result of wide-spread industrial capital construction undertaken by local authorities. Take iron and steel for example. The amount of iron to be produced by local enterprises this year will reach 1,730,000 tons (as against the 593,000 tons produced last year) and that of steel will reach 1,410,000 tons (as against the 790,000 tons of last year). The rapid growth of the local industries is one of the outstanding features of this year's industrial upswing.

* * *

In agriculture, the most striking leap took place in the campaign of the cooperative farmers to build irrigation works. From last October to April this year, the irrigated acreage throughout the country increased by 350 million *mou*, that is, 80 million *mou* more than the total added during the eight years since liberation and 110 million *mou* more than the total acreage brought under irrigation in the thousands of years before liberation.

* * *

Karl Marx prophesied that the proletarian revolution would usher us into a great epoch when "20 years are concentrated in a day." If in past revolutionary struggles we experienced such great times, then is not our present socialist construction another great time again? Here one can see how the courageous and hard-working Chinese people, under the leadership of the great Chinese Communist Party and its leader Comrade Mao Tse-tung, have poured forth their history-making strength and wisdom in endless measure.

II

The current mighty leap forward in socialist construction is the product not only of the successful development of the antirightist struggle and the rectification campaign but also of a correct implementation of the party's general line—to build socialism by exerting our utmost efforts, and pressing ahead consistently to achieve greater, faster, better, and more economical results.

Comrade Mao Tse-tung has often said that there are two methods of carrying on socialist transformation and construction: One will result in doing the work faster and better; the other slowly and not so well. Which method shall we adopt? This has been an issue. In his work *On the Question of Agricultural Co-operation* published in 1955, Comrade Mao Tse-tung provided a theoretical solution to the struggle between these two methods regarding the socialist revolution in the ownership of the means of production. Furthermore, this struggle was decided in practice by the upsurge in socialist transformation which took place between the autumn of 1955 and the spring of 1956. There was also a conflict between the two methods in connection with the socialist revolution on the political and ideological fronts, and this too was worked out theoretically by Comrade Mao Tse-tung in his article *On the Correct Handling of Contradictions Among the People* published last year, and was resolved in practice by the rectification campaign and antirightist struggle which began last year. In connection with socialist construction too, the Central Committee of the Party and Comrade Mao Tse-tung have always taken a clear-cut stand, insisting that the method of working faster and better be adopted and the other method, of working slowly and not so well, be rejected. However, on this question some comrades still clung to such outmoded ideas as "keeping to the right is better than keeping to the left," "it's better to go slower than faster" or "it's better to take small steps than to go striding forward." The struggle between the two methods in dealing with this question was not fully decided until the launching of the rectification campaign and the antirightist struggle.

* * *

On the proposal of Comrade Mao Tse-tung, the party in January, 1956, put before the people a "Draft National Program for Agricultural Development, 1956 to 1967." This is a program for developing socialist agriculture by achieving "greater, faster, better, and more economical results." Not only did it set great goals for rural work throughout the country but it gave a correct orientation for development of the entire work of socialist construction.

In April of the same year, at an enlarged meeting of the Political Bureau of the Central Committee of the Party, Comrade Mao Tse-tung made a report on "Ten Sets of Relationships" in which he called the whole party's attention to the correct handling of the relationships.

*   *   *

These guiding lines and policies formulated by Comrade Mao Tse-tung have played a tremendous role in our work. In 1956, every phase of China's economy and culture made a mighty leap forward.

*   *   *

There were individual defects in our work during the leap forward in 1956, mainly because of the difficulty of supplying the market caused by an excessive number of new workers and staff and excessive increases in certain categories of wages. These defects paled before the tremendous achievements made at the time and the problems arising from these defects were solved after a few months of efforts by the people throughout the country in a campaign launched at the call of the party to increase production and practice economy. However, some comrades at the time magnified these defects and underestimated the great achievements attained, and hence regarded the leap forward of 1956 as a "reckless advance." In a flurry of opposition to this so-called "reckless advance," some people even had misgivings about the principle of "achieving greater, faster, better, and more economical results" and the 40-article Program for Agricultural Development. This dampened the initiative of the masses and hampered progress on the production front in 1957, and particularly on the agricultural front. But the party soon corrected this error. The Third Plenary Session of the Central Committee of the Party held in September last year reaffirmed the need to adhere to the principle of achieving "greater, faster, better, and more economical results" in building socialism. Following that, the Central Committee made public a revised version of the Draft Program for Agricultural Development, and Comrade Mao Tse-tung issued a militant call to overtake and surpass Britain in the output of iron and steel and other major industrial products in 15 years. Such correct guidance by the Central Committee, combined with the initiative of the masses evoked by the rectification campaign and the antirightist struggle, gave rise to the all-round forward leap which is currently developing on an even larger scale in our socialist construction. Many of those comrades who expressed misgivings about the principle of building socialism by achieving "greater, faster, better, and more economical results," have learned a lesson from all this. But some of them have not yet learned anything. They say: "We'll settle accounts with you after the autumn harvest." Well, let them wait to settle accounts. They will lose out in the end!

The development is U-shaped, i.e., high at the beginning and the end, but low in the middle. Didn't we see very clearly how things developed on the production front in 1956—1957—1958 in the form of an upsurge, then an ebb, and then an even bigger upsurge or, in other words, a leap forward, then a conservative phase, and then another big leap forward?

The party and the masses have learned a lesson from this U-shaped development.

Now the people everywhere are full of confidence in the forward leap in production; they are determined to further speed up socialist construction. They are eager to remove the obstacles placed in their way by technical and cultural backwardness. In view of the basic victory of the socialist revolution already achieved on the economic, political, and ideological fronts, the Central Committee of the Party and Comrade Mao Tse-tung consider that the time is ripe to set new revolutionary tasks before the party and the people, that now is the time to call for a technical revolution and, along with it, a cultural revolution.

Marx, Engels, and Lenin often pointed out that the watchword of the working class should be "uninterrupted revolution." In putting forward new revolutionary tasks at the proper time so that there is no halfway halt in the revolutionary advance of the people, the revolutionary fervor of the masses will not subside during interruptions of the revolution; and party and state functionaries will not rest content with the success won and grow arrogant or apathetic. The Central Committee of the Communist Party and Comrade Mao Tse-tung have always guided the Chinese revolution by this Marxist-Leninist theory of uninterrupted revolution. Already on the eve of the victory of the democratic revolution, the Seventh Central Committee of the Party, in a resolution adopted in March, 1949, at its Second Plenary Session, clearly put forward the task of "transforming the new-democratic state into a socialist state." After the founding of the People's Republic of China and immediately following the completion of land reform, the Central Committee, in December, 1951, pointed out the road to collective farming through the mutual-aid and cooperative movement, and in 1953 carried out extensive publicity and education among the people for the socialist transformation of agriculture, handicrafts, and private industry and commerce. After the socialist revolution in the ownership of the means of production had been basically won, the Central Committee launched the socialist revolution on the ideological and political fronts. All this has enabled the revolution to advance at the opportune moment from one stage to another, scoring one victory after another.

The issuance of the call for the technical and cultural revolution means that our constantly developing revolution must now advance to a new stage. The broad masses of workers, peasants, and intellectuals have given an immediate and enthusiastic response to this timely call of the party. In fact, the masses have already swung into action. In many places, the great march to overcome our technical and cultural backwardness has already started with vigor and vitality.

* * *

By vigorously carrying out the party's general line for socialist construction and bringing about a technical revolution and a cultural revolution, we shall achieve an enormous development of our social productive forces and a great increase in our labor productivity. This will enable our industry to catch up with and surpass Britain within 15 years or less in the output of iron and steel and other major industrial products, will enable our agriculture, on the basis of carrying out the National Program for Agricultural Development ahead of schedule, to surpass quickly the agricultural achievements of the capitalist countries, and will enable our science and technology, on the basis of carrying out the 12-year Program for the Development of Science, to catch up with the world's most advanced levels in the shortest possible time.

* * *

Some people do not recognize the importance of increasing the speed of construction; they do not approve of the policy of consistently achieving greater, faster, better, and more economical results; and they have raised various objections.

Some say that speeding up construction makes people feel "tense," and so it's better to slow down the tempo. But are things not going to get tense if the speed of construction is slowed down? Surely one should be able to see that a really terribly tense situation would exist if more than 600 million people had to live in poverty and cultural backwardness for a prolonged period, had to exert their utmost efforts just to eke out a bare living, and were unable to resist natural calamities effectively, unable to put a quick stop to possible foreign aggression, and utterly unable to master their own fate. It was to pull themselves out of such a situation, that the hundreds of millions of our people summoned up their energies to throw themselves, full of confidence, into the heat of work and struggle. This is simply normal revolutionary activity to which we should give our heartiest approval. This kind of "tension" is nothing to be afraid of.

It goes without saying that we should guide the workers and peasants to direct their efforts to improve their technique, tools, methods of work, and labor organization so as to bring about a forward leap in production. We should see to it that the masses enjoy necessary rest periods as production surges ahead, so as to alternate hard battles with necessary rest and enable production and construction to advance in a rhythmic manner; in addition, we should pay attention to safety measures.

During this great movement in which hundreds of millions of people have been mobilized, it is inevitable that there should be some defects in our work even while great successes are being scored, and that, as we advance, we should meet with some difficulties—even great, unforeseeable difficulties. We should make provision for all this. The broad masses of our people who have forged a solid unity among themselves will certainly not be frightened by these defects and difficulties, and they will surely be able to overcome them in good time. Some people criticize us for "craving greatness and success," for seeking "quick success and instant benefits." What they say about us is right! And shouldn't we crave greatness for our 600 million people and the success of socialism? Should we rather crave smallness and court failure, reject success and benefits, and rest content with lagging behind and doing nothing?

Some people wonder whether the implementation of the policy of consistently achieving greater, faster, better, and more economical results won't lead to waste. Of course, if this policy is followed out piecemeal and if we merely go in for quantity and speed and neglect quality and economy, or vice versa, then of course there will be waste. "Greater" and "faster" results are concerned with quantity and speed; "better" and "more economical" with quality and cost. They supplement and condition each other. Facts have proved that by implementing the policy of achieving greater, faster, better, and more economical results in a comprehensive way, the initiative and potentialities of the people can be brought into fullest play, and the greatest economies can be effected in developing production and construction. Conversely, opposition to this policy and restriction of the initiative and potentialities of the people will certainly result in great wastes of manpower, money, materials, and precious time.

Others are worried that implementation of this policy will throw the various branches of production off balance as well as financial revenue and expenditure. There is bound to be imbalance. Even if we do not carry out this policy, there will always be imbalance, because any balance is temporary and conditional, and hence relative. There is no absolute balance.

* * *

Thus, none of the criticisms directed against the policy of increasing the speed of construction and of achieving greater, faster, better, and more economical results, can hold water.

Why is it that, to increase the speed of construction, industry and agriculture must be developed simultaneously? This is correct because ours is a large agricultural country, and of our over 600 million people, more than 500 million are peasants who constitute a most powerful force both in the revolutionary struggle and construction. Only by relying on this powerful ally and giving full play to the peasants' initiative and creativeness can the working class of our country achieve victory. The paramount importance of the peasantry as an ally is just the same in the period of construction as it was in the period of revolution. Whenever political mistakes were made they invariably had something to do with this question. While giving priority to the growth of heavy industry, we must make great efforts to develop agriculture, which means, first, to get the greatest domestic market in the world to place immense orders for heavy and light industrial products, including farm machinery, chemical fertilizers, building materials, fuels, electrical power, and transport facilities; and, second, to mobilize the biggest labor force in the world to increase the production of foodstuffs, meat, vegetables, etc., and the output of cotton and other industrial crops, to contribute its astonishing labor power to produce enormous wealth, accumulate large amounts of funds for national industrial construction, and itself to build small industrial enterprises in the villages. The energetic development of agriculture, therefore, will certainly speed up the industrialization of our nation and growth of the entire national economy; it will help greatly to improve the livelihood of the people throughout the country and consolidate the worker-peasant alliance. Without the rapid development of agriculture, there can be no rapid development of light and heavy industries, or of the national economy as a whole. The facts in the past eight years, and in this year in particular, have fully proved this.

Some comrades are worried that, though the development of agriculture can accumulate funds for industrialization, it will for the present at least divert some funds which could be used by the state for industrialization. The upsurges in agriculture in 1956 and 1958 have proved such worries unnecessary. So long as we know how to rely on this great force of our 500 million peasants, we can greatly expand the scope of agricultural construction even if there is no increase in state investments in agriculture.

*   *   *

Why is it necessary to undertake the simultaneous development of national and local industries, and of large, small, and medium-sized enterprises in order to increase the speed of construction? Since the development of industrial production is the universal demand of the whole population, it is necessary to follow the principle of building industries by the efforts of the whole party and population, and completely explode the myth that industry can be run only by the few. "The fire burns high when everybody adds wood to it"—it is only when all central and local authorities at every level down to the cooperatives get going at it, only when there is a division of labor and cooperation between big, small, and medium-sized enterprises, that we can achieve greater, faster, better, and more economical results. It is necessary for the central, provincial, municipal, and autonomous region authorities to build a certain number of big enterprises. Big enterprises which have a big output and a high technical level can solve key problems having a decisive bearing on the national economy. They form the backbone of the force that pushes forward the industrial development of the country. But small and medium-sized enterprises have the advantages which big enterprises do not have: they require less investments and can more easily absorb funds from scattered sources; they require less time to build and produce quicker results; they can be designed and equipped locally; they can make do with various simple types of equipment which are readily available in the localities. They can be set up over a wide area so as to facilitate industrialization of the country as a whole, promote the training of technical personnel throughout the country and a balanced development of the economies of the various regions. They can produce a great variety of goods and can be flexibly adapted to produce new types of goods. Close to the sources of raw materials and markets, they can reduce transport costs and make flexible use of available resources, making it easier to bring about a satisfactory relation between supply, production, and sales. It is easier for them to make flexible use of the labor power available in the countryside and of casual labor, depending on the amount of work to be done, and thus help reduce the differences between city and countryside, between workers and peasants.

*   *   *

A big development of local industries, and of small and medium-sized enterprises, will give rise to many new problems which it is difficult for us to foresee at the moment. But here it must be especially emphasized that this growth of local industries and small and medium-sized enterprises which we encourage must be placed under centralized leadership and overall planning, with a proper division of labor and coordination of efforts; there must be no blind development nor development through free competition. To prevent or reduce any possible waste in resources and funds and idle stocks of products, the Central Government and local authorities at all levels must seriously improve the work of coordination and balance, firmly oppose capitalist ideas in management, and any tendency to localism or departmentalism. At the same time, whether in national or local industries, in giant enterprises or small and medium-sized enterprises, it is necessary to oppose resolutely any tendency to chase only after the latest technical equipment, while failing to make full use of all that is on hand; oppose any tendency to overemphasize the role of experts to the disparagement of the great role that can be played by the workers and peasants in developing new production techniques. All such tendencies which lead away from reality and from the masses, no less than the tendency to resign oneself to backwardness and make no attempts to advance, are detrimental to the nation's progress in construction.

* * *

III

The tasks of the party at present are, on the basis of the rectification campaign, to continue to handle contradictions among the people, systematically improve the work of the state, strengthen the work of party organizations at all levels, and work unswervingly for the implementation of the general line for socialist construction.

As mentioned above, the rectification campaign which started in May, 1957 has achieved great results. But, we would be making a big mistake to become dizzy with the successes already won and think that now everything is all right. We must not overlook the fact that the development of the campaign is not even. In some units, in some places, and among some people, it has not been carried out thoroughly enough; it has not got down to the roots of things. In some units, styles of work marked by bureaucracy, commandism, sectarianism, and subjectivism have not been shaken; there are even cases where leading positions are still occupied by bourgeois rightists and rotten elements; and the initiative of the masses is still being hampered. Even in places where the campaign has been carried out fairly throughly, not all the problems brought up by the masses that must be solved have received satisfactory solutions. The leading organizations must undertake a thorough checkup, make energetic efforts to strengthen weaker units, give serious consideration to the suggestions of the masses, and persist in carrying through the rectification campaign to complete victory.

* * *

Under all circumstances, a strict distinction must be drawn between the methods used to handle contradictions among the people and those used to handle contradictions between the enemy and ourselves. So far as ideological problems among the people are concerned, no matter whether it is a case of a few against the many, or of the many against a few, they must be tackled by means of persuasion and education, not by means of force and coercion. In the fields of culture and academic studies, we must continue to carry out the policy of "letting a hundred flowers blossom and a hundred schools of thought contend." This is a method, a scientific Marxist method, of promoting constant progress in the sciences and arts. It is also a method of resolving contradictions among the people. As to the utterances and activities of those who aim to undermine socialism and restore capitalism, we have never sanctioned such utterances and activities, because they are not permitted under the socialist system. But we allow the antisocialist poisonous weeds to grow and confront the people with contrasts, so that by way of comparison, the people can see clearly what they really are, and roused to indignation, rally together to uproot them. In this way, the fighting ability of the masses will be tempered, and it will open up bright prospects for the socialist blossoming of a hundred flowers. This policy has been publicly announced. It was followed in the past and will be followed in the future. The existence of poisonous weeds is an objective phenomena. They will keep cropping up ten thousand years hence. But the poisonous weeds which will emerge in the far distant future will not wear the stamp of class struggle as they do now. Since poisonous weeds exist objectively, if we did not allow them to grow as they are, they would have appeared in disguise, and poisoned the people in secret. We had better tell them openly: "Poisonous weeds are illegal; they've got to be uprooted when they grow. But we do not stop you from sprouting if you want to. Whoever wants to come out and fight, let them do so!" This policy has proved very effective. Large numbers of poisonous weeds furiously attacked the people, and were uprooted by them. Those which have not been uprooted have learned nothing from those which have been eradicated; they still come out and fight. They will certainly come out if they are given the chance, and we shall have to uproot them again. To uproot poisonous weeds is a question between the enemy and ourselves. To let a hundred flowers blossom is a question among the people. These are two different kinds of contradictions and there are two different methods of handling them. The reactionary rightists of the bourgeoisie claimed to be one of the hundred socialist flowers. But that was simply a fraud. They can't be recognized as such.

⁂   ⁂   ⁂

We are now in a great period in the history of our country, the period of development by leaps and bounds. Our party and our country now need a host of people who think, speak, and act with courage and daring; who dare to topple the old idols, to make innovations, and create new things; who dare to uphold the truth, conquer ever new positions for the truth, and raise the banner of progress and revolution. Only by relying on such people can we lead the people of the whole country in making one forward leap after another and complete the great work of socialist construction by achieving greater, faster, better, and more economical results.

For more than a hundred years our country suffered from the oppression of foreign aggressors which made us backward in many respects. Although China has been liberated and has made rapid advances in every field, the mentality of quite a few of our people still bears the imprint of the oppressed, their minds are still filled with all kinds of shibboleths, fears, and feelings of inferiority. Instead of exerting themselves to the utmost, they are apathetic; and instead of pressing ahead consistently, they are resigned to backwardness. The proletariat and the people's militants must rid themselves lock, stock, and barrel of such states of mind; they should cultivate the noble way of firmly believing in the truth, resolutely relying on the masses, and being fearless of any authority. We must remember that modesty helps one to make progress, whereas conceit makes one lag behind. But the practical modesty we advocate has nothing to do with any sense of inferiority. We have a population of more than 600 million and our party has ties of flesh and blood with this vast population. By relying on this great force we can, or soon can, do anything within the realms of human possibility. It is true that for the time being this population of 600 million and more is economically poor and culturally is like a clean sheet of white paper. But what does this matter to Marxist-Leninist revolutionaries? Comrade Mao Tse-tung has put it well: "In addition to other characteristics, our more than 600 million people are characterized by poverty and 'whiteness.' This appears to be a bad thing, but in fact it is a good thing. Poor people want to change, to work hard, and make a revolution. A clean sheet of white paper has nothing written on it and is therefore well suited for writing the newest and most beautiful words on and for drawing the newest and most beautiful pictures." Isn't this a fact? Our 600 million and more people have already far surpassed the most advanced capitalist countries in the West in the speed of the upsurge of their revolutionary consciousness and of the victories of their revolutionary struggles and will definitely far surpass them too in the speed of economic and cultural growth. In history, it is always the newcomers who outstrip the old, always the newborn things, which for a time appear weak and small but represent what is progressive, that defeat the moribund things, which appear powerful but represent what is conservative. Within a very short historical period we shall certainly leave every capitalist country in the world far behind us. And so, shouldn't we have confidence in ourselves and discard everything that smacks of superstition, fear, and feelings of inferiority?

The inevitable victory of our cause is also grounded in the fraternal aid of the countries in the socialist camp headed by the great Soviet Union—which is internationally the most important factor in our favor. We shall continue to draw on the advanced experience of the Soviet Union and other countries, continue to strengthen mutual assistance and cooperation with the other countries in the socialist camp, and, shoulder to shoulder with our fraternal parties in all countries, raise still higher the banner of Marxism-Leninism and reinforce the militant solidarity of the international communist movement. We resolutely support the peace proposals of the Soviet Union, the efforts of the peoples of all lands to safeguard peace, and all national movements which oppose aggression, defend their sovereign rights, and seek independence. The struggles of the people of all countries support our cause and through our work we in turn support the people of all countries.

Comrades! Let us, on the basis of the party's general line for socialist construction, strengthen ceaselessly the unity of the entire party and unity between the party and all the people. Let us strengthen ceaselessly our solidarity with the Soviet Union and other countries in the socialist camp and with all the peoples of the world in the common cause of peace, democracy, and socialism. Victory will surely be ours!

THE GREAT LEAP FORWARD

"The Strength of the Masses Is Limitless" by Yin Tse-ming, excerpted from a pamphlet, *Six Hundred Million Build Industry*, prepared by the editors of Foreign Language Press, Peking, 1958.

The "Great Leap Forward" upon which China embarked in the spring of 1958 involved the greatest and most intense mobilization of manpower that has ever occurred. The masses in the Chinese cities and countryside were recruited, organized and dispatched all over China according to military directives. As Mao was to admit, the Great Leap Forward was contemptuous of the institutions, experience, and accomplishments of the past. This was to him a completely new development, new in China and new in the pages of history.

But the tools that the Chinese were to use were those of China's past: the spade, the basket, human hands. To these were to be added the indispensable ingredient of revolutionary enthusiasm.

Thousands of accounts such as the one reproduced here, told how joyfully the populace responded to the party's new campaign. "The people felt elated and stimulated." "In honor of the anniversary of the Communist Party (July 1), 67,000 people in Hsinhua County worked for three days and nights on end and built 1025 blast furnaces. Many people hearing the news came from as far as 100 li away to join the work. . . . There was a 50-year-old woman who voluntarily contributed more than 200 yuan, her savings of many years, for local industry. . . . To solve the housing problem, the people of Tienping Township, in one morning, spontaneously vacated more than 500 rooms," etc., etc.

Though the "voluntary" and "spontaneous" aspects of the occurrences are to be regarded with quite a few grains of salt, there can be no doubt that an effort of herculean proportions was being undertaken in China.

Most of the factories, mines, and "power stations" in the process of construction required no investment by the central government. The plans were simple. Even so the elementary know-how or equipment required was usually lacking. The populace was encouraged to "innovate." Nothing was to be allowed to stand in the way of the campaign to achieve "faster, better." "It doesn't matter" read one account, "if you're poor, or lack technical skill. These problems can be overcome. The main thing is to break through the aura of mystery that has been built up around scientific processes. Liberate your thinking."

The stated objective of the great leap was overtaking British production in steel and many other areas within 15 years. As "enthusiasm" mounted, the goal became 15 years "or less." And finally one official claimed that the decade and a half aimed at would be shortened by five years. Of course, even if the goal were attained, Great Britain's per capita production would still exceed China's by many times, but the propaganda value would be incalculable.

By the end of 1958, fantastic claims of the successes attained by the "blue ant hills" of Chinese workmen were being made. It was reported that in one special administrative region in Szechuan province alone, 43,000 new factories had been constructed in two months. At another place, a smelter began producing iron 35 days "after the first brick was laid." Baby tractors and ball bearings were being mass-produced by hitherto unskilled and uneducated peasants and workmen. It was boasted that production for 1958 had doubled that of the preceding year. The Great Leap Forward was proclaimed an overwhelming success.

But when the huge stocks supposedly produced failed to appear in the cities, foreign observers began to doubt the accuracy of the government's statistics. Nevertheless the blatant claims of the party propagandists continued and the initial impression of almost unbelievable advancement prevailed.

However, by mid-August, 1959, the "miscalculations" had become so obvious, both inside and outside China, that the party leadership found it necessary to revise the statistics abruptly downward, and to announce that the "backyard" steel had been found unsuitable for modern industrial purposes. Three years later, it was moved to concede that the Great Leap Forward program had, in general, been in error.

Iron smelting and steel making in the Shaoyang Special Administrative Region, Hunan Province, are rapidly developing on a mass scale. In a short period in the autumn of 1958, 12,378 local blast furnaces were built in this area. Of these, 4816 went into immediate operation, with a daily output of more than 2400 tons. The highest daily output has reached the 2438 ton mark, which is an average of half a ton a day for each local furnace in operation. In the first ten days of September, 1958, daily output of iron more than trebled (the daily output on September 1 was 595 tons). Now this region has already produced 50,000 tons of iron. Not only is there a "bumper harvest" in many places but the Chinhua Iron Works in Shaotung County, "king" of local blast furnaces, has produced the remarkable record of almost three tons (5836 catties) a day.

At present, people in many districts are working with increasing enthusiasm to produce iron and steel, and as more and more effective measures are taken, it is anticipated that there will be even greater achievement in steel and iron production in the near future.

The main reason for this remarkable progress in iron and steel production in such a short time in Shaoyang region is the fact that this region has fully carried out the Communist Party's directive to let the whole party and all the people work in iron and steel production, in keeping with the party's general line of socialist construction.

Iron and steel production is not simply a technical job; it is also a political task that has an important bearing on all other activities. Therefore, the first condition for the rapid development of production is for the party secretaries to take the lead and have the entire party membership mobilized. The party committees of Shaoyang region are all clearly convinced of the importance of the guiding principle of making steel production the first task, in order to hasten the progress of industry and agriculture and they gave iron and steel production priority. The first secretaries of different party committees all took personal charge, leading more than ten thousand government functionaries and nearly one million workers in this battle for iron and steel. Many government functionaries organized experimental units in the factories and workshops and they all took part in actual production. By joining the movement first the leaders not only set an example for the masses and hastened its progress, but they also learned much and became experienced workers. By the beginning of September, 1958, government functionaries in this region had set up a total of 2352 experimental blast furnaces and 500 experimental coal pits. In Lienyuan County 15 members of the county party committee and 29 township party secretaries have already mastered the technique of smelting iron.

In Lunghui County, deputy secretary of the county party committee, Hsieh Kuo, set up experimental furnaces at Shihmen, but failed to produce iron in 22 successive attempts. He persisted, studying and trying again and again and finally he produced iron in all the five local furnaces. In Shaotung County, the head of Niumasze Township, Chao Lin-fu, stayed by the furnace, sleeping and eating on the spot. After 21 experiments he finally increased the daily output of each furnace from 300 to 2250 catties. Leaders of co-ops, peasants, men and women of all ages, workers, government officials, and soldiers are all trying their skill with experimental furnaces. Many peasants want to be capable of running agricultural co-ops and factories, capable of farming as well as smelting iron.

When they first began to work in iron and steel production, many people wanted to have big "foreign" blast furnaces. They were not interested in these small native furnaces. They thought it necessary to wait for elaborate equipment. Actually that line of thinking would result in producing less, slower, more expensively, and not so well; and it would not lead to production on a mass basis. Under the timely guidance of the Central Committee and the provincial committee of the Communist Party, that policy was firmly rejected and the policy of putting iron and steel production on a mass basis, of mobilizing all the party members, and letting politics take the lead was carried out. From the beginning, Shaoyang region initiated a gigantic propaganda campaign. All the people were encouraged to voice their opinions in a general debate on such subjects as the following: Why must iron and steel production be developed? How can it be done? What is the relationship between the production of iron and steel and agriculture? Through voicing different opinions and public debates the masses achieved a clearer understanding and became convinced; thus their enthusiasm was aroused. Within a few days more than half a million written pledges were sent to the party in support of the campaign. The people felt elated and stimulated; millions of hearts had only one wish—to fight hard to achieve and surpass the goal of producing 300,000 tons of iron in 1958.

The strength of the masses is tremendous. All the problems of funds, raw materials, equipment, fuel, and geological survey of resources, which seemed hard to solve in the past, disappeared before the resourcefulness of the people. In honor of the anniversary of the Communist Party (July 1), 67,000 people in Hsinhua County worked for three days and nights on end and built 1025 blast furnaces. Many people hearing the news came from as far as 100 *li* away to join in the work, carrying timber and bamboo and their food and clothes. In Szetu Township, 53 couples came to put their names down offering to help in industrial production. Within a few days this county collected a fund of more than 1.6 million yuan. There was a 50-year-old woman who voluntarily contributed more than 200 *yuan*, her savings of many years, for the local industry. The people contributed 1280 pigs, more than 700,000 catties of vegetables, and 180,000 pairs of straw sandals for the people who were taking part in this industrial construction project. To solve the housing problem, the people of Tienping Township, in one morning, spontaneously vacated more than 500 rooms. The contributions from the masses became a mighty torrent, and the blast furnaces were set up very quickly. The people composed a song describing this event:

> The Communist Party is really wonderful.
> In three days more than a thousand furnaces were built.
> The masses' strength is really tremendous.
> The American imperialists will run off, tails between legs.
> The Chinese people will now surpass Britain.
> The East wind will always prevail over the West wind.

*   *   *

THE COMMUNE COMES—AND GOES

Resolution Adopted by the Eighth Central Committee of the Chinese
Communist Party, Peking, December 10, 1958.

In the midst of the turmoil created by the industrial Great Leap
Forward in 1958, the CCP instituted a radical new agricultural policy
designed to sweep the peasantry into the main line of China's alleged
rapid advance. The new policy, that of "communizing" agriculture,
(later all China, urban as well as rural, was to be organized into communes) was first widely implemented in August, 1958.

The commune was to be a step beyond the collectivization of agriculture which had been only recently carried out in China. Under
it the remaining private possessions of the peasants were to be con-
fiscated. Payment for labor was to be mostly in kind and services and
according to need rather than to ability. The great body of Chinese
were to be placed under military organization and discipline in order
to unite them as one man to instantaneously and unquestioningly
carry out the orders of the party.

The commune was a radical move and the leftist leaders of the
CCP now in charge were aware that it was. But they had to a degree
been carried away by the successes already reported in the great leap.
Daring and the involvement of popular enthusiasm had paid off in
industry, they believed. It would do the same in agriculture. Moreover, the recruitment of huge amounts of manpower to substitute
for the machinery that China lacked had denuded the collectives of
their labor force. Communization was seen as a form of reorganizing
the remaining peasant population to secure its maximum utilization
in the forthcoming harvest and beyond.

And so, in the late summer of 1958, the "new social organization
appeared, fresh as the morning sun, above the broad horizon of east
Asia." Much was hoped for from the commune. Under it, promise
was given that China's food problem would be permanently solved
by 1959. And the peasants were guaranteed the realization of a
"happy, prosperous" life within three years. These claims for the
commune, which the Chinese regarded as distinctively theirs, aroused
great animosity among the Russians, who felt that their own long,
drawn-out labors were being downgraded, by the Chinese assertion
that their superior organization and enthusiasm would quickly succeed in achieving for China what it had taken the Russians long
decades to accomplish.

Even more were the Soviets outraged by the Chinese introduction of a semifree-supply system. The Russian Marxist position is that the free-supply system must await a much higher level of economic development than currently exists even in the Soviet Union. The Russian comrades felt certain that the Chinese steps in the direction of free supply would stumble badly. And they were infuriated by what they considered Chinese presumption in introducing this latter-day innovation at such an early stage of industrial development.

According to the Chinese party accounts, the masses were overjoyed at the institution of the commune. They quickly "volunteered" to be included in them. And when the local party officials did not act with sufficient dispatch, then the peasants communized themselves and "beat gongs and drums, went to them (the CCP officials) to report the good news." It was the party line that the people demanded the changes effected by the communes.

In fact, however, it is quite certain that the masses did not react very favorably to the seizure of the small parcels of land that remained to them, to the general expropriation of their private possessions, to having their families separated and their ancestral burying grounds plowed under, to being moved from job to job and place to place in the commune at the leaders' orders. There was more than scattered resistance to communization; but nevertheless by December, 1958, at the meeting of the Central Committee, it was possible to announce that—probably on paper anyway—99 percent of all China's peasant households had been communized. The communes were declared to be a success.

But the very same pronouncement that declared the victory of the communes also ordered their end. For the Central Committee resolution of December 10, 1958, in effect states that the communes had been instituted too quickly, without sufficient preparation, and that far too much had been expected of them.

Even though the commune is cited as having a "profound and far reaching significance," the attempt to make it the basic unit of Chinese rural, to say nothing of urban, organization is dropped. The peasant is told he can keep his clothing, bedding and furniture, trees, his small livestock and poultry, the home in which he lives, his bank savings; and he can again pursue his trade, so long as it does not interfere with his assigned task. The resolution again and again uses such terms as "impetuous," "premature," "hastily," or "Utopian" to describe the actions surrounding the implementation of the commune. It warns against "wishful thinking." Finally it states: "Three years of hard battle plus several years of energetic work may bring about a great change in the economic face of the county. But even then there will still be a considerable distance to go to reach the goals of a high degree of industrialization . . . and there will be an even longer distance to go to reach the goals of an enormous abundance of social products. . . ." "For the present," the Chinese party admits, "the scope of free supply should not be too wide."

Thus, at the end of 1958, the Chinese, for reasons that still are not completely clear, in essence abandoned the communes. However, it would still be three years, the spring of 1962, before it would be acknowledged by the CCP that the commune, as the Great Leap Forward, in general, had been undertaken in error.

I

In 1958, a new social organization appeared, fresh as the morning sun, above the broad horizon of east Asia. This was the large-scale people's commune in the rural areas of our country which combines industry, agriculture, trade, education, and military affairs and in which government administration and commune management are integrated. Since their first appearance, the people's communes with their immense vitality have attracted widespread attention.

The movement to set up people's communes has grown very rapidly. Within a few months starting in the summer of 1958, all of the more than 740,000 agricultural producers' cooperatives in the country, in response to the enthusiastic demand of the mass of peasants, reorganized themselves into over 26,000 people's communes. Over 120 million households, or more than 99 percent of all China's peasant households of various nationalities, have joined the people's communes. This shows that the emergence of the people's communes is not fortuitous; it is the outcome of the economic and political development of our country, the outcome of the socialist rectification campaign conducted by the party, of the party's general line for socialist construction and the great leap forward of socialist construction in 1958.

Although the rural people's communes were established only a short while ago, the mass of the peasants are already conscious of the obvious benefits they have brought them. Labor power and the means of production can, on a larger scale than before, be managed and deployed in a unified way to ensure that they are used still more rationally and effectively, and consequently to facilitate the development of production. Under the unified leadership of the commune, industry, agriculture (including farming, forestry, animal husbandry, side-occupations, and fisheries), trade, education, and military affairs have been closely coordinated and developed rapidly. In particular, thousands and tens of thousands of small factories have mushroomed in the rural areas. To meet the pressing demands of the masses, the communes have set up large numbers of community dining rooms, nurseries, kindergartens, "homes of respect for the aged," and other institutions for collective welfare, which have, in particular, completely emancipated women from thousands of years of kitchen drudgery and brought broad smiles to their faces. As the result of the bumper crops, many communes have instituted a system of distribution that combines the wage system with the free supply system; the mass of peasants, both men and women, have begun to receive their wages; and those families which in the past constantly worried about their daily meals and about their firewood, rice, oil, salt, soya sauce, vinegar, and vegetables are now able to "eat without paying." In other words they have the most important and most reliable kind of social insurance. For the peasants, all this is epoch-making news. The living standards of the peasants have been improved and they know from practical experience and the prospects of the development of the communes that they will live still better in the future.

The development of the system of rural people's communes has an even more profound and far-reaching significance. It has shown the people of our country the way to the gradual industrialization of the rural areas, the way to the gradual transition from collective ownership to ownership by the whole people in agriculture, the way to the gradual transition from the socialist principle of "to each according to his work" to the communist principle of "to each according to his needs," the way gradually to lessen and finally to eliminate the differences between town and country, between worker and peasant, and between mental and manual labor, and the way gradually to lessen and finally to eliminate the internal function of the state.

All this has proved the correctness and historic significance of the Resolution on the Establishment of People's Communes in the Rural Areas adopted on the basis of the creativeness of the masses by the Political Bureau of the Central Committee of the Chinese Communist Party at its Peitaiho meeting in August 1958.

People's communes have now become the general rule in all rural areas inhabited by our people of various nationalities (except in Tibet and in certain other areas). Some experiments have also begun in the cities. In the future, urban people's communes, in a form suited to the specific features of cities, will also become instruments for the transformation of old cities and the construction of new socialist cities; they will become the unified organizers of production, exchange, and distribution and of the livelihood and well-being of the people; they will become social organizations which combine industry, agriculture, trade, education, and military affairs, organizations in which government administration and commune manangement are integrated. There are, however, certain differences between the city and the countryside.

Firstly, city conditions are more complex than those in the countryside.

Secondly, socialist ownership by the whole people is already the main form of ownership in the cities; and the factories, public institutions, and schools, under the leadership of the working class, have already become highly organized in accordance with socialist principles (with the exception of some of the family members of the workers and staffs). Therefore, the transition in cities to people's communes inevitably involves some requirements different from those in the rural areas.

Thirdly, bourgeois ideology is still fairly prevalent among many of the capitalists and intellectuals in the cities; they still have misgivings about the establishment of communes—so we should wait a bit for them.

Consequently, we should continue to make experiments and generally should not be in a hurry to set up people's communes on a large scale in the cities. Particularly in the big cities, this work should be postponed except for the necessary preparatory measures. People's communes should be established on a large scale in the cities only after rich experience has been gained and when the sceptics and doubters have been convinced.

The rural people's communes which have already been established have not had time to consolidate their organizations, perfect their working systems, or systematically settle the new questions concerning production, distribution, livelihood and welfare, management and administration which have arisen with the establishment of the communes. This has happened because the communes were only recently set up and most of them, immediately after their establishment, threw themselves into the heavy work of the autumn harvest, ploughing, and sowing and the nationwide campaign for iron and steel. There is as yet insufficient experience in successfully running and developing the people's communes. Different approaches to certain questions are unavoidable. The urgent tasks at present are to quickly achieve a unity of views on the communes among all members of the party and among the people, strengthen the leadership over the communes, check up on and consolidate their organization, define and perfect their working systems, and improve the organization of production and life in the communes. Energetic efforts must be made to strengthen those communes which have already been set up, so that they will be in a position to carry out ever more successfully their great mission of promoting the development of the productive forces and the relations of production.

II

The people's commune is the basic unit of the socialist social structure of our country, combining industry, agriculture, trade, education, and military affairs; at the same time it is the basic organization of the socialist state power. Marxist-Leninist theory and the initial experience of the people's communes in our country enable us to foresee now that the people's communes will quicken the tempo of our socialist construction and constitute the best form for realizing, in our country, the following two transitions.

Firstly, the transition from collective ownership to ownership by the whole people in the countryside; and,

Secondly, the transition from socialist to communist society. It can also be foreseen that in the future communist society, the people's commune will remain the basic unit of our social structure.

From now on, the task confronting the people of our country is to develop through such a form of social organization as the people's commune, and on the basis of the general line for socialist construction laid down by the party, the social productive forces at high speed, to advance the industrialization of the country, the industrialization of the communes, and the mechanization and electrification of agriculture, and to effect the gradual transition from socialist collective ownership to socialist ownership by the whole people, thus fully realizing ownership by the whole people in the socialist economy of our country and gradually building our country into a great socialist land with a highly developed modern industry, agriculture, science, and culture. During this process, the elements of communism are bound to increase gradually and these will lay the foundation of material and spiritual conditions for the transition from socialism to communism.

This is a gigantic and extremely complex task. In the light of experience already gained, as conditions now stand in our country, it is possible that socialist ownership by the whole people may be fully realized at a somewhat earlier date, but this will not be very soon. Though the pace at which we are advancing is fairly rapid, it will still take a fairly long time to realize, on a large scale, the industrialization of the communes, the mechanization and electrification of agriculture, and the building of a socialist country with a highly developed modern industry, agriculture, science, and culture. This whole process will take 15, 20, or more years to complete, counting from now.

The imperialists and those who parrot them say that this is too short a time for us to build a highly developed modern industry, agriculture, science and culture, and that we won't be able to achieve our aim. We've got used to such tunes; we needn't pay any attention to them; the facts are bound to batter these people down time and time again. But there will be other people who will say that this time is too long. They are good-hearted people in our own ranks, but they are overeager. They think that the building of a highly developed modern industry and so on, full realization of socialist ownership by the whole people, and even the attainment of communism, are very easy things. They think that ownership in the rural people's communes is even now of the nature of ownership by the whole people and that very soon or even now they can dispense with the socialist principle of "to each according to his work" and adopt the communist principle of "to each according to his needs." Consequently, they cannot understand why the socialist system will have to continue for a very long time. Their view, of course, is a misconception, which must be cleared up.

It should be pointed out that the switch from agricultural producers' cooperatives to people's communes, the transition from socialist collective ownership to socialist ownership by the whole people and the transition from socialism to communism are processes which are interconnected but at the same time distinct from each other.

First of all, the switch from the agricultural producers' cooperatives to the people's communes has expanded and strengthened the existing collective ownership and contains certain elements of ownership by the whole people. But this is not to say that collective ownership in the countryside has been transformed into ownership by the whole people. The whole Chinese countryside has now switched over to people's communes, but a certain time will have to pass before ownership by the whole people is realized throughout the countryside.

True, the establishment of the people's communes has added certain elements of ownership by the whole people to the collectively owned economy. This has happened because the rural people's communes and the basic organizations of state power have been combined into one; because the banks, stores, and some other enterprises owned by the whole people, originally existing in the countryside, have been placed under the management of the communes; because the communes have taken part in establishing certain undertakings in industrial and other construction which are by nature owned by the whole people; because in many counties the county federations of communes, exercising unified leadership over all the people's communes in these counties, have been formed and have the power to deploy a certain portion of the manpower, material, and financial resources of the communes to undertake construction on a county or even bigger scale (this has already started in many areas), and so on. But at the present time the means of production and the products of the rural people's communes are in the main still collectively owned by the communes and differ from those of the state-owned enterprises which belong to the whole people. Both collective ownership and ownership by the whole people are socialist ownership; but the latter is more advanced than the former because the state, representing the whole people, can directly make a unified and rational distribution of the means of production and the products of enterprises owned by the whole people according to the requirements of the national economy as a whole, while this cannot be done by enterprises run under collective ownership, including the existing rural people's communes. To say that ownership by the people's communes as they now exist in the country-side is already ownership by the whole people does not conform to reality.

To gradually promote the transition from collective ownership to ownership by the whole people, every county should set up its federation of communes. In coming years, and on the basis of the energetic development of production and the raising of the people's political understanding, such federations should take suitable steps gradually to increase the proportion of their means of production that is owned by the whole people and the proportion of their products that is subject to unified distribution by the state, and, when conditions mature, should change collective ownership into ownership by the whole people. If timely steps are not taken to promote and complete this change and if the existing collective ownership is kept intact indefinitely with the result that commune members confine their attention to the relatively narrow scope of the interests of their collective, the continuous development of the social productive forces and the continuous development of the people's political understanding will be impeded. This is not appropriate. However, it must be pointed out that collective ownership still plays a positive role today in developing production in the people's communes. How soon the transition from collective ownership to ownership by the whole people will be effected will be determined by the objective factors—the level of development of production and the level of the people's political understanding—and not by mere wishful thinking that it can be done at any time we want it. Thus this transition will be realized, by stages and by groups, on a national scale only after a considerable time. Those who, because they fail to understand this, confuse the establishment of people's communes with the realization of ownership by the whole people, making impetuous attempts to abolish collective ownership in the countryside prematurely, and trying hastily to change over to ownership by the whole people, will not be doing the right thing and therefore cannot succeed.

Furthermore, the change from socialist collective ownership to socialist ownership by the whole people is not the same thing as the change from socialism to communism. Still less is the change from agricultural producers' cooperatives to people's communes the same thing as the change from socialism to communism. The change from socialism to communism will require much more time than the change from socialist collective ownership to socialist ownership by the whole people.

True, the free-supply system adopted by the people's communes contains the first shoots of the communist principle of "to each according to his needs"; the policy carried out by the people's communes of running industry and agriculture simultaneously and combining them has opened up a way to reduce the differences between town and countryside and between worker and peasant, and when the rural people's communes pass over from socialist collective ownership to socialist ownership by the whole people, these communist factors will grow further. All this must be acknowledged. Moreover, with social products becoming plentiful thanks to the continuous advance of industry and agriculture throughout the country; with the proportion of what is supplied gratis under the distribution system of the people's communes gradually growing larger and the standards of free supply being gradually raised; with the consistent raising of the level of the people's political understanding; with the constant progress of education for the whole people; the gradual reduction of the differences between mental and manual labor; and with the gradual diminution of the internal function of the state power, etc., the conditions for the transition to communism will also gradually mature. It is of course not proper to ignore or even impede this course of development and relegate communism to the distant future.

Nevertheless every Marxist must soberly realize that the transition from socialism to communism is a fairly long and complicated process of development and that throughout this entire process society is still socialist in nature. Socialist society and communist society are two stages marked by different degrees of economic development. The socialist principle is "from each according to his ability and to each according to his work"; the communist principle is "from each according to his ability and to each according to his needs." The communist system of distribution is more rational; but it can be put into effect only when there is a great abundance of social products. In the absence of this condition, any negation of the principle of "to each according to his work" will tend to dampen the working enthusiasm of the people and is therefore disadvantageous to the development of production and the increase of social products, and hence to speeding the realization of communism. For this reason, in the income of commune members, the portion constituting the wage paid according to work done must occupy an important place over a long period and will, during a certain period, take first place. In order to encourage the working enthusiasm of commune members and also to facilitate the satisfaction of their complex daily needs, the communes must strive gradually to increase the wages of their members and, for a number of years to come, must increase them at a rate faster than that portion of their income which comes under the heading of free supply. Even after the transition from collective ownership to ownership by the whole people, the people's communes will, during a necessary historical period, retain the system of "to each according to his work" owing to the fact that there is not as yet an abundant enough supply of social products to realize communism. Any premature attempt to negate the principle of "to each according to his work" and replace it with the principle of "to each according to his needs," that is, any attempt to enter communism by overreaching ourselves when conditions are not mature—is undoubtedly a Utopian concept that cannot possibly succeed.

Both the transition from socialist collective ownership to socialist ownership by the whole people and the transition from socialism to communism must depend on a certain level of development of the productive forces. Production relations must be suited to the nature of the productive forces and only when the productive forces develop to a certain stage will certain changes be brought about in production relations—this is a fundamental principle of Marxism. Our comrades must bear in mind that the present level of development of the productive forces in our country is, after all, still very low. Three years of hard battle plus several years of energetic work may bring about a great change in the economic face of the country. But even then there will still be a considerable distance to go to reach the goals of a high degree of industrialization of the entire country and the mechanization and electrification of our country's agriculture; and there will be an even longer distance to go to reach the goals of an enormous abundance of social products, of a great lightening of labor and of a sharp reduction of working hours. Without all these, it is, of course, impossible to talk about entering a higher stage of development in human society—communism. Therefore, since we are devoted to the cause of communism, we must first devote ourselves to developing our productive forces and working energetically to fulfill our plan for socialist industrialization. We should not groundlessly make declarations that the people's communes in the countryside will "realize ownership by the whole people immediately," or even "enter communism immediately," and so on. To do such things is not only an expression of rashness, it will greatly lower the standards of communism in the minds of the people, distort the great ideal of communism and vulgarize it, strengthen the petty-bourgeois trend towards equalitarianism, and adversely affect the development of socialist construction.

On the question of transition from socialism to communism, we must not mark time at the socialist stage, but neither should we drop into the Utopian dream of skipping the socialist stage and jumping over to the communist stage. We are advocates of the Marxist-Leninist theory of uninterrupted revolution; we hold that no "Great Wall" exists or can be allowed to exist between the democratic revolution and the socialist revolution and between socialism and communism. We are at the same time advocates of the Marxist-Lenist theory of the development of revolution by stages; we hold that different stages of development reflect qualitative changes and that these stages, different in quality, should not be confused. The Political Bureau of the Central Committee has pointed out clearly in its August Resolution on the Establishment of People's Communes in the Rural Areas:

in the case of the people's communes, "the transition from collective ownership to ownership by the whole people is a process, the completion of which may take less time—three or four years—in some places, and longer—five or six years or even more—elsewhere. Even with the completion of this transition, people's communes, like state-owned industry, are still socialist in character, i.e., the principle of 'from each according to his ability and to each according to his work' prevails. Some years after that, the social product will increase greatly, the communist consciousness and morality of the entire people will be raised to a much higher degree, universal education will be instituted and developed, the differences between worker and peasant, between town and country, between mental and manual labor—the legacies of the old society that have inevitably been carried over into the socialist period—and the remnants of unequal bourgeois rights which are the reflection of these differences—will gradually vanish; and the function of the state will be limited to protecting the country from external aggression; it will play no role internally. At that time Chinese society will enter the era of communism in which the principle of 'from each according to his ability and to each according to his needs' will be practiced." In order to clear up misconceptions about the people's communes and ensure the healthy development of the people's commune movement, extensive and repeated publicity and education based on this Marxist-Leninist point of view must be carried out seriously throughout the party and among all the people of China.

III

The people's communes must plan their production, exchange, consumption, and accumulation. Their plans should be subordinated to the state plans and to the administration of the state. In working out their plans, the people's communes should at the same time fully develop their own characteristic features and their initiative.

Development of production is the key to the consolidation and elevation of the people's communes. The correct policy of the people's communes for the development of production should be to insure the simultaneous development of industry and agriculture and of production for their own use and for exchange, in accordance with the principles of unified state planning, of adaptation to local conditions, and of running the communes industriously and thriftily. In every aspect of production and capital construction, thrift must be observed; careful plans must be worked out; and manpower, material, and financial resources must be used as rationally as possible; production costs must be reduced; expenditures must be cut down and income increased; extravagance and waste among some functionaries of the communes following bumper harvests should be prevented and opposed.

In agricultural production, shallow ploughing, careless cultivation, and "big acreage with small output" should be gradually replaced by deep ploughing, intensive cultivation, and "small acreage with big output." Farming should be carried on as meticulously as gardening, and agricultural production should be mechanized and electrified to bring about a big increase in per *mu* yields and labor productivity and to gradually reduce the area under cultivation and manpower engaged in agriculture. We should strive to reach a yearly average of two to three thousand *jin* or one ton to one and a half tons of grain per capita within a comparatively short period. As the grain problem is solved, the proportion of the total agricultural output occupied by cotton, flax, and jute, silk, soya beans, oil-bearing crops, sugar-bearing crops, tea, tobacco, medicinal, and other industrial crops must be gradually increased. In addition, great attention should be paid to speeding the development of forestry, animal husbandry, farm side lines, and fisheries. In short, as on the industrial front, a great revolution must be carried out on all the fronts of agriculture, forestry, animal husbandry, farm side lines, and fisheries so as to thoroughly transform the face of agriculture.

People in the past often worried about our "overpopulation" and relatively small amount of available arable land. But this idea has been overturned by the facts of our 1958 bumper harvest. Insofar as we succeed in seriously popularizing the rich experience gained in getting high yields through deep ploughing, intensive cultivation, layer-by-layer fertilization, and rational close planting, it will be found that the amount of arable land is not too small but very considerable, and that the question is not so much overpopulation as shortage of manpower. This will be a very big change. In the next several years, local conditions permitting, we should try to reduce the area sown to crops each year to about one-third of what it is at present. Part of the land so saved can be used for fallow rotation, pasturage, and the growing of green manure; the rest can be used for afforestation, reservoirs, and the extensive cultivation of flowers, shrubs, and trees to turn our whole land with its plains, hills, and waters into a garden. By these means:

Firstly, it will be possible to greatly economize the use of water, fertilizer, and manpower, and to considerably increase the fertility of the soil;

Secondly, full use can be made of every mountain, river, forest, and the pasture; and the comprehensive management of agriculture, forestry, animal husbandry, farm side lines, and fisheries can be greatly developed.

Thirdly, our natural environment will be transformed and the whole country beautified.

This is a great ideal that can be realized. People's communes throughout the land should work to realize this aim.

People's communes must go in for industry in a big way. The

development of industry by the people's communes will not only accelerate the industrialization of the whole country but also promote the realization of ownership by the whole people in the rural districts, and reduce the differences between town and country. According to the differing conditions in each people's commune, an appropriate part of the labor force should be transferred, step by step, from agriculture to industry so as to develop, according to plan, the production of fertilizer, insecticides, farm implements, and machinery and building materials; the processing and many-sided utilization of agricultural produce; the manufacturing of sugar, textiles, and paper; the expansion of mining, metallurgy, electric power, and other light and heavy industries. Industrial production in the people's communes must be closely linked with agricultural production; it should first of all serve the development of agriculture and the mechanization and electrification of farming; at the same time it should serve to meet the demands of commune members for staple consumer goods, and serve the country's big industries and the socialist market. The principles of adaptation to local conditions and obtaining raw materials locally should be fully taken into consideration; in order to avoid increased costs and waste of labor power, industries should not be set up in places where there are no raw materials or where these have to be brought from very far away. With regard to production techniques, the principle should be carried out of linking handicraft with mechanized industry, and indigenous methods with modern methods of production. All handicraft industries which have good foundations and prospects for expansion must continue to be developed, and gradually carry through the necessary technical transformations. The mechanized industries must also make full use of indigenous methods and iron, steel, machine tools, other raw materials and equipment produced by indigenous methods; they will gradually advance from indigenous to modern, from small to large, and from a low to a high level.

Whether in industry or agriculture, people's communes should develop production for their own use which directly meets their own needs, and they should also develop commodity production on as wide a scale as possible. Every people's commune, according to its own characteristics and under the guidance of the state, should carry out the necessary division of labor in production and exchange of commodities with other people's communes and state-owned enterprises. Only in this way can the economy of our whole society expand at a faster rate, and every commune obtain through exchange the machinery and equipment required for the mechanization and electrification of farming, as well as the consumer goods and ready cash required to meet the needs of commune members and pay them wages, and make it possible to raise wages step by step. To ensure fulfillment of trading plans, an extensive system of contracts should be set up between the state and the communes and among the communes themselves.

It must be stressed that during the course of a necessary historical period, commodity production by the people's communes and the exchange of commodities between the state and communes and among the communes themselves must be greatly developed. Such production and exchange of commodities are different from those under capitalism, because they are conducted in a planned way, on the basis of socialist public ownership and not in an anarchic way on the basis of capitalist private ownership. Continued development of commodity production and continued adherence to the principle of "to each according to his work" are two important questions of principle in expanding the socialist economy. The whole party should have a uniform understanding of them. Some people, attempting to "enter communism" prematurely, have tried to abolish the production and exchange of commodities too early, and to negate at too early a stage the positive roles of commodities, value, money, and prices. This line of thinking is harmful to the development of socialist construction and is therefore incorrect.

IV

The people's communes in rural districts should distribute their own incomes properly on the principle of running the communes industriously and thriftily. To speed up production, the proportion of accumulation should be appropriately increased after production costs, administrative expenses, and taxes have been deducted from the gross income. But on the basis of the development of production, the portion of the income used to meet the individual and collective expenses of commune members (including the portion spent on public welfare, culture, and education) should be increased annually in order to improve the livelihood of the people year by year.

The introduction of a distribution system which combines the wage system and the free-supply system in the part of the commune's income allotted to its members for consumption is a form of socialist distribution created by China's people's communes, and at the present time it represents what the broad mass of members earnestly demand. As stated above, this distribution system includes the first shoots of communism but in essence it is still socialist—based on the principle of "from each according to his ability and to each according to his work."

The proportions of wages and free supplies in the total amount allotted to members should be determined in the light of the varying levels of the development of production in the communes. At present, in fixing the ratio between wages and free supplies, care should be taken as far as possible to avoid reducing the income of households which have relatively few members but are strong in labor power;

in general, it should be made possible for more than 90 percent of the members to increase their income as compared with the previous year while the rest should get no less than in the previous year.

For the present, the scope of free supply should not be too wide. The application of the free-supply system does not seek to make the life of the people uniform. Under the systems of socialism and communism, the needs of the people are on the whole similar while varying according to the individual. Therefore in the future, as well as at present, care should be taken to insure, as far as possible, that members have suitable freedom of choice within the framework of the free-supply system.

Wages must be increased gradually as production expands. For the present, after deducting the items freely supplied, wage scales in the rural areas can be divided into six to eight grades, and the highest grade may be four or more times as much as the lowest grade. But the differences should not be too great; for if they were, they would not conform to the existing differences in laboring skills in the rural areas. Certain differences between the wage levels in different areas are permissible. For the present the differences between wage grades in the city are greater than those in the countryside, and this is necessary. In the future, as a result of the tremendous rise in production, everyone will be much better off and whether in city or countryside such differences between wage grades will be unnecessary and will gradually disappear. That will be nearing the era of communism.

The reasons why wage levels in the city are generally higher than those in the countryside are manysided (including the factor of living costs being higher in the city), and this is also a temporary situation which should be explained to the peasants. Some commune members, apart from working in the villages, also receive money sent home by their relatives who are away in cities or elsewhere (such as workers, soldiers, functionaries, and Chinese living abroad). Work should be done to dissuade other members from wrangling about this. In distribution within the commune, members with such receipts should be treated the same as others without discrimination in regard to free supplies and wages, and they should not be urged to make special investments or contributions to the commune. If they rely on family members away from home for the whole of their livelihood, the commune should not interfere, but it may stop supplying them with the usual allotments. Those who leave home for study, apart from those whose needs are covered by the state or can be covered by their own families, should be supported by the county federation of communes according to the standards laid down by the schools.

The more socialism develops and the more abundant social products become, the more abundant too will become the means of livelihood allotted to each individual. Some people think that the switch to communes will call for a redistribution of existing property for personal use. This is a misconception. It should be made known among the masses that the means of livelihood owned by members (including houses, clothing, bedding, and furniture) and their deposits in banks and credit cooperatives will remain their own property after they join the commune and will always belong to them. When necessary, the commune may borrow the surplus housing space of members with their consent, but the ownership still belongs to the owners. Members can retain odd trees around their houses, small farm tools, small instruments, small domestic animals, and poultry; they can also continue to engage in some small domestic side-line occupations on the condition that these do not hamper their taking part in collective labor.

Debts incurred before the people's communes were established should not be declared cancelled irrespective of whether these are between individuals, between the commune and its members, or debts contracted by commune members with banks or credit cooperatives. These debts should be repaid where conditions permit and where the conditions do not allow repayment for the time being, they should be held over.

V

The people's commune is the organizer of the production and livelihood of the people and the fundamental purpose of the development of production is to satisfy to the maximum extent the constantly growing material and cultural needs of all members of society. In leading the work of the commune, the party must give all-round attention to the ideological development, production, and livelihood of commune members. It must care for the people and correct the tendency to see only things and not human beings. The greater the working enthusiasm of the masses, the greater the attention the party should pay to their well-being. The more attention the Party pays to the livelihood of the masses, the greater their enthusiasm will be in work. It is wrong to set production and people's livelihood against each other and to imagine that attention to the livelihood of the masses will hamper production. Of course, it is also wrong to put a one-sided and excessive stress on the improvement of the people's livelihood without regard to the raising of their level of political consciousness and the development of production, and not to advocate working hard for long-term interests.

Communists have always held that in a communist society labor will be changed "from a heavy burden into a pleasure" and will become the "primary necessity of life." There is no doubt that the working day will be greatly shortened in future. With the development of mechanization and electrification, we must strive to introduce the six-hour workday within a certain number of years. Our intensive work at the present time is precisely to create conditions for the six-hour workday and even shorter working hours in future. At present, the system of eight hours of actual work and two hours of study should be put into effect in both city and countryside. During the busy farm season or when other work in the rural areas is particularly heavy, working hours may be appropriately extended. But, in any event, eight hours for sleep and four hours for meals and recreation, altogether twelve hours, must be guaranteed every day and this must not be reduced. It is true that there is a labor shortage at present, but the way out must be found in stressing the successful implementation of the reform of tools and improvement of labor organization and not in extending working hours. Special attention must be paid to safety in production and labor conditions must be improved as far as possible in order to reduce to the minimum or completely eliminate work accidents. Adequate rest must be insured to women both during pregnancy and after childbirth and they should also get the necessary rest during menstruation when they should not be asked to do heavy work, to get their feet wet in cold water, or work at night.

Community kitchens should be well run. All commune members must be assured of plenty of good, clean food suited to their national and local habits. The communal eating establishments should have dining rooms, and they should efficiently run their own vegetable gardens, bean-curd mills, bean-noodle mills, and condiment shops; they should raise pigs, sheep, chickens, ducks, and fish. The food should be varied and appetizing. Nutrition specialists should be consulted to make sure that the food contains enough calories and the nutriments needed by the human body. Where necessary and possible, special food should be provided for the aged, children, invalids, pregnant women, and nursing mothers. It is permissible for some commune members to cook at home. Community dining rooms should be managed democratically. Their administrative staffs and cooks should be chosen from among those who are politically reliable. It is best that they be elected democratically.

Nurseries and kindergartens should be run well so that every child can live better and receive a better education in them than at home, and so that the children want to stay there and the parents want to put them there. The parents may decide whether it is necessary for their children to board there, and may take them home at any time. In order to run nurseries and kindergartens well, communes should train a large number of qualified child-care workers and teachers.

The "homes of respect for the aged" should be run well so as to provide better dwelling places for those old people who have no children to take care of them (those who are eligible for the "five guarantees"—food, clothing, fuel, the bringing up of children, and burial).

Communes must ensure the successful running of primary and secondary schools and adult education. Universal primary school education should be instituted in the rural areas throughout the country. Full-time secondary schools and half-time secondary agricultural schools, or other secondary vocational schools, should be well run; and universal secondary education should be introduced step by step. Earnest efforts should be made to wipe out illiteracy, organize various kinds of spare-time schools, and conduct political education, cultural classes, and technical education for adults. In reducing the differences between manual and mental labor, the institution of universal education among the working people and the gradual raising of their educational level is an important step which must be carried out conscientiously. The communes, in addition, must also select and send a number of young people to study in senior secondary schools, secondary vocational schools, and institutions of higher learning in the cities so as to train fairly well-educated working personnel for the state and the communes. The principle of combining education with productive labor must be carried out thoroughly in all schools, without exception. Children above the age of nine may take part in some labor to an appropriate extent so as to cultivate the habit of work in childhood and stimulate their physical and mental development; but full attention must be paid to the health of the children—they must only be given light work for short periods of time, suited to their physical strength and their aptitude.

Ideological and political work among the staffs in community dining rooms, nurseries, kindergartens, "homes of respect for the aged," primary schools, public health centers, clubs, and shops must be strengthened and efforts must be made to give positive guidance to public opinion so that the whole of society and the whole communes regard the successful running of community dining rooms, nurseries, kindergartens, and other collective welfare undertakings and satisfactory work in the personal services as noble work of service to the people. The attitude of the exploiting classes in looking down on work which concerns the daily life and welfare of the masses and work in the personal services, must be criticized and corrected.

The existing old-style houses must be reconstructed step by step; townships and village housing estates with parks and woods must be built by stages and in groups: these will include residential quarters, community dining rooms, nurseries, kindergartens, the "homes of respect for the aged," factories, threshing floors, livestock sheds, shops, post and telecommunications offices, warehouses, schools, hospitals, clubs, cinemas, sports grounds, baths, and public lavatories. The construction plans of townships and village housing estates should be thoroughly discussed by the masses. We stand for the abolition of the irrational patriarchal system inherited from the past and for the development of family life in which there is democracy and unity. This stand has been warmly received by the masses. Therefore, in building residential quarters, attention must be paid to building the houses so that the married couples, the young and the aged of each family can all live together.

There is now a big bunch of fools in the world who are attacking the people's communes with all their might and main and among them is Mr. Dulles of the United States. This Dulles knows nothing about things in our country but likes to pretend to be a China expert and madly opposes the people's communes. What breaks his heart especially is that we have supposedly destroyed the marvellous family system which has been handed down for thousands of years. True, the Chinese people have destroyed a feudal, patriarchal system. This patriarchal system, it must be noted, generally disappeared long ago in capitalist society and that was a progressive step in capitalist society. But we go a step further and establish a democratic, united family and this is generally rare in capitalist society. Only in the future, when the socialist revolution has been carried out and when the capitalist system of exploitation of man by man has been eliminated, will it be possible to establish such families there universally. As to nurseries, kindergartens, and workers' canteens in the factories, these also first appeared in capitalist society. But under capitalism, all such undertakings established by the bourgeoisie are capitalist in nature and are aimed at facilitating the exploitation of men and women laborers by the capitalists. On the other hand, such undertakings run by us are socialist in nature and they facilitate the development of the socialist cause and the emancipation of the individual personality of man. They have truly and completely emancipated the mass of women and enabled the children to receive better education and care. That is why they are warmly welcomed by all the working people, and first of all by the masses of women.

VI

The organizational principle of the people's commune is democratic centralism. This principle must be applied in the management of production, in the distribution of income, in the livelihood and welfare of commune members, and in all other aspects of work.

Unified leadership and management at different levels should be put into effect in the people's commune. The administrative setup of the commune in general can be divided into three levels, namely: the commune administrative committee, the administrative district (or production brigade), and the production team. The administrative district (or production brigade) is in general the unit which manages industry, agriculture, trade, education, and military affairs in a given area and forms an economic accounting unit, with its gains and losses pooled in the commune as a whole. The production team is the basic unit of labor organization. Under the unified leadership of the commune administrative committee, the necessary powers should be given to the administrative district (or production brigade) and the production team over such matters as the organization of production work and capital construction, finances, and welfare, in order to bring their initiative into full play.

The various levels of organizations of the county federation of communes and of the people's commune must learn to make reasonable distributions and deployments of manpower for the different branches of production (agriculture, industry, transport) and for routine production work, shock production tasks, and service work, so as to avoid situations where there is work without men in one place and there are men without work in another. The organization of labor must be constantly improved, the system of responsibility for a given task at a given level must continue to be applied and reinforced in production and other tasks, the system of labor inspection and labor awards must be perfected in order to guarantee effectively the steady improvement of labor efficiency and the quality of work.

There must be both discipline and democracy in the organization of labor in the people's commune. What we describe as getting organized along military lines means getting organized on the pattern of a factory. It means that the organization of labor in the people's commune should be as organized and disciplined as in a factory or the army; this is necessary in large-scale agricultural production. The forces of large-scale agricultural production, like the forces of large-scale industrial production, constitute an industrial army. The modern industrial army was organized by the bourgeoisie, each factory being like a military camp. The discipline for the worker standing before the machine is as rigid as that in the army. The industrial army in socialist society is an industrial army of a single class, the working class, which has got rid of the capitalists who squeezed surplus value out of the workers and which has put into force in the working class a vigorous and lively democratic centralism based on the voluntary principle. We are now applying this system to the rural areas, thus establishing a socialist industrial army for agriculture based on democratic centralism, which is free from exploitation by the landlords and rich peasants and is elevated above the level of small-scale production.

Militia organizations should be set up at corresponding levels of the production organizations in the people's commune. The leading bodies of the militia and production organizations should be separate and, in principle, the commanding officers of the various levels of the militia such as regimental, battalion, and company commanders, should not be concurrently directors of communes and administrative districts (leaders of production brigades) and leaders of production teams. These commanders should take part in the administrative organizations of the same levels in the commune as their members, and they will receive dual leadership: from the administrative organizations of the same level and the superior commanding organizations of the militia. The militia should be equipped with the necessary arms produced by arsenals set up locally. The basic units of the militia should undergo military training according to a set schedule, while the ordinary militiamen should also get appropriate training after work; this is to prepare conditions for turning the whole nation into soldiers. The broad mass of working people in our country greet the militia system warmly, because, in the course of their protracted revolutionary struggle against imperialism, feudalism, and their running dogs, the Kuomintang reactionaries, they came to realize that only by arming themselves would they be able to overcome the armed counterrevolution and become masters of the land of China. After the victory of the revolution, they have come to see further that there are still imperialist pirates abroad who are clamoring every day about wiping out this people's state. Therefore, the whole of our people are determined to continue to arm themselves, and they declare: Be warned, you pirates bent on plundering us; do not dare to make a vain attempt to harm our people engaged in peaceful labor; we are fully prepared! Should the imperialists dare to unleash an aggressive war against our country, then we will turn the whole nation into soldiers; the militia will cooperate with the People's Liberation Army and at any time replenish it to crush the aggressors utterly.

There should be both centralism and democracy in all organizations of the people's communes, including the militia organizations. The people's communes should not only organize the people's production work but the people's livelihood as well. In order to do their work well, the communes must practise a high level of democracy, consult the masses on all matters, faithfully represent their interests, and reflect their will. Therefore, while "organizing along military lines, working as if fighting a battle and living the collective way," the communes must fully implement democratic management. It is absolutely impermissible to use "getting organized along military lines" as a pretext or to make use of the militia system—which is directed against the enemy—to impair, in the least, democratic life in the commune and the militia organizations. The people's commune is the basic organization of our country's state power; only by ensuring democracy in the commune will it be possible to create throughout the country a vigorous and lively political situation in which there are both centralism and democracy, both discipline and freedom, both unity of will and personal ease of mind.

VII

In running a people's commune well the fundamental question is to strengthen the leading role of the party. It is only by strengthening the party's leading role, that the principle of "politics in command" can be realized, that socialist and communist ideological education among the cadres and commune members and the struggle against all kinds of erroneous tendencies can be conducted in a thoroughgoing way and that the party's line and policy can be implemented correctly. There are some people who think that with the emergence of the commune the party can be dispensed with, and that they can practise what they call "merging the party and commune in one." This kind of thinking is wrong.

In its work in the people's commune, the party, besides its task of insuring that the correct line and policy are put into effect, should also pay attention to educating the commune staffs to develop good styles of work—first of all the mass line and a practical and realistic style of work.

Following the 1957–1958 rectification campaign, the party's mass line achieved a new, great victory. The great leap forward in socialist construction and the setting up of people's communes throughout the rural areas are two signal marks of this victory. The mass-line working method of the party is the lifeblood of the people's communes. The setting up and consolidation of the people's communes is impossible without the mass line, without the full faith of the people in the party and in the People's Government, and without an upsurge in the revolutionary zeal of the masses. Therefore, leading functionaries of all levels in the commune must put the mass line thoroughly into practice in every type of work tackled. They must look upon themselves as ordinary working people, and treat the commune members in a comradely way. Kuomintang and bourgeois styles of work which coerce the masses are strictly prohibited. Because of the big leap forward in production and the victory in setting up communes, some cadres are beginning to get dizzy with success; and, unwillng to do the patient work of educating the masses by persuasion, they are exhibiting certain rude attitudes. Though these are individual cases, they should make us keenly vigilant.

In all its work, the party should hold fast to the principle of combining revolutionary zeal with a scientific spirit. The great leap forward in 1958 has won an unprecedented victory for socialist construction in our country. Now even our enemies find it impossible to deny the significance of this victory. But we must never overlook our small weak points because of big achievements. On the contrary, the bigger the achievement, the more we need to remind our cadres to keep cool-headed and not be carried away by the flood of news of victory and become unable or even unwilling to see the weak points in their work. One tendency to which we must pay attention in the present work of socialist construction is exaggeration. This is incompatible with the practical working style of our party, and is harmful to the development of our socialist construction. We must do our economic work in a more thoroughgoing way. Our leading personnel at all levels must be good at differentiating between the reality and the false appearance of things and between demands which are justified and those which are not; in assessing conditions, they must strive to keep close to objective reality. Only by doing so can we work out and carry through our plans on a reliable and solid basis.

VIII

In order to promote the consolidation of the people's communes and ensure an even bigger leap forward in industry and agriculture in 1959, the Communist Party committees of the provinces, municipalities, and autonomous regions should, in accordance with the requirements set forth in this resolution and in close integration with the production tasks of the winter and spring seasons, make full use of the five months from December, 1958, to April, 1959, to carry out, within the people's communes in their areas, educational work, checkup and consolidation, that is the work of checking up on the communes.

In the course of checking up on the communes, it is necessary, in the first place, for leading personnel to make serious self-criticisms and listen with modesty to the masses' opinions, and on this basis, mobilize the masses with great daring to air their views freely and frankly, carry out debates and post up *dazibao* (written opinions in big Chinese characters posted publicly for everybody to read—*Ed.*), to commend good persons and deeds, criticize wrong ideas and bad styles of work, sum up experiences, clarify the line of work, and develop a thoroughgoing socialist and communist ideological education movement.

In the course of checking up on the communes, it is necessary to carry out an overall and thorough inspection of the production plan, distribution, welfare, management, financial work, organization, and leadership in the communes. The organizations of the Communist Party and communes should be carefully checked over at the same time to guarantee that the leading personnel of the Communist Party and communes at various levels are activists, loyal to the interests of the people and to the cause of communism. In addition, the finest people who have been tested in the big leap forward and people's commune movement and are qualified for Communist Party membership, should be enrolled in the party.

Problems related to the style of work of Communist Party members and cadres should be dealt with through party education and frank airing of views by the masses. In dealing with these problems, attention should be paid to safeguarding the zeal and initiative of the cadres and masses, and the principles of "unity—criticism—unity" and "taking warning from the past in order to be more careful in the future" and "treating the illness in order to save the man" must be observed. Those who have committed errors but are willing to correct them should be criticized seriously but treated with leniency. The masses should be mobilized to purge the leadership in the communes of those alien class elements who have smuggled themselves into the leadership and the very few who display a very bad style of work and have never corrected their errors even after being repeatedly admonished.

Complex class struggles not only develop sharply abroad, in the capitalist world, but also exist at home. It is necessary to educate the masses to increase their revolutionary vigilance to prevent disruptive enemy activities. Whether ex-landlords, rich peasants, and counter-revolutionaries and other people formerly deprived of political rights should be accepted as members or probationary members of the communes, or remain to work under the communes' supervision, should be discussed and decided by the masses dealing with each case on its merits in the course of checking up on the communes.

The work of checking up on the communes should first be carried out in one or two communes in each county as an experiment. That is to say help should be given to the comrades in one or two people's communes to get things going well in a fairly short space of time, so as to acquire experience, set examples and then popularize the experience gained generally. Every province, municipality, and autonomous region should organize its inspection team consisting of a thousand, several thousands, or ten thousand people for the checkup, and the first secretaries of the Communist Party at the provincial, regional, and county levels should personally lead the work of checking up on the communes. These inspection teams should compare different special administrative regions, counties, and communes, organize mutual visits, call on-the-spot meetings to develop the good points found and overcome the shortcomings discovered, rouse the drive of the people, and find ways of concretely solving current problems and promptly popularizing successful experience. In short, through these checkups, the work of the people's communes in the country must be generally carried one step forward.

THE CULT OF MAO

"Under the Banner of Comrade Mao Tse-tung" by Chen Po-ta, delivered at a meeting at Peking University in honor of the 37th anniversary of the founding of the CCP. Published in *Hung Chi* (*Red Flag*) July 16, 1958.

One of the imponderables in the Sino-Soviet conflict is the personal enmity that exists between the Chinese and Soviet leadership. To a degree this personal element will pass when Mao and Khrushchev leave the scene. But even then it will continue to play a role if only because of the rival claims of Russian and Chinese chauvinism.

The great early figures of international Communism—Marx, Engels, Lenin—were noted for their ability as theoreticians. And so Stalin, when he had climbed over his competitors to the pinnacle of power, felt it necessary to parade himself as a great theoretical genius, poverty-stricken though his literary capabilities in this direction were. Khrushchev, even less than Stalin, is inclined towards theory. He is primarily an actor. He couldn't read until he was past 20 and he is far from being the greatest Marxist scholar alive. But with his position as supreme leader of the Soviet Union and the entire Communist world, goes the responsibility of being supreme theoretician as well. It is a job for which Khrushchev probably has little appetite, but he cannot maintain his own prestige and that of the U.S.S.R. unless he assumes it.

On the other hand there is Mao, who not only presumes to be a theoretician but is in fact one of ability. Mao considers himself a man of culture, a mandarin of the modern era; he shows not inconsiderable pride in the bits of poetry which he has written. As a theoretician, as the representative of an ancient people, as well as in the role of tactician, he has contempt for the gross ex-factory hand who heads the Soviet government.

It must indeed be remembered that Mao's position in China is considerably different from that of Nikita Sergeyevich in the Soviet Union. Khrushchev came to power· in a country that had already been Communist for almost four decades. In the Russian revolution he played an entirely negligible role. When the Revolution broke out, he was not a party member. Even his predecessor who had ruled in paranoic isolation for greater than a quarter of a century had not been one of the major figures of October. But Mao Tse-tung made the Chinese revolution. It was he who had picked up the party after its humiliating defeats of the 1920s, outfitted it with new dogma, led it to victory and brought five hundred million Chinese into the Communist camp. Mao is not just a skilled politician and theorist, and an exceptionally able administrator. He is a world-renowned and immensely successful revolutionary. He is the Chinese Lenin.

As such, Mao's reputation is a powerful influence, at home and in the Communist world in general. His stature is towering. Khrushchev has a difficult time trying to cast as large a shadow.

And so we have the picture of the nontheoretically minded Khrushchev in competition with the prestigious and much more theoretically oriented Mao. Mao is contemptuous of his rival. Khrushchev is jealous of his prerogatives. He opposes attempts to build the image of Mao any taller than it is already.

Thus Khrushchev, on a personal basis, is understandably put on edge by Mao's assertion of having found a new way to communism, much shorter than the Russian path and with far fewer sacrifices.

Still another facet of the Mao-Khrushchev rivalry that has rankled Nikita Sergeyevich was the renewed launching in 1958 of the "cult of Mao," which was being propagated in China at a time when the Soviet Union was waging a campaign against the "Stalin cult." The "cult of Mao" had its origins in the years immediately after the establishment of the People's Republic, but for the most part in deference to Stalin it was toned down. However, in early 1958, with the commencement of the Great Leap Forward and communization it was again turned on and has with minor variations in volume continued to blare forth. Mao has been portrayed as all-wise sage, as the personification of "spirituality," as "perfection" itself. At times it has even been implied that for China the order of importance had been changed from Marxism-Leninism-Maoism to Maoism and Marxism-Leninism.

"Under the banner of Comrade Mao" is one of the prime examples of the cult of Mao in operation. Note here that Mao's name is mentioned in almost every paragraph and Stalin's and Khrushchev's appear in none. Also note that the occasion for the article is the party's birthday, but it is not the party but Mao who is being discussed—and lauded.

The Chen Po-ta speech, which was apparently conceived after the decision to communize had been taken but not yet put into effect, is also important for the argument it presents to let China go her own way. The time is July, 1958, and Khrushchev is about to visit Peking and there is evidently the necessity to convince him that Soviet experience is not definitive in all cases. Marx and Engels "could only show us the general direction," Chen says. The same is true of Lenin. "Therefore, in applying the general principles of Marxism-Leninism, the advanced representatives of the working class of each country must *independently think of their concrete problems in the light of the conditions of their county."*

July 1 is the birthday of our party. It has been 37 years since the founding of our party. In these 37 years, the Chinese people and our party have traversed a tortuous path and won a series of great victories under the banner of Comrade Mao Tse-tung. Thirty-seven years is not a long time in the history of China but one can see that under the leadership of our party and the banner of Comrade Mao Tse-tung the Chinese people have realized an epoch-making revolution on their land and are creating their own life by leaps and bounds at such a rate that "twenty years are concentrated in one day." The productive force built in the past eight years since liberation is, in a certain sense, far in excess of the productive force built over the past thousands of years. This is merely the beginning of thawing of our productive force. It may be divined beforehand that guided by the general line of the party for socialist construction—achieving better, more, faster, and economical results by exerting utmost efforts and pressing ahead consistently—the productive force will undergo a more rapid change day by day.

What has been accomplished by party leadership is most striking. Our party is a political party of the working class, a political party guided by Marxism-Leninism and a political party which creatively applies Marxism-Leninism under the direction of Comrade Mao Tse-tung. Such a party, being closely bound to the people, will constantly work miracles, either in revolution or in construction, that will dumbfound the vulgar. In particular, with the exploitation of man by man eliminated and the six hundred million working people taking their destiny into their own hands, the emergence of a mass of new things is inevitable and cannot be entirely anticipated at present.

The oppressed class had long been under a primitive communist illusion in the past thousands of years as to the elimination of exploitation and the creation of a life free of class. The history of China knows many peasant wars and many heroes whose ideal was to build a society "in which all share joys and sorrows." But since there was no modern industry or the modern working class, one could not possibly understand the law of the development of society and consequently could not possibly translate their illusion into reality, whether in the case of slavery riots or in the case of peasant wars.

Those who hold aloft the banner of scientific communism were great revolutionaries and thinkers of the working class, first Marx and Engels and then Lenin. Under the new historical conditions they summed up the experiences of the workers' movement and the results of human knowledge, discovered the law of the development of society, and proved the inevitable extinction of capitalist system and its substitution by the socialist and communist systems. Our party is armed with this Communist science and with Marxist-Leninist thinking. The correctness and the invincible force of this great science of revolution are borne out daily by a mass of facts in world countries, as well as by the experience of our country. Imperialists hate it to the bone, curse it; revisionists represented by the Tito clique echo the imperialist curse and distort it in the most despicable ways. All this does not detract a dot from its brilliance. An ancient Chinese said aptly: "One is simply taking an improper measure of himself if he thinks his self-destruction will obscure the moon and the sun."

Needless to say, Marx and Engels could only show us the general direction of struggle and give us the general principles for directing the struggle; they could not write out a prescription for each nation and each country that will cure all kinds of diseases, and insure victory of revolution and realization of communism. It was impossible for them to arrange all things well in the world and to provide each nation and each country with a detailed and ready-made scheme. Lenin developed Marxism at the new historical stage, but we could not present him with this demand either.

Marx and Lenin are our great teachers. We must learn from them seriously. But revolution must depend on the people of each country. Therefore, in applying the general principles of Marxism-Leninism, the advanced representatives of the working class of each country must independently think of their concrete problems in the light of the conditions of their country. Not that one might stop using his brains when Marx and Lenin had come to the world. On the contrary, Marx, Engels, and Lenin, devoted to revolutionary dialectics, frequently called upon the fighters of the working class to keep their heads sober, to contemplate and ponder over things deeply and thoroughly, and to discriminate different kinds of concrete facts; they expected the figures of the working class to examine critically the experiences of other countries, to sum up the new experiences of struggle with seriousness, and to solve the new problems presented by history. In short, they held that the Marxist theory could not be allowed to remain where it was but should be constantly enriched and developed according to life and the different historical conditions.

The revisionists, denying the general guiding principle of Marxism, sink into the quagmire of renegades; the doctrinaires, losing sight of the new things appearing on the horizon, deny the development of Marxism. Marxists-Leninists must fight on two fronts.

The Chinese Communist Party has called for, from the time of its birth, solution to the problem of integrating the universal truth of Marxism-Leninism with the practice of the Chinese revolution. As we know, the reason why Comrade Mao Tse-tung becomes the greater banner-bearer of the Chinese revolution is that he constantly resolves this problem correctly in theory and practice and along with the change in the conditions of the revolutionary struggle, thereby guiding the Chinese people from one victory to another.

Can it be said that it is a very easy and common thing to solve such a problem in this country known for its backward economic conditions and large population? Of course not. If we recollect what Lenin told the communists of the East during 1919, we will understand that the complex problems confronting us here were not encountered by the communist movements of the past and we will realize how important it is to the international communist movement as a whole to solve this problem. Lenin said:

You are confronted with a task never before encountered by the Communists of the world, that is, you must, in the light of special conditions unknown to the European countries, apply the general Communist theory and Communist measures and realize that peasants are the principal masses and that it is not the capital but the survivals of the Middle Ages that is to be opposed. You must apply the general Communist theory and Communist measures on the basis of these conditions. This is a difficult and special task as well as an extraordinarily noble task. . . . You must find special forms to unite the proletarians of the world with the working masses of the East who are constantly subjected to exploitation under the living conditions of the Middle Ages. . . .

This passage was part of Lenin's report to the second congress of the Communist Party organizations of nationalities in Eastern Russia and was addressed to the Communists of various nationalities in the eastern parts of Russia. But the contents of these words actually went beyond the frontier of the Soviet Union. The eastern countries beyond the frontier of the Soviet Union were more or less in the same position, that is, the peasants were the principal masses. Thus, the task presented by Lenin—"extremely momentous task" in his words —was in fact likewise placed before the Communists of eastern countries.

Comrade Mao Tse-tung achieved this extremely momentous task courageously and magnificently in the Chinese revolution.

Comrade Mao Tse-tung is able to examine and explore the characteristice of China without being the least bound by formulism. Practice instead of formula is his point of departure. The most striking feature of Comrade Mao Tse-tung's thought is his ability to integrate the universal truth of Marxism-Leninism closely with the creativeness of the masses. He puts faith in the masses, relies on the masses, and respects the intelligence of the ordinary masses, thereby to increase the invincible power of Marxist-Leninist theory under new conditions and in new surroundings.

In the struggle for integrating the universal truth of Marxism-Leninism with the concrete practice of the Chinese revolution and in the struggle for victory of two revolutions and socialist construction,

Comrade Mao Tse-tung waged irreconcilable and violent struggle against all sorts of anti-Marxist-Leninist and non-Marxist-Leninist trends, against all sorts of opportunism, revisionism, and adventurism and closed-doorism that came from the left. He won because truth was with him and because he laid down the correct line of the party and set forth a great ideal that accorded with the interests of the Chinese people and constantly pressed forward the advance of the Chinese people.

It is clear that without the proper solution to the problem of integrating the universal truth of Marxism-Leninism with the practice of the Chinese revolution, without the victory of the Mao Tse-tung thought in the struggle against all sorts of erroneous thoughts, and without the progress of the Chinese revolution under the banner of Mao Tse-tung thought, there can be no victory of the Chinese people's revolution and socialist construction.

The problems solved by Comrade Mao Tse-tung were many sided. Here I will take up several problems that were important to the cause of the Chinese people as a whole.

The primary and outstanding construction Comrade Mao Tse-tung made to the Democratic Revolution was his theory of building and developing revolutionary bases in the countryside as the main form of alliance between the working class and the peasantry under the leadership of the Communist Party in the political, military, and economic fields, and of taking such bases as the starting points of revolution and nation-wide victory. In the past, many people, basing their view on the French bourgeois revolution of the eighteenth Century and on the 1911 revolution and Northern Expedition in China, established the idea that revolution always began from big cities. And it was generally held that guerrilla warfare was merely a supplement of regular warfare. Comrade Mao Tse-tung rejected these old ideas that were not applicable to the conditions of the Chinese revolution. He set forth the new idea of encircling the cities by revolutionary countryside, the new idea of placing guerrilla warfare in a strategic position in the Chinese revolution, and the new idea of arming all the people in revolution. These new ideas put forward by Comrade Mao Tse-tung gave the party leadership a new direction of struggle after the 1927 revolutionary failure. Later, during the period of anti-Japanese war Comrade Mao Tse-tung developed and enriched these ideas, and eventually the Chinese people and our party were enabled to win a nation-wide victory during 1949.

During the period of socialist revolution in our country, Comrade Mao Tse-tung creatively solved a series of fundamental problems of socialist transformation arising from transition from individual ownership to collective ownership, from capitalist ownership to popular ownership. During the time of establishing revolutionary bases, Comrade Mao Tse-tung had summed up the experiences of the mutual-aid organizations of the peasant masses. He saw germs of socialism in such mutual-aid organizations and popularized these mutual-aid organizations in his belief that such mutual-aid organizations could raise labor productivity to a considerable degree. After the nation-wide liberation, Comrade Mao Tse-tung continued to sum up new experiences of this type and, shortly after conclusion of the agrarian reform, urged widespread establishment of temporary mutual-aid teams and year-round mutual-aid teams on a voluntary basis, and the gradual and massive development of agricultural producer cooperatives semisocialist in character (land share, common labor, and unified administration) on the basis of mutual-aid teams. He took the view that such agricultural producer cooperatives semisocialist in character were the main form of guiding the peasants voluntarily to full socialism, thereby breaking down the old view of some comrades that without agricultural machinery large-scale cooperativization of agriculture could hardly be realized.

On the question of capitalist ownership, Comrade Mao Tse-tung drew a distinction between ownership by bureaucratic capitalists and ownership by the national capitalists. Towards the former, a policy of expropriation was adopted at the time of liberation; towards the latter, methods of gradual transformation and various forms of state capitalism were adopted in order to transform capitalist enterprises steadily into socialist enterprises.

In short, whether in the case of agriculture and handicrafts or in the case of capitalist industry and commerce, coordination was achieved between revolution from the top and revolution from the bottom, and diversified forms of transition and different methods of transition were massively adopted. As a result, the socialist transformation of economy won an unexpected and rapid victory.

Comrade Mao Tse-tung broke down the old view that solution to the problem of ownership would answer the question of outcome of struggle between socialism and capitalism. He held that, beside solving the question of outcome of struggle as regards ownership, we must go a step further and solve the question of the outcome of struggle on the political and ideological fronts—otherwise the results of socialist transformation as regards ownership could not be consolidated. The big debate held by the people over socialism and capitalism during 1957, when the bourgeois rightists launched a ferocious attack on the party, bore out Comrade Mao Tse-tung's viewpoint. When the masses have waged an all-out struggle against the rightists and the people have distinguished right and wrong through the rectification campaign, contention, and blossoming, a new situation has arisen in which the Communist ideology is set free.

As far back as the time when Kiangsi was used as a revolutionary base, Comrade Mao Tse-tung laid down a correct policy of combining revolution and construction. During the Anti-Japanese War, Comrade

Mao Tse-tung continued to adhere to this policy. Following the rectification campaign which began in 1942, Comrade Mao Tse-tung promoted a large-scale production drive during 1943, which considerably
increased the material strength of the people in liberated areas and
provided a material basis for wiping out Chiang Kai-shek's counterrevolutionary army during the liberation war. Over the economic and
financial problems Comrade Mao Tse-tung always placed the mass
development of production in the leading position and criticized the
error of one-sided financial and distribution viewpoints divorced
from the development of production.

After the nation-wide liberation, socialist transformation and socialist construction are interlocked in their progress. In the course of
socialist transformation, observing the signs that began in agricultural
cooperation, Comrade Mao Tse-tung pointed to the inexhaustible and
immense latent power of the Chinese working people to develop the
productive force. Comrade Mao Tse-tung said in his comments in the
Upsurge of Socialism in China's Countryside: "There will appear
various things never conceived before and high yield of crops several,
ten and scores of times greater than at present. The development of
industry, communications, and exchange will be beyond the imagination of the predecessors. This will also be the case with science, culture, education, and public health." Therefore, he pointed out in the
preface to the *Upsurge of Socialism in China's Countryside* that the
questions confronting the party and the whole nation after solution
of the problem of socialist transformation were the question of scale
and rate of economic and cultural construction, the question of doing
things regarded as impossible, and the question of criticizing the
rightist conservative ideas.

Comrade Mao Tse-tung set forth the general line of building socialism more, faster, better, and more economically. And in order to
carry out this general line, Comrade Mao Tse-tung raised the question
of correctly handling the contradictions among the people and the
question of mobilizing all positive factors to serve socialist construction.

Some of our comrades seem to think that no contradictions exist
during the period of socialist construction, particularly among the
people, and that during the period in question the task is very simple,
that is, the productive force will be developed if we do things in the
usual way. They admit that the mass line is necessary during the
period of revolution, but over the question of socialist construction
they think that the question of socialist construction no longer exists.
It is their belief that if administrative orders are issued from above and
if professional jobs are done and experts and facilities are available,
everything will be all right. They pay attention only to technology and
not to political leadership, only to cadres and not to the masses, only
to the center and not to the localities, only to selective construction and

not to widespread construction, only to heavy industry and not to agriculture and light industry, only to big enterprises and not to medium and small enterprises, only to the most up-to-date technology and not to the mass technological revolution which seems "common." In particular, a rightist view is held which is disadvantageous to construction and is very harmful. Persons holding such a rightist view simply confine themselves to financial problems while neglecting the enthusiasm and creativeness of the masses in increasing production and practicing economy. They seem to take the view that instead of governing consumption, distribution, and exchange, production is governed by consumption, distribution, and exchange. Such a harmful rightist viewpoint was essentially a point of departure for the so-called "opposition to reckless advance" thinking in the winter of 1956.

Comrade Mao Tse-tung repudiated the erroneous ideas mentioned above, pointing out that such erroneous views could only serve to restrict the productive force. Comrade Mao Tse-tung sets forth his new and profound conception, i.e., correct handling of contradictions among the people. He divides the social contradictions into two types of contradictions different in character: (1) contradictions between the enemy and ourselves which are antagonistic in character, (2) contradictions among the people which are nonantagonistic in character. He regards it as erroneous to deny the existence of contradictions during the period of socialism. Contradictions always exist. With old contradictions resolved, new contradictions will arise. The point is that the social contradictions are different in character and should be resolved in different ways. At present, imperialists hostile to us abroad, remnant counterrevolutionaries at home, and bourgeois rightists opposed to the people and socialism—all such represent contradictions between the enemy and ourselves. New contradictions arise among the people but such contradictions are developed among our people in their advance. The main contradictions in our country during the transition period are still contradictions between the proletariat and the bourgeoisie, between socialism and capitalism; these contradictions manifest themselves as contradictions between the enemy and ourselves in the relations between the bourgeois rightists and the working people; they manifest themselves as contradictions among the people in the relations between the national bourgeoisie which accepts the socialist transformation and the working people and the relations between different sections of the working people. Comrade Mao Tse-tung takes the view that in a socialist society contradictions exist in the relationship of production to productive force and between the superstructure and the economic base, but that these contradictions are entirely different from these contradictions in a capitalist society. Capitalist contradictions cannot be resolved by the capitalist system itself and can only guide the capitalist system to extinction, whereas the socialist contradictions can be gradually resolved by the socialist system itself and thereby lead the society to a new stage of prosperity, i.e., a new stage of communism. The basic method proposed by Comrade Mao Tse-tung to resolve the contradictions among the people is the method of rectification. Its formula is: "Unity-criticism-unity." Here, new contradictions may be resolved through debate and appropriate readjustment so as to achieve new unity and press forward the development of the productive force. How to resolve the contradictions among the people, for example, between politics and technology, between cadres and the masses, between the center and localities, between improvement and popularization, between heavy industry and agriculture and light industry, between big enterprises and medium and small enterprises, between the most up-to-date technology and innovated technology, etc., etc.? To tackle one to the neglect of another is a one-sided way of solving the problem. Some comrades even neglect the main stream of socialist construction and only tackle the side issues. For instance, they give up political leadership and tackle only the professional problem; instead of relying on the enthusiasm and creativeness of the masses, they place reliance only on administrative orders and impractical regulations and institutions. Needless to say, such methods are erroneous.

Comrade Mao Tse-tung's great contribution consists not only in his creative formulation of the general line—building socialism more, faster, better, and more economically by exerting utmost efforts and pressing ahead consistently—but also in his creative selection of several basic points of the general line: gradually carrying out technological revolution and cultural revolution simultaneously with the continual completion of the socialist revolution on the economic, political, and ideological fronts; developing industry and agriculture simultaneously with priority given to the development of heavy industry; developing central industry and local industry and developing big enterprises and medium and small enterprises simultaneously under centralized leadership and over-all planning and in coordination. This is his main summation of the experiences in our socialist construction. It is a general principle that runs through the socialist construction of our country. This general principle will resolve all problems. Thanks to this general line for socialist construction, the creativeness of the people and local and central departments is brought into full play. The general big leap forward of the productive force since last winter has been taken under these conditions.

*   *   *

To cope with the big leap forward in agriculture and industry and technological revolution and in order to meet the needs of cultural revolution, we should not only wipe out illiteracy but also popularize primary school education and open middle schools in all *hsiang* areas.

Some *hsien* have already set up comprehensive or specialized institutes of higher learning and even some agricultural cooperatives have set up spare-time universities. The Chiachuan APC in Mengtsin *hsien* of Honan is a pioneer in setting up a cooperative-operated spare-time university. This spare-time university has 17 departments with 519 students. The press reported that "the teaching is characterized by close coordination between education and production." In classrooms, book knowledge is studied and theory is grasped; in the field, crops are used as teaching materials and on-the-spot work and experiments are carried out. This new type of spare-time university has begun to make useful contributions to the agricultural production carried on by the cooperative. The worker masses are striving to raise their cultural level, study science, and attain the summit of world technology. They have begun to achieve a series of success in a short time. Factories in many cities have set up various types of schools. For instance, the Taiyuan Iron and Steel Works has set up a cultural-educational organization embracing all grades from primary school to university: it includes a steel and iron college; 10,000 workers and office employees of the Works are enrolled in the cultural-educational organization. Workers of Peking, Taiyuan, and Chungking are breaking down the idea that "comprehensive knowledge and specialized knowledge cannot be acquired at the same time"; they are striving to become communist-type workers politically red and professionally proficient. The workers of some localities, primarily the workers of the Shanghai Chiuhsin Ship Building Factory, have begun an upsurge of philosophical studies. They are studying Comrade Mao Tse-tung's *On the Correct Handling of Contradictions Among the People, On Practice, On Contradictions*, etc. Tientsin workers remarked: "Technology alone is not enough." Their objective of study is raised to the plane of principle. The masses of Honan have this to say: "After studying philosophy the *hsiang* cadres show three new attitudes: conducting more investigations, showing less inclination towards subjectivism and commandism, placing more reliance on the masses." This shows that Comrade Mao Tse-tung's philosophical writings on Marxism-Leninism will gradually turn a key to the wisdom of the working masses.

*   *   *

It is obvious that under the direction of Mao Tse-tung thought, under the banner of Comrade Mao Tse-tung, and at a time when the national economy and culture are developed at such a rate that "twenty years are concentrated in one day," one can visualize the gradual transition of our country from socialism to communism.

By the series of facts showing the great effect of the Mao Tse-tung thought on our revolution and socialist construction, we are reminded of Lenin's words: "Without a revolutionary theory there will be no revolutionary movement" and "only the party guided by advanced theory can play the role of advanced fighter." It is under the great banner of Comrade Mao Tse-tung that the Chinese people are forging ahead.

Mao Tse-tung's banner is a banner of combining the Chinese Communists and the people, a banner integrating the universal truth of Marxism-Leninism with the concrete practice of the Chinese revolution, and a banner of creatively developing Marxism-Leninism under the conidtions of China. Therefore, Mao Tse-tung's banner is a banner of victory of the Chinese people's revolution and socialist construction.

Mao Tse-tung's banner is a red flag held aloft by the Chinese people. Guided by this great red flag the Chinese people will in the not distant future enter on the great Communist society.

THE NEW STRATEGY

Comrade Mao Tse-tung on "Imperialism and All Reactionaries Are Paper Tigers," compiled and edited by the editorial department of *Shijie Zhish (World Culture)* and *Jenmin Jihpao (People's Daily)* Peking, 1958.

The victory of the left in China in mid-1957 was expressed not only in domestic issues, but also in the foreign policy of the People's Republic. Radical innovations in industry and agriculture were paralleled by abrupt changes of position in intrabloc relations and in the attitudes expressed towards the non-Communist world. It is to be questioned, as some observers have done, whether China could have pursued a militantly revolutionary course in one area and followed a conservative path in the others. In any event, Chinese leadership in 1957 simply had no intention of being conservative, of going slow. It was out for "better, quicker" in all spheres, at home and abroad.

The change in China's external policy first became clear through the debates at the meeting of the Communist parties in power, which followed the celebration of the 40th anniversary of October in Moscow in November, 1957. Throughout 1956 and most of 1957 Peking had sided with the liberals of the bloc, arguing for the right of every socialist country to follow its own path to communism. China was regarded as pro-Gomulka, as a leading disciple of polycentrism. But in November, 1957, Mao makes an about-face. He argues determinedly for the predominant role of the Soviet Union and for the validity of Soviet experience for all Communist countries. Mao, the revisionist, suddenly reverts to orthodoxy. As Khrushchev later admitted, Mao forced upon the meeting a far stronger statement* of Russian primacy than the Soviet leadership had sought or wanted.

Probably several factors induced Mao's about-face, not the least of which was the working out on the international scene of Peking's reaction to the fiasco of the "hundred flowers." Peking had observed at first hand the violent repercussions which had resulted from permitting divergence at home. And suddenly she saw what she feared was an equal peril to the Communist bloc arising from divergence

* For the "Declaration of the Twelve Communist Parties in Power," see D. N. Jacobs, Ed., The New Communist Manifesto, 2nd ed., Harper & Row, New York, 1962.

within it. Thus unity, and the orthodoxy of Soviet domination, had to be enforced.

As abrupt as was the change in stance made by China in intrabloc relations, even more dramatic and far-reaching in effect was the new pose assumed in foreign relations. For it was the Chinese demand for more dynamic, revolutionary, and provocative behavior—first openly expressed by Mao in Moscow during the same November, 1957, meeting—that gave rise to the far-ranging Sino-Soviet conflict over strategy which stretched out into the next decade.

Whether Mao was merely seeking a reason to justify the more aggressive foreign policy that he believed the situation of international communism required, or whether he was sincerely convinced of the reality of the newly developed "superiority" of the Communist bloc, there can be no doubt that the point of departure taken by Mao as the rationale for his new external aims was the Soviet announcement of the launching of the Sputnik-ICBM just prior to the November meetings. Mao in his now famous meteorological metaphor declared that this new development meant that "the East wind has prevailed over the West wind."

A most emphatic statement of Mao's new views on Communist relations with the West was contained in a statement which he made in Moscow on November 18, 1957. No complete text of this statement has ever been published. However, excerpts from it are available in the compendium of Maoisms published in Peking in 1958 under the title Comrade Mao Tse-tung on "Imperialism and All Reactionaries Are Paper Tigers." In the November 18 speech, Mao gives the history of the term "paper tiger." He had applied it to Chiang Kai-shek almost a dozen years previously, while Chiang still held the upper hand in China. And Chiang did fold up, like a "paper tiger." The tsar had been a "paper tiger." So were the Chinese emperor and Japanese imperialism. So are all imperialists "paper tigers." And so is the United States.

It is always a mistake to overestimate the strength of the enemy, says Mao. It is particularly so now, that the socialist forces, with their ICBM's, "are overwhelmingly superior to the imperialist forces."

Let the capitalists bring on their warfare, as Mao said in Moscow, on November 2, "there is no other result they can achieve but bringing about the complete destruction of the world capitalist system."

Moscow never has claimed the overall superiority that China has attributed to her. Moreover, since the Autumn of 1957, a succession of Soviet spokesmen have warned that a nuclear war would not only destroy capitalism but would inflict horrible damage on the Soviet state as well, exacting a price for victory that the Russians are unwilling to pay.

I

* * *

On November 6, 1957, Comrade Mao Tse-tung declared at the meeting of the Supreme Soviet of the U.S.S.R. celebrating the 40th anniversary of the October Revolution:

The socialist system will replace the capitalist system in the end. This is an objective law independent of human will. No matter how hard the reactionaries try to prevent the wheel of history from advancing, revolution will take place sooner or later and will surely triumph. "Lifting a rock only to have his own toes squashed" is a Chinese saying to describe the action of some fools. The reactionaries of every country are just such fools. Their varied persecution of revolutionary people can only end in arousing the people to wider and more intensive revolution. Didn't the various persecutions of the revolutionary people by the Russian tsar and Chiang Kai-shek serve precisely to stimulate the great Russian and Chinese revolutions?

* * *

The reactionaries are bound to collapse and the revolution is bound to triumph. In his concluding speech at the Seventh National Congress of the Communist Party of China, Comrade Mao Tse-tung called on the people to be confident in the certain victory of the revolution. He cited the ancient Chinese fable, "How the Foolish Old Man Removed the Mountains," to show that as long as the revolutionary people have confidence, do not fear the reactionaries and have the determination to persist in the struggle to the end, the revolution will certainly triumph:

To popularize the line of the Congress is to inspire the whole party and the whole people with confidence that the victory of the revolution is certain. First of all, we must inspire the vanguard of the revolution so that, resolute and ready for self-sacrifice, they will overcome all difficulties in the struggle for victory. This, however, is not enough; we must also inspire the mass of the people throughout the country so that they too will wholeheartedly join us in the common struggle for victory. We must instill into them the belief that China belongs to the Chinese people and not to the reactionaries. In ancient China there was a fable called "How the Foolish Old Man Removed the Mountains." It is the story of an old fellow in North China in ancient times, known as the Foolish Old Man of the North Mountain. His house faced south and its doorway was blocked by two big mountains, Taihang and Wangwu. With great determination, he led his sons to dig away the mountains with pickaxes. Another greybeard known as the Wise Old Man watched their attempts and laughed, saying: "What fools you are to attempt this! To dig away two huge mountains is utterly beyond the capacity of you and your sons." The Foolish Old Man replied: "When I die, there are my sons; when they die, there will be their sons, and so on to infinity. As to those two mountains, high as they are, they cannot become higher but, on the contrary, with every bit dug away they will become lower and lower. Why can't we dig them away?" He thus refuted the Wise Old Man's mistaken view and resolutely went on digging day after day. His perseverance finally touched the heart of God in heaven who sent down two celestial beings to carry the mountains away on their backs. Today there are two big mountains lying like a dead weight on the Chinese people: imperialism and feudalism. The Chinese Communist Party has long made up its mind to remove them. We must persevere and work unceasingly, and we too may touch the heart of God in heaven. This God is none other than the mass of the Chinese people. And if they rise and dig together with us, why can't we dig away these two mountains?

*   *   *

II

In the editorial "The Turning-Point in World War II" that he wrote for the Yenan *Jiefang Ribao* (*Liberation Daily*) on October 12, 1942, Comrade Mao Tse-tung analyzed the essential nature of the reactionary forces which are outwardly strong but inwardly weak, and reminded the revolutionary people not to be misled by superficial phenomena. He wrote:

In the history of mankind all reactionary forces on the verge of extinction invariably exert themselves to give a dying kick at the revolutionary forces, and some revolutionaries are likely to be deluded for a while by this display of strength cloaking actual exhaustion and so fail to grasp the essential point that their enemy is nearing extinction while they themselves are approaching victory. The rise of the fascist forces and the war of aggression they waged for some years are precisely an example of such a dying kick, while in the war the dying kick took the form of the attack on Stalingrad. At this turning-point in history many people in the world antifascist front are misled by the ferocious appearance of fascism and fail to see its real substance.

The reactionaries are always boasting of their seemingly powerful military strength. Among the people themselves, there are a certain number who, in varying degrees, entertain a fear of the military strength of the reactionaries. This is the viewpoint that "weapons decide everything." In his well-known treatise *On the Protracted War* written in May, 1938, Comrade Mao Tse-tung made a profound criticism of this viewpoint:

. . . The so-called theory of "weapons decide everything". . . is a mechanistic theory of war, a subjectivist and one-sided view. Our view is contrary to this; we see not only weapons but also the power of man. Weapons are an important factor in war but not the decisive one; it is man and not material that is decisive. The contest of forces is not only a contest of military and economic power, but also one of the power and morale of man. Military and economic power must be controlled by man.

In August, 1946, Comrade Mao Tse-tung gave an interview to the American journalist Anna Louise Strong and expressed his famous viewpoint that all reactionaries are paper tigers. Following is the full text of the interview:

Strong asks: Do you think there is hope for a political and peaceful settlement of the Chinese question in the near future?

Mao answers: That depends on the attitude of the government of the United States. If the American people hold back the hands of the American reactionaries that are helping Chiang Kai-shek fight the civil war, there is hope for peace.

Q. Suppose the United States gives Chiang Kai-shek no more aid than it has already done, how long can Chiang Kai-shek keep on fighting?

A. Over a year.

Q. Can Chiang Kai-shek possibly last that long economically?

A. Yes, he can.

Q. What if the United States makes it clear that it will give Chiang Kai-shek no more aid from now on?

A. At present, there is no sign as yet to indicate that the United States Government and Chiang Kai-shek have any desire to stop the war at an early date.

Q. How long can the Communist Party keep going?

A. As far as our desires are concerned, we don't want to fight even for a day. But if the circumstances force us to fight, we are able to fight to the finish.

Q. Suppose the American people ask why the Communist Party fights the war, what should I answer?

A. Because Chiang Kai-shek wants to massacre the Chinese people and the people have to defend themselves if they want to survive. This the Americans can understand.

Q. What do you think of the possibility that the United States will go to war against the Soviet Union?

A. The propaganda about an anti-Soviet war consists of two aspects. On the one hand, U.S. imperialism is really preparing a war against the Soviet Union; the current talk about an anti-Soviet war and other anti-Soviet propaganda are the political preparation for an anti-Soviet war. On the other hand, this propaganda is a smokescreen put up by the U.S. reactionaries to cover up the many real contradictions U.S. imperialism is now facing. These are the contradictions between the U.S. reactionaries and the American people and the contradictions between U.S. imperialism and other capitalist countries and colonial and semicolonial countries. At present the U.S. slogan of waging an anti-Soviet war actually means the oppression of the American people and the expansion of its aggressive forces in the capitalist world. As you know, Hitler and his partners, the Japanese warlords, used the anti-Soviet slogan for a long time as an excuse for enslaving the people in their own countries and carrying out aggression against other countries. Now the U.S. reactionaries are doing precisely the same thing.

To start a war, the U.S. reactionaries must first launch an attack against the American people. They are already attacking the American people. They have been oppressing the American workers and democratic elements politically and economically, and are preparing to institute fascism in the United States. The American people should rise to resist the attacks of the U.S. reactionaries and I believe they will.

Between the United States and the Soviet Union there stretches a vast territory, consisting of many capitalist countries and colonial and semicolonial countries on the continents of Europe, Asia, and Africa; before the U.S. reactionaries have subjugated these countries, an attack against the Soviet Union is out of the question. In the Pacific, the U.S. now controls more than all of the former British spheres of influence. It controls Japan, Kuomintang-ruled China, half of Korea, and the South Pacific; it has long dominated Central and South America; it also seeks to control the entire British Empire and Western Europe. Under various pretexts the United States is conducting large-scale military preparations and establishing military bases in many countries. All the naval bases they have established and are preparing to establish all over the world, the U.S. reactionaries say, are directed against the Soviet Union. True, these military bases are directed against the Soviet Union. But, at present, it is not the Soviet Union but those countries where military bases are established which suffer U.S. aggression first. I believe it won't be long before these countries come to realize who is really oppressing them, the Soviet Union or the United States. The U.S. reactionaries will one day find themselves opposed by the people throughout the world.

Of course, I do not mean to say that the U.S. reactionaries do not intend to attack the Soviet Union. The Soviet Union is the defender of world peace, the powerful factor in obstructing the establishment of world domination by the U.S. reactionaries. With the Soviet Union in existence, the ambitions of the U.S. and world reactionaries cannot be realized at all. That is why the U.S. reactionaries hate the Soviet Union intensely and are actually dreaming of wiping out this socialist country. But, today, not long after the end of World War II, all the high-pitched loose talk about a U.S.-Soviet war by the U.S. reactionaries and the foul atmosphere they create cannot but make one take a look at their real aims. It turns out that under the anti-Soviet slogan, they are frantically attacking the American workers and democratic elements and turning all the countries which are the objects of U.S. expansion abroad into U.S. appendages. I think the American people and the peoples of all countries menaced by U.S. aggression should unite to repel the attacks of the U.S. reactionaries and their lackeys in various countries. Only victory in this struggle can avert a third world war; it cannot be averted otherwise.

Q. This is an excellent explanation. But suppose the United States uses the atom bomb? And suppose the United States bombs the Soviet Union from its bases in Iceland, Okinawa, and China?

A. The atom bomb is a paper tiger with which the U.S. reactionaries try to terrify the people. It looks terrible, but in fact is not. Of course, the atom bomb is a weapon of mass destruction, but the outcome of a war is decided by the people, not by one or two new weapons.

All reactionaries are paper tigers. In appearance, they are frightening, but in reality their strength is not so great. From the long-term point of view, the really powerful strength lies not with the reactionaries, but with the people. Before the February Revolution (1917) in Russia, which side in Russia was really strong? Superficially, the tsar at the time was powerful; but he was swept away by one blast of the February Revolution. In the final analysis, the strength of Russia was on the side of the Soviets of workers, peasants, and soldiers. The tsar was only a paper tiger. Wasn't Hitler once considered very powerful? But history proved him to be a paper tiger. So were Mussolini and Japanese imperialism. On the other hand, the Soviet Union and the democracy and freedom-loving people of all countries are more powerful than expected.

Chiang Kai-shek and his supporters, the U.S. reactionaries, are also paper tigers. Speaking of U.S. imperialism, people seem to feel that it is exceedingly powerful, and the Chinese reactionaries are using the "power" of the United States to frighten the Chinese people. But the U.S. reactionaries, like all reactionaries in history, will be proved to be not strong at all. In the United States, there are people of another kind who really have strength—they are the American people.

Take the situation in China for instance. What we rely on is only millet-plus-rifle, but history will finally prove this millet-plus-rifle stronger than Chiang Kai-shek's aircraft-plus-tanks. Although many difficulties still confront the Chinese people, although the Chinese people will suffer hardships for a long time under the joint attacks of U.S. imperialism and the Chinese reactionaries, one day these reactionaries will fail and we shall win. The reason is none other than the fact that the reactionaries represent reaction, while we represent progress.

* * *

In the article "Revolutionary Forces of the World Rally to Combat Imperialist Aggression," which he wrote for the journal *For a Lasting Peace, for a People's Democracy* in November, 1948, Comrade Mao Tse-tung pointed out that "it would be a very big mistake to overestimate the strength of the enemy and to underestimate the strength of revolution."

After the victory in World War II, U.S. imperialism, which has taken the place of fascist Germany, Italy, and Japan, together with its stooges in various countries, are frantically preparing for a new world war and are menacing the whole world. This reflects the extreme decay of the capitalist world and its fear of impending doom. This enemy still has strength. Therefore, all the revolutionary forces within each country and the revolutionary forces of all countries must be united. An anti-imperialist united front headed by the Soviet Union must be formed and a correct policy pursued, otherwise, victory cannot be achieved. The foundation of this enemy is weak. It is collapsing internally, is divorced from the people, and is confronted with an inextricable economic crisis. Therefore, it can be defeated. It would be a very big mistake to overestimate the strength of the enemy and to underestimate the strength of revolution.

On January 18, 1948, in the directive "Concerning Several Important Questions in the Present Party Policy" which he wrote for the Central Committee of the Chinese Communist Party to be issued within the party, Comrade Mao Tse-tung told us that as a whole and strategically we should slight the enemy, while at the same time we should be attentive to the art of struggle and in regard to each individual part and in each concrete struggle, we should take full account of the enemy.

We are against overestimating the strength of the enemy. For example, the fear of U.S. imperialism; the fear of going to fight in the Kuomintang-controlled area; the fear of abolishing the comprador feudal system, distributing the land of the landlords and confiscating bureaucratic capital; the fear of protracted war, etc.—all these are incorrect. Capitalism throughout the world and the rule of the reactionary Chiang Kai-shek clique in China are already rotten, without any future. We have reasons to slight them. We are certainly able and have the confidence to defeat all the enemies of the Chinese people at home and abroad. But in regard to each individual part and in each concrete struggle (whether military, political, economic, or ideological), we must never slight the enemy. On the contrary, we should take full account of the enemy, concentrate all our efforts on the fight. Only in this way can victory be achieved. While we correctly point out that as a whole and strategically we should slight the enemy, we must never slight the enemy in regard to each individual part as well, and in each concrete struggle. If as a whole we overestimate the enemies' strength and consequently do not dare to overthrow them and do not dare to gain victory, we shall be committing the mistake of "right" opportunism. If in regard to each indvidual part and in each concrete struggle we are not careful, are not attentive to the art of struggle, do not concentrate all our efforts on the struggle and do not pay attention to winning over all the allies whom we should win over (middle peasants, independent industrialists and merchants, the middle bourgeoisie, students, teachers, professors and the intellectuals in general, the general run of public functionaries, the professionals, and the enlightened gentry), we shall be committing the mistake of "left" opportunism.

On November 18, 1957, in his speech at the meeting of representatives of the Communist and Workers' Parties of the socialist countries held in Moscow, Comrade Mao Tse-tung said:

In 1946 when Chiang Kai-shek launched his attacks against us, many of our comrades and people throughout the country were very much worried: Could the war be won? I myself was also worried about this. But of one thing we were confident. At that time an American journalist named Anna Louise Strong came to Yenan. We discussed many questions in our talks, including Chiang Kai-shek, Hitler, Japan, the United States, the atom bomb, etc. I said that all the reputedly powerful reactionaries were merely paper tigers. The reason was that they were divorced from the people. You see, wasn't Hitler a paper tiger? Wasn't Hitler overthrown? I also said that the tsar was a paper tiger, the Chinese emperor was a paper tiger, Japanese imperialism was a paper tiger. You see they were all down and out. U.S. imperialism has not yet fallen and it has the atom bomb. I believe it will also fall. It is also a paper tiger. Chiang Kai-shek was very powerful. He had more than four million regular troops. At that time we were in Yenan. What was the population of Yenan? Seven thousand. How many troops did we have? We had 900,000 guerrillas, all divided by Chiang Kai-shek into scores of bases. But we said Chiang Kai-shek was only a paper tiger and we would certainly defeat him. In order to struggle against the enemy, we have formed the concept over a long period, namely, that strategically we should slight all enemies, and tactically we should take full account of all enemies. That is also to say, we must slight the enemy as a whole but take full account of him so far as each and every concrete question is concerned. If we do not slight the enemy as a whole, we shall be committing the mistake of opportunism. Marx and Engels were only two people. In their time they already said that capitalism throughout the world would be overthrown. But on concrete questions and on questions concerning each and every particular enemy, if we do not take full account of the enemy, we shall be committing the mistake of adventurism. In war, battles can only be fought one by one and the enemy can only be annihilated bit by bit. Factories can only be built one by one. The peasants can only plough the land plot by plot. The same is true of eating a meal. Strategically, we slight the eating of a meal: we can finish the meal. But when actually eating, we do it a mouthful at a time. It would be impossible for you to swallow the entire feast in a single mouthful. This is called the one-by-one solution. And in military literature, it is called smashing the enemy one by one.

III

Speaking at the Moscow meeting of representatives of Communist and Workers' Parties of socialist countries, on November 18, 1957, Comrade Mao Tse-tung analysed the international situation at that time and pointed out that the socialist forces have surpassed the imperialist forces and that the East wind has prevailed over the West wind. He said:

I am of the opinion that the international situation has now reached a new turning point. There are two winds in the world today: the East wind and the West wind. There is a Chinese saying: "Either the East wind prevails over the West wind or the West wind prevails over the East wind." I think the characteristic of the situation today is the East wind prevailing over the West wind. That is to say, the socialist forces are overwhelmingly superior to the imperialist forces.

Addressing Chinese students studying in the Soviet Union on the day before he made the above-mentioned speech, that is on November 17, Comrade Mao-Tse-tung said:

The direction of the wind in the world has changed. In the struggle between the socialist camp and capitalist camp, either the West wind prevails over the East wind; or the East wind prevails over the West wind. The whole world now has a population of 2700 million, of which the various socialist countries account for nearly 1000 million; the independent, former colonial countries make up more than 700 million; and the capitalist countries now struggling for independence or for complete independence and capitalist countries with neutral tendencies have 600 million. The population of the imperialist camp is only about 400 million; moreover, they are divided internally. "Earthquakes" may occur there. At present, it is not the West wind which is prevailing over the East wind but the East wind that is prevailing over the West wind.

On November 6, 1957, speaking at a meeting of the Supreme Soviet of the U.S.S.R. in celebration of the 40th anniversary of the October Revolution, Comrade Mao Tse-tung said:

The imperialists pin their hope on war, in addition to staking their fate on the oppression of the peoples at home and in the colonial and semicolonial countries. But what can they expect from war? In the past half century, we have experienced two world wars. After World

War I, the Great October Socialist Revolution took place in Russia. And after World War II, more revolutions took place in eastern Europe and in the East. If the imperialist warriors are determined to start a third world war, there is no other result they can achieve but bringing about the complete destruction of the world capitalist system.

On February 27, 1957, Comrade Mao Tse-tung delivered his speech *On the Correct Handling of Contradictions Among the People* at the 11th enlarged session of the Supreme State Conference. In Part 10 of his speech, under the subheading "Can Bad Things Be Turned into Good Things?" he said:

People in all countries of the world are now discussing whether or not a third world war will break out. In regard to this question, we must be psychologically prepared, and at the same time take an analytical view. We stand resolutely for peace and oppose war. But if the imperialists insist on unleashing another war, we should not be afraid of it. Our attitude on this question is the same as our attitude towards all disturbances: firstly, we are against it; secondly, we are not afraid of it. The first world war was followed by the birth of the Soviet Union with a population of 200 million. The second world war was followed by the emergence of the socialist camp with a combined population of 900 million. If the imperialists should insist on launching a third world war, it is certain that several hundred million more will turn to socialism; then there will not be much room left in the world for the imperialists, while it is quite likely that the whole structure of imperialism will utterly collapse.

Given specific conditions, the two aspects of a contradiction invariably turn into their respective opposites as a result of the struggle between them. Here, the conditions are important. Without specific conditions, neither of the two contradictory aspects can transform itself into its opposite. Of all the classes in the world the proletariat is the most eager to change its position; next comes the semiproletariat, for the former possesses nothing at all, while the latter is not much better off. The present situation in which the United States controls a majority in the United Nations and dominates many parts of the world is a transient one, which will eventually be changed. China's situation as a poor country denied her rights in international affairs will also be changed—a poor country will be changed into a rich country, a country denied her rights will be changed into a country enjoying her rights—a transformation of things into their opposites. Here, the decisive conditions are the socialist system and the concerted efforts of a united people.

On June 28, 1950, when U.S. imperialism openly launched the aggressive war against Korea and invaded China's territory of Taiwan by armed force, Comrade Mao Tse-tung made the following statement in his address to the Eighth Meeting of the Central People's Government Council:

The Chinese people have already affirmed that the affairs of the various countries throughout the world should be run by the peoples of these countries, and that the affairs of Asia should be run by the peoples of Asia and not by the United States. U.S. aggression in Asia will only arouse widespread and resolute resistance by the peoples of Asia. Truman stated on January 5 this year that the United States would not interfere in Taiwan. Now he has proved his own statement to be false, and has torn to shreds all the international agreements regarding noninterference by the United States in the internal affairs of China. The United States has thus openly exposed its own imperialist face, and this is beneficial to the people of China and of all of Asia. There is no reason at all for U.S. intervention in the internal affairs of Korea, the Philippines, Vietnam, or other countries. The sympathy of the people throughout China, as well as of the broad mass of the people everywhere in the world, is on the side of the victims to aggression, and most decidedly not on the side of U.S. imperialism. The people will neither be bought by imperialism nor cowed by it. Imperialism is outwardly strong but feeble within, because it has no support among the people. People throughout China and the world! Unite and prepare fully to defeat any provocation by U.S. imperialism.

On February 14, 1955, at a banquet given by the Soviet Embassy in Peking celebrating the 5th anniversary of the signing of the Sino-Soviet Treaty of Friendship, Alliance and Mutual Assistance, Comrade Mao Tsetung said:

With the cooperation between our two great countries, China and the Soviet Union, I am convinced that the aggressive plans of imperialism will be smashed.

We can all see that with the great cooperation between China and the Soviet Union, there are no aggressive plans of imperialism which cannot be smashed. They will certainly be smashed thoroughly. Should the imperialists start a war of aggression, we, together with the people of the whole world, will certainly wipe them off the face of the earth.

On September 8, 1958, at the Supreme State Conference, Comrade Mao Tse-tung said:

The present situation is favorable for the people the world over who are fighting for peace.

The general trend is that the East wind prevails over the West wind.

U.S. imperialism invaded China's territory of Taiwan and has occupied it for the past nine years. A short while ago it sent its armed forces to invade and occupy Lebanon. The United States has set up hundreds of military bases in many countries all over the world. The

Chinese territory Taiwan, Lebanon, and all U.S. military bases on foreign territories are like nooses tied round the necks of the U.S. imperialists. The Americans themselves, and nobody else, made these nooses, and they themselves put them round their own necks and handed the ends of the ropes to the Chinese people, the peoples of the Arab countries, and all the peoples of the world who love peace and oppose aggression. The longer the U.S. aggressors remain in these places, the tighter the nooses round their necks will become.

The U.S. imperialists have been creating tension in all parts of the world in attempts to achieve their aggressive ends and to enslave the peoples of various countries. The U.S. imperialists calculate that they will always benefit from tense situations, but the fact is that the tense situations created by the United States have led to the opposite of what the Americans wish. They serve, in effect, to mobilize the people of the world to oppose the U.S. aggressors.

If the U.S. monopoly capitalist group is bent on carrying out its policy of aggression and war, the day will certainly come when humanity will hang it by the neck. A similar fate awaits the accomplices of the United States.

On September 29, 1958, Comrade Mao Tse-tung returned to Peking after a tour of inspection in several Yangtse valley provinces. In an interview with a correspondent of *Hsinhua News Agency* he said:

Imperialism will not last long because it has been consistently doing all sorts of evil things. It makes a point of grooming and backing up reactionaries against the people in various countries. It seizes and occupies by force many colonies and semicolonies and establishes many military bases. It threatens peace with atomic warfare. In this way, imperialism has forced more than 90 percent of the people of the world to rise against it or prepare to fight it. Imperialism is still alive and kicking, still blustering its way in Asia, Africa, and Latin America. The imperialists are still oppressing the people of their own countries in the West. But such a situation has to be changed. It is the task of the people of the world to put an end to the aggression and oppression perpetrated by imperialism, especially by U.S. imperialism.

WAR AND PEACE

"Answers to Readers' Queries on War and Peace" by Sung Tu, in *Chungkuo Ch'ingnien (China Youth)*, Peking, February 16, 1960.

Presenting the Central Committee report to Party Congress XX in February, 1956, Khrushchev made some addenda to Marxism-Leninism that have since figured pre-eminently in the Sino-Soviet conflict. Peaceful coexistence, Khrushchev told the assembled faithful in the Great Hall of the Kremlin, is a basic principle of Soviet foreign policy and not just a "tactical move." Today says Khrushchev, "there are only two ways: either peaceful coexistence or the most destructive war in history. There is no third way."

Many in the West, with good reason, doubted Khrushchev's sincerity in abjuring war as a means of extending communism, but evidently the Chinese, shortly thereafter, if not in 1956, took Khrushchev's statement at its face value.

Khrushchev certainly did not mean that communism was surrendering her goal of world conquest, but that this was to be obtained through "the decisive superiority" which the socialist mode of production is to increasingly gain over the capitalist mode. "We believe," said the Soviet party First Secretary, "that all the working people on earth, once they have become convinced of communism's advantages will sooner or later take the road of struggle for the construction of a socialist society." Thus, the masses were to be brought to communism through attraction and not through force.

But the Chinese were aware that the history of communism's expansion has been not through the "attraction" of the masses to superior Communist productive, moral, and social capacities, but through war and force. Moreover, granting the plausibility of Khrushchev's "attraction" thesis, they saw for themselves little possibility of soon developing a "personality" which would entice "all the working people on earth." For the Chinese, surrendering war as an offensive weapon was tantamount to crippling their revolutionary capability.

At the time that Khrushchev made the statement that "war is not a fatalistic inevitability," the Chinese went along; but when the abrupt shift to the left occurred in Peking in 1957-1958, Khrushchev's statement of February, 1956, became a focal point of disagreement.

The frankest and most succinct Chinese answer to Khrushchev to that date appeared in February, 1960, in a series of questions and answers on "war and peace" in the journal China Youth. While the Russians are not specifically mentioned, it is apparent that the arguments are directed at them.

In February, 1960, Khrushchev was fairly recently back from the United States and the U-2 incident had not yet occurred. It was an era of "good feeling" in Soviet-American relations. There was an approaching summit conference. There was increased talk of disarmament. And so Peking felt it necessary to warn Moscow not to trust the capitalists: So long as imperialism exists there will be wars. It is true that as socialism advances, the imperialists will find it "still more difficult" to start a war. But, the greater the menace to capitalism becomes, the greater its desperation. Every cornered beast fights—and so will imperialism. The imperialists talk of peace, but it is false talk, designed "to cover up their true intention to prepare for war." The West's primary goal in negotiating is to gain time.

In 1959, Khrushchev extended his 1956 remarks on the evitability of war by implying that war—even local wars—can be permanently removed from the "life of society" even before the complete victory of socialism throughout the world. To this the CCP replied that "the so-called 'warless world'—if it is not a childish fantasy—can only be a world where there is no imperialism." As the plight of capitalism grows worse, its desperation and readiness to take chances mounts. "At a time when the imperialists not only still exist but are even armed to the teeth, any thought that there is a short cut to realizing a 'warless world' will only disarm the people's vigilance against the imperialists."

It is interesting to note that the Chinese Communists picture the West as both impotent "paper tigers" and "cornered beasts" ready to spring. Which of the portrayals is to be used depends upon whether the Chinese are arguing for a more militant Soviet policy, in which case the imperialists are "paper tigers," or against disarmanent negotiations, wherein the imperialists are bloodied but ferocious carnivores.

Question: At the present moment, the force of socialism is unprecedentedly strong and the international situation has eased to a certain extent. Could we say that the imperialists would find it still more difficult to start a world war?

Answer: Yes, it is unquestionably so. The current international situation is characterized by the ever more solidification and expansion of the socialist camp. In Asia, Africa, and Latin America the tide of nationalist, democratic movement is on the flow whereas the imperialist camp is splitting into many factions and facing myriads of difficulties. The East wind prevails over the West wind, and the forces of peace with the socialist camp as their nucleus have far surpassed the forces of war of the imperialists. As all the people yearn for peace, even the imperialists cannot but use peace as their signboard. We have every reason to believe that the imperialists would find it more and more difficult to start a world war.

Question: When you say that the forces of peace with the socialist camp as their nucleus have far surpassed the forces of war of the imperialists, do you chiefly mean that the Soviet Union is far superior to the United States in the technique of rockets and guided missiles?

Answer: When I say this I mean the comparison of total strength, militarily, economically, as well as politically. As to the decisive factor, I would rather say political force than military strength. For what decides a war is, after all, the will of the people.

Judged from the current situation, that the imperialists dare not start a war is of course true, to a very large extent, because the Soviet Union is overwhelmingly superior in the field of rockets and guided missiles. But the deciding factor is the people. The history of mankind has proved this point long ago.

After the Soviet Union had repelled the military offensive of the international bourgeoisie, Lenin said: "Workers and peasants who have freed themselves from the oppression of the capitalists can create real miracles as long as they remain united. From here we have seen a concrete example: if a revolutionary war can genuinely attract the oppressed masses to participate in it and care for it, if the masses can be made to realize that they are opposing the exploiters, then the revolutionary war will be able to arouse the enthusiasm and talent for creating miracles." He continued: "The side who has more reserves, more manpower, and a firmer grasp on the masses will invariably win the battle."

Take the personal experience of us Chinese people as an example. With rifles and millet only, we defeated the joint attack of Chiang Kai-shek and the American imperialists.

Quite a few examples can also be found in practical international life in the past two or three years. After landing in Lebanon and meeting both the resistance of the Lebanese people and the reprimand of the people of the whole world, American soldiers could not but make a hasty and "inglorious" retreat. Also, was it not because of the heroic resistance of the Egyptian people and the righteous support rendered to this resistance by the people of the whole world that the joint Anglo-French invasion of Egypt ended in failure?

This shows that it is the people who can hold the arm of the imperialists and stop them from starting a war.

Now, as the people's peace movement is ever gaining momentum, the imperialists dare not go against the will of the people and start a war; as the tide of nationalist, democratic movement is on the flow in Asia, Africa, and Latin America, the imperialists have no solid rear and reserve force at all. On the other hand, the ever expanding forces of the socialist camp have stirred up the fighting will of the people of the whole world, and our policy of opposing imperialism and striving for lasting peace is winning more and more sympathy and support.

Question: Since it is because we are strong and the enemy is weak that war is averted, is it not true that a continuation of this situation means there will be no war forever?

Answer: Such a view is incorrect. First of all, it should be pointed out that although the forces of socialism become ever stronger and the imperialists find it ever more difficult to start a war, they have never abandoned their expansion of armament and preparations for war but are doubling their efforts at armament expansion and war preparations instead. For instance, recently the United States has entered into military alliance with Japan; in Europe it is actively reviving German militarism; it is also trying to strengthen the North Atlantic Treaty Organization, the Southeast Asia Treaty Organization, and the Central Treaty Organization, as well as to form other military cliques. In its budget for the fiscal year of 1961, military expenditure occupies 57.1 percent of the total disbursement. Besides, it has declared that it would restore nuclear tests at any moment. All these serve as examples, which we can easily pick up at random, to prove that the imperialists are working double time to prepare for a new war. As long as such a situation exists, we should not ignore the danger of war.

Of course, time is to our advantage. Following the further growth of socialist forces—for instance, after the Soviet Union completes her Seven-Year Plan and our country completes its Third Five-Year Plan; when the industrial production of the socialist world surpasses that of the entire capitalist world—the imperialists will then find it still more difficult than today to start a war. This is an absolute certainty; it is also the aim we are striving for. However, even if it be so, we still cannot say that there will never be a war. For war is actually a form of class struggle conducted internationally by the imperialists against the socialist countries and the people of the whole world; and, as Chairman Mao said, "in human history, all reactionary forces that are about to be extinguished invariably fight desperately against the revolutionary forces." Isn't there a Chinese saying that says: "A cornered beast will put up a desperate fight"? It is precisely because the imperialists are sinking fast that we should evaluate the possibility that they might run the risk as "a cornered dog would try to jump over the wall." Chairman Mao once said: "The imperialists follow a logic that is entirely different from the logic of the people. The logic which the imperialists and all reactionaries in the world will follow and never desert is to cause trouble and end in failure, to cause trouble again and end in failure again until destruction. This is a Marxist definition. When we say that 'imperialists are fierce,' we mean they will never change their true character, never lay down their butcher's knife, and never become Buddhas, not even until the day they meet their final destruction."

At the same time, even though in the beginning the imperialists dare not fight the socialist countries, there is still the possibility that they might fight among themselves; and under certain conditions such a war among the imperialists might turn into a war against the socialist countries. For instance, World War II was started by a fight among the imperialists themselves; when the fight reached a certain stage, Hitler turned the direction of his gun and attacked the Soviet Union.

From here we return to Lenin's old proposition, that is, as long as imperialists live, there exists the danger of war. This is the truth. On the one hand, we acknowledge that the strength of the socialist camp becomes stronger and stronger and the imperialists find it more and more difficult to start a war; but on the other hand, we have no reason whatsoever to believe that because of the ever-growing strength of the socialist camp the imperialists will yield willingly and abandon their hope in war, and that therefore there will be no war forever.

Question: I still do not quite understand your meaning. Since to start a war is more and more to the disadvantage of the imperialists, why can't we suppose that the imperialists would resort to peaceful means to realize their aims? Isn't it true that at present the American imperialists also advertise for peaceful coexistence and adopt peaceful measures to solve international disputes?

Answer: The peace advertised by the imperialists is false. Fact is the best answer for this. Apart from their empty talks, can you name one fact to prove they really long for peace? They say they agree to solving international disputes by peaceful means and not by force; but why don't they show their sincerity in peace by withdrawing their armed forces from Taiwan and the Taiwan Straits areas? It is impossible for others to believe their peaceful intentions if their swords are resting on others' throats.

The purpose of the imperialists in advertising false peace is to cover up their true intention to prepare for war. Their "brinkmanship policy" and "policy of strength" have met with repulsion everywhere and cannot be carried out any longer as before. In order to avert the situation of becoming more isolated day after day, they have to assume a peaceful attitude in an attempt to get the things which they could not get by old methods. Using peace as a camouflage, they try to get enough time to reinforce their armament; at the same time, they try to use peace to bewilder the people, slacken the people's will of fighting against imperialism, disarm the people's vigilance, and thereby clear the way for them to start an aggressive war.

In the long run, is it possible for the imperialists to use peaceful means to realize their aims? In spite of their high-sounding words about so-called "to-win-by-peaceful-means" strategy, what they are actually doing is, on the one hand, to arm themselves up to the teeth and, on the other, to sabotage socialism and preserve capitalism by such "peaceful" means as erosion, infiltration, and subversion. The word "peace," nevertheless, is utterly incompatible with the true character of the imperialists. During the 15 years after the end of War II, though the people of the world have never slackened their efforts in pursuit of peace, the imperialist countries have never stopped in expanding their armament. There have been more and more military bases and larger and larger military expenditures; new military blocs have been set up after old ones were overthrown, and the scope of militarization of economy has no limit in its expansion. After atomic bombs came hydrogen bombs; a few were not enough but the more the better; and after the U.S. and Britain got them, France and West Germany want to have them too. Are these accidental phenomena? No, they are absolutely not. They are the inevitable results of the development of imperialism at the present stage.

Question: Aren't we advocating all-round, thorough disarmament? Isn't it true that one day when this advocacy is successful there will be a lasting peace in the world?

Answer: Yes, we socialist countries advocate all-round, thorough disarmament; we are making persistent efforts to realize our advocacy, and we will continue to work for this. This is only one side of the picture, however. We must also take note of the other side, namely, that the imperialists have not taken even one step toward disarmament. What the imperialists are interested in is not disarmament but expansion of armament. Hence, to fight for all-round, thorough disarmament is a long-term, complicated struggle against the imperialists, from which we cannot get any result at one stroke. Fundamentally speaking, as long as they live the imperialists will never disarm themselves. Therefore, it is a kind of impractical fantasy to pin our hope for a lasting world peace on the possibility that the imperialists might agree to, and actually execute, an all-round, thorough disarmament.

Question: Please explain why it is that as long as the imperialists exist we cannot rest assured that there will be no war.

Answer: We must first study what a war is. Chairman Mao said: "Ever since the beginning of class society and private ownership of property, war is the highest form of struggle which has been employed to solve the contradiction between class and class, nationality and nationality, state and state, and political group and political group in a certain stage of development." Lenin said: "War is the continuation of policy by a different means. No war can be separated from the political system which begets it. The policy enforced by a certain country or certain class during wartime is invariably a continuation of the policy that country or class has long been enforcing before the war; the only difference is in the style of action. . . . Imperialist war is a continuation of the policy of the imperialists, the ruling class, the landlords, and the capitalists." This shows that war and class are inseparable.

Ever since capitalism reached the stage of imperialism, aggression and war have become two inseparable, constituent parts of the imperialist system. This can be proved by the fact that two world wars had taken place within less than half a century. Why? The policy of the imperialists is to seize colonies, to oppress peoples of foreign nationalities, and to suppress peoples of their own countries. Such a policy inevitably leads to aggression and war. Aggression and war are therefore the unavoidable results of imperialism.

After World War II, due to the emergence of the socialist camp and the expansion of the movement for nationality independence, imperialism has been rapidly declining. Some people see the decadence of imperialism and think it will abandon war; but the fact is that the more downfallen it is, the more vicious it becomes. It is exactly because of their downfall that the imperialists depend still more closely on the use of naked violence to enforce their domestic and international policies of opposing socialism, seizing colonies, suppressing their own people, and enslaving the whole world; that they desperately expand their armament in preparation for war. All this has still more strongly verified Lenin's analysis concerning imperialism's inevitably heading for war.

Question: Since there is always the danger of war so long as imperialism exists, isn't it true, then, that our efforts in pursuit of a lasting peace have lost their significance?

Answer: We should not put it this way. Under definite historical conditions, it is still possible for us to maintain peace for a relatively long period. This is precisely what we are fighting for. Judged from the situation at present, this aim of ours can be realized so long as we continue to reinforce ourselves, insist on Marxist-Leninist policies and principles, constantly expose the tricks and schemes of the imperialists, encourage the fighting will of the people of the whole world, and fight shoulder to shoulder with the people of the whole world to the very end.

Question: In what way can we realize a "warless world," then?

Answer: The so-called "warless world"—if it is not a childish fantasy—can only be a world where there is no imperialism, or, putting it succinctly, where there is no class. To realize this ideal, the human race must necessarily undergo a long-term, sinuous, complicated and violent struggle so as to eliminate imperialism and class. At a time when the imperialists not only still exist but are even armed to the teeth, any thought that there is a short cut to realizing a "warless world" will only disarm the people's vigilance against the imperialists.

Question: Can it be said that to fight for peace is the fundamental foreign policy of us socialist countries?

Answer: It is definitely so. This is decided by the nature of our socialist system. We socialist countries are countries of a new style, where the laboring people are the masters and where the system of one man exploiting another no longer exists. The laboring people do not exploit their fellow men; what they want is peace so that they can work in peaceful surroundings. This is also true with the state of the laboring people.

As early as 1870, Marx had already pointed out the direction of foreign relations of a socialist state. At that time he said: "Opposite to that economically poor and politically stupid old society, a new society is being born. The international principle of this new society will be *peace,* because people of all nations will be ruled by labor!" To spare no effort in striving for peace with respect to international relations—this is exactly what the Soviet Union has been doing ever since the October Revolution; this is also what our country has been doing since the year 1949. In fact, this has been and is being done by each and every socialist country.

To strive for peace is the fundamental foreign policy of us socialist countries. On the other hand, however, we cannot but take note of the fact that imperialist countries beside us are hostile to us, that they are armed to the teeth, and that as soon as there is a chance they will jump upon us like a wild beast. This has been proved by the war of interference conducted by the imperialists against the Soviet Union after the October Revolution, by the attack of Fascist Germany against the Soviet Union, as well as by the American imperialists' aggression in Taiwan and their attack on Korea after the Chinese Revolution. Hence, to effectively safeguard peace, we must necessarily resist aggression, constantly expose the imperialists' secret plots, always remain vigilant, and be prepared to resolutely counterattack the aggressors. Only by using great, righteous war to crush the unrighteous war of the imperialists can we effectively maintain peace. We are in pursuit of peace; but we never harbor any illusion about peace or beg for peace from the imperialists.

Question: It is understandable that, as you said, we must counterattack the imperialists when they start any aggressive war against us socialist countries. But why are we to support the war in certain other countries?

Answer: The war in those countries is a righteous war against the imperialists. We oppose the unrighteous war started by the imperialists, but we support all righteous wars conducted by oppressed peoples against the imperialists. All anti-imperialist peoples in the world are our good friends, and we support all the righteous wars against the imperialists' interference and aggression in Asia, Africa, and Latin America. Only by determinedly supporting all righteous, revolutionary wars can we effectively weaken imperialism and strive for peace.

Question: By so doing, aren't we provoking the imperialists? Since our fundamental foreign policy is to strive for peace, why can't we compromise a little?

Answer: With the imperialists we should not compromise; for the imperialists are a bunch of creatures that submit to force but never listen to persuasion. When dealing with the imperialists, there is no such question as provoking or not. Speaking from the stand of the people of various countries in the world, there can never be a question of their interfering with the imperialists or taking any act of aggression against the imperialists. When the question of provocation is mentioned, we should, in fact, ask why the imperialists are so ruthless as to provoke the people. For instance, soldiers of the American imperialists have recently landed in the Dominican Republic. Since this is an act of provocation against the Dominican people, can it be called provocation when we voice our support to the Dominican people? On the contrary, if the people do not stand up and fight but compromise with the imperialists, then the latter will "ask for a mile after you give him an inch." The shameful Munich pacification policy had paved the way for Fascist Germany to start a world war. Was it not that Chiang Kai-shek's "nonresistance" policy had led to the war of Japanese aggression against the whole country of China? In sharp contrast, the heroic resistance of the Korean people and the efforts of our people in resisting the U.S. and aiding Korea had repelled the American imperialists' mad attacks and safeguarded both the security of Korea and China and the peace in the Far East.

This shows that peace will be preserved if we fight for it, and it will be lost if we resort to compromise. This is the truth that has stood many tests.

Question: Some people say that since we now have nuclear weapons we can no longer use war as a means to solve international dispute, and that we therefore can eliminate war from the life of mankind forever. What do you think about such a view?

Answer: I think that such a view is unfounded. Nuclear weapons are very destructive weapons, the appearance of which will certainly bring about a series of great changes to the war in future; however, it has not changed, and will not change either, the class nature of war or the fundamental principle of war. He who uses war to plunder or to keep his plunder is always an imperialist. To say that because of the appearance of nuclear weapons the imperialists will cease using war or the threat of war to solve international disputes is merely the talk of a man in his dream. The best proof of this is the fact that the American imperialists are enthusiastically preparing for conventional wars or small wars at the same time that they are readying themselves for a so-called nuclear war. Isn't this sufficient to prove that the imperialists will never abandon war as a means to plunder and enslave others? No matter whether nuclear weapons will be used in a future war or not, what can be affirmed is that aggression and war will always exist so long as imperialists exist.

In fact, that the American imperialists put up a show of nuclear weapon is actually to "scare" people. As the socialist camp will not be scared, the chief intention of the American imperialists is to scare the rebellious people in the capitalist world itself and also other imperialist countries in competition with the U.S. By this method, the American imperialists try to monopolize the vast intermediate area between the U.S. and the socialist camp, thereby attacking the socialist camp. For this reason, to expose that the U.S. is a paper tiger, to have no fear of its nuclear threat, and to stir up the fighting will of the people in the whole world constitutes an extremely important step we should take in our struggle for peace.

Furthermore, whether there will be a third world war, whether nuclear weapons will be used or not, is not to be decided by us but by the imperialists. If the imperialists should start the war, it is certain that they would bring about their own destruction.

Question: Facing the current international situation, what attitude do you think we young people should take toward the question of war and peace?

Answer: We are Chinese youths who have grown up in the great Mao Tse-tung era among the violent storm of revolutionary war. The policy of peace is originally the fundamental foreign policy of our great, socialist motherland. In order to build up our glorious, new life, we are in particular need of peaceful international surroundings. Judged from the international situation at present, it is entirely possible for us to strive for a comparatively lasting peace. We should spare no effort in striving for this aim. Nevertheless, we must not forget that imperialists still exist, that they are armed to the teeth, and that they are working double tides to prepare for war. We must not forget that the American imperialists still occupy our territory Taiwan and that their armed forces have been frequently violating our territorial waters and air. We must not forget either that the imperialists are still bullying people in many parts of the world, and that in every hour and every minute there are myriads of people fighting a life-and-death struggle against the imperialists. On this account, though we are in pursuit of peace, we must neither beg for peace from the imperialists nor harbor any fantasy about the so-called eternal peace. We are determinedly against imperialist war, but whether to start a third world war or not is not to be decided by us. Hence, in spite of our resolute opposition to war, we are not afraid of war. We should be prepared for any sudden change of event. As we were born during a storm, we are not afraid of any storm from whatever direction it may come.

CRESCENDO

Unite Under Lenin's Revolutionary Banner by Lu Ting-yi, delivered before the Central Committee of the Chinese Communist Party, Peking, April 22, 1960.

Although the Russo-Chinese differences over strategy began in late 1957, the dispute was carried along in rather cryptic and subdued tones until the beginning of 1960. Then, in the wake of years of frustration, apprehensive about the arrangements that might be negotiated, in their absence, at the forthcoming summit conference between Eisenhower and Khrushchev, the Chinese heated up the argument. They used the occasion of Lenin's 90th birthday to launch their· heaviest and most biting attack against the Soviets.

In a series of articles and speeches, of which Unite Under Lenin's Revolutionary Banner is the most vituperative, the CCP identifies itself and its policies with Lenin. And it uses his words to castigate the "modern revisionists" (read Khrushchev and the CPSU).

And castigate it does. The modern revisionists are accused of "revising, emasculating, and betraying revolutionary Marxism-Leninism." They are depicted as being "panic-stricken by the imperialist policy of nuclear-war blackmail." They try to kill the revolutionary spirit of Marxism. Indeed, "they are the agents of imperialism and the enemies of the proletariat and working people of all countries."

The point of departure for the Chinese attacks is again Khrushchev's Central Committee Report to Party Congress XX in 1956. The Chinese counter Khrushchev's arguments that war is not "fatalistically inevitable" by stating that local wars and wars of national liberation can and must not be prevented. "No force on earth can hinder or restrain the peoples of the colonies and semicolonies from rising in revolution," nor can the proletariat in capitalist countries be kept down. Moscow fears that such revolutionary outbursts will develop into civil wars in which both the United States and the U.S.S.R. will become involved, leading to world war. The Chinese have no such qualms. "All revolutionary Marxist-Leninists should likewise support these just revolutionary struggles, resolutely and without the slightest reservation." By implication, those who hesitate to do so, who are irresolute or have reservations, are not revolutionary Marxist-Leninists. They are modern revisionists, and the greatest danger to the international communist movement.

As for Khrushchev's assertion that the prospects for peaceful achievement of socialism have greatly improved, the Chinese hold that imperialism will not "step down from the stage of history of its own accord, without a revolution." There can be no peace until imperialism has been completely eliminated.

The main arguments of the modern revisionists for introducing their alien concepts, says Lu Ting-yi (Member of the Politburo of the CCP), is that "Lenin's analysis of imperialism has become 'outmoded,' that the nature of imperialism has 'changed,' and that imperialism has 'renounced' its policies of war and aggression." But, the modern imperialists, he continues, are the same old imperialists. They increase their arms, they carry out nuclear-war blackmail; they cry "peace" and use "sugar-coated cannon balls"—but all the while they relentlessly prepare for war.

It was these same imperialists, led by the United States, "the last pillar of international imperialism," with whom the Russians were then negotiating, and the Chinese Communists feel it necessary to remind the Soviet comrades of what Lenin had to say about imperialists and their inclinations. He "pointed out long ago that U.S. imperialism is the most vicious enemy of the people of the whole world playing the role of gendarme. Now, U.S. imperialism has gone ever further, appointing itself world gendarme, everywhere strangling the revolution, suppressing the national liberation movement and the revolutionary struggle of the proletariat in the capitalist countries." And these are the men with whom the Russian Communists are discussing peace.

As for the Russian accusation that the Chinese are "rigid dogmatists," Lu answers that to the modern revisionist "whoever persists in fighting against imperialism and for revolution is hindering peace and peaceful coexistence and is a 'rigid dogmatist.' " What these modern revisionists are actually doing, say the Chinese, is slandering real Marxism-Leninism as dogmatism and, in so doing, corroding "the revolutionary soul of Marxism-Leninism."

The series of Chinese diatribes in the spring of 1960 had little effect upon the Russians. The Soviets did cancel the summit conference, but for reasons probably having nothing to do with the Chinese. Even after the U-2 incident, Khrushchev continued to make the same arguments as before in favor of peaceful coexistence; Russian policy did not change appreciably. However, from April, 1960, on, Russia could have no doubt as to the intensity of Chinese feeling on these matters of international Communist strategy, and as to China's determination to adhere to her position.

Comrades, Friends:

Today, April 22, is the 90th anniversary of the birth of the great Lenin.

Lenin, following on Marx and Engels, was a great revolutionary teacher of the proletariat, the working people, and the oppressed nations of the whole world. Under the historical conditions of the epoch of imperialism and in the flames of the proletarian socialist revolution, Lenin resolutely defended and developed the revolutionary teachings of Marx and Engels. Leninism is Marxism of the epoch of imperialism and proletarian revolution. In the eyes of the working people of the world, the name of Lenin is the symbol of the triumph of the proletarian revolution, the symbol of the triumph of socialism and communism.

Ninety years ago, when Lenin was born, mankind was still under the dark rule of capitalism. Lenin and the Russian Bolshevik Party led the Russian proletariat and working people to break the chain of world imperialism, overthrow the bourgeois rule of violence by using revolutionary violence, win victory in the Great October Socialist Revolution, found the first state of the dictatorship of the proletariat, and open up a new era in the history of mankind.

❈   ❈   ❈

Now, the Soviet Union has entered the historical period of the extensive building of communism. Under the leadership of the Central Committee of the Communist Party of the Soviet Union and the Soviet Government, headed by Comrade N. S. Khrushchev, brilliant achievements have been scored in Soviet economic construction, and Soviet science and technology have advanced by leaps and bounds. The Soviet Union launched the world's first batch of artificial earth satellites and space rockets, opening up a new era in man's conquest of nature. These great achievements have greatly inspired the people of the world in their struggles against imperialism; for national liberation, people's democracy, and socialism; and for a lasting world peace.

The life of Lenin was the life of a great proletarian revolutionary, spent in bitter struggle against imperialism, against all sorts of reactionaries and opportunists. Leninism developed in the struggles against imperialism and opportunism. The special characteristic, the essence, of Leninism lies in its thorough proletarian revolutionary character. Leninism not only wholly revived the revolutionary content of Marxism which had been emasculated by the revisionists of the Second International, and restored the revolutionary keenness of Marxism once dulled by them, but further developed the revolutionary content and sharpened the revolutionary keenness of Marxism in the light of new historical experience under new historical conditions.

❈   ❈   ❈

Lenin taught us that without a proletarian revolutionary party tempered in repeated struggles, it is impossible to vanquish powerful enemies. Such a party should take Marxism-Leninism as its ideological basis, it should have a proletarian revolutionary program and have close links with the broad masses of laboring people. Our Chinese

Communist Party is exactly such a proletarian revolutionary party. Our party grew to maturity in the struggles against powerful enemies, at home and abroad, and against right and left opportunism. It was after repeated struggles against right and left opportunism that the Marxist-Leninist leadership of our party's Central Committee headed by Comrade Mao Tse-tung was firmly established. Precisely because our party has such a leadership, it has been able, in the period of the democratic revolution, to firmly secure proletarian leadership, carry the democratic revolution to thorough victory, and quickly turn the victory of the democratic revolution into that of the socialist revolution.

In our party's struggles against right and left opportunism, such works of Lenin as *Two Tactics of Social-Democracy in the Democratic Revolution*; *The State and Revolution*; *"Left-Wing" Communism, an Infantile Disorder*; and *The Proletarian Revolution and the Renegade Kautsky* have been our most important ideological weapons.

Our party applied in the practice of the Chinese revolution the Marxist-Leninist doctrines of uninterrupted revolution and the development of revolution by stages, and correctly and concretely solved a series of problems in turning the democratic revolution in our country into a socialist revolution.

* * *

Under the guidance of our party's general line for socialist construction, our country has seen big leaps forward in industrial and agricultural production, the emergence of the rural and urban people's communes, the movement for technical innovations and technical revolution, the combining of education with productive labor, and big leaps forward in the work of commerce, scientific research, culture and art, public health and physical culture.

Our party's general line for socialist construction has not only been attacked by the imperialists and modern revisionists, but has also been slandered by some philistines as "petty-bourgeois fanaticism." But facts remain facts. Our general line for socialist construction is a Marxist-Leninist general line. With the advance of our cause of socialist construction under the guidance of this general line, the face of our country is undergoing a rapid change in all its aspects.

* * *

The victories scored by our people in the new democratic revolution, socialist revolution, and socialist construction have all been achieved under the leadership of the Chinese Communist Party headed by Comrade Mao Tse-tung and under the guidance of Mao Tse-tung's thinking which integrates the universal truths of Marxism-Leninism with the concrete practice of the Chinese revolution. We have received help from the great Communist Party of the Soviet Union, the Soviet

Government, and the Soviet people, from all the socialist countries and from the Communist and workers' parties, from the laboring people and progressives of all countries. The Chinese people will always cherish this great spirit of internationalism and never forget it.

We are living in the great new epoch in which the collapse of the imperialist system is being further accelerated, and there is a constant growth in the victories and awakening of the people throughout the world.

On this situation, the Marxist-Leninists and the modern revisionists, starting from fundamentally different stands and viewpoints, draw fundamentally different conclusions. The Marxist-Leninists regard this as an unprecedentedly favorable new epoch for the proletarian revolution in the various countries of the world and for the national revolution in the colonies and semicolonies. The forces of peace have grown greatly, and there is already a practical possibility of preventing war. The people of the whole world must further intensify the struggle against imperialism, promote the development of revolution, and defend world peace. The modern revisionists, on the other hand, regard this as a "new epoch" in which the proletarian revolution in various countries and the national revolution in the colonies and semicolonies have disappeared from the world agenda. They think that imperialism will step down from the stage of history of its own accord, without a revolution; and that a lasting peace will come of itself, without waging anti-imperialist struggles. Thus, whether or not to carry out revolution and whether or not to oppose imperialism have become the fundamental difference between the Marxist-Leninists and the modern revisionists.

The main arguments of the modern revisionists in revising, emasculating, and betraying revolutionary Marxism-Leninism are based on their allegations that under the historical conditions of the new epoch, Lenin's analysis of imperialism has become "outmoded," that the nature of imperialism has "changed" and that imperialism has "renounced" its policies of war and aggression. Under the pretext of a so-called "historical, nondogmatic" approach to the theoretical legacy left by Lenin, they have attacked the revolutionary content and revolutionary spirit of Marxism-Leninism.

In the circumstances in which the East wind has prevailed over the West wind and the forces of socialism and peace have got the upper hand over the imperialist forces of war, there is a multitude of difficulties within the ranks of the imperialists who are falling on harder and harder times. The imperialists are putting up all sorts of desperate struggles in an attempt to save themselves from their doom. Recently, the imperialists, especially the U.S. imperialists, have tried hard to use even more cunning and deceptive tactics to pursue their aggressive and predatory policies, and benumb the people of the world. Even the U.S. imperialists themselves sometimes make no secret of their intention to adopt what they call more "flexible" tactics. They have employed multifarious means, adopting alternately tactics of war and tactics of peace. While stepping up arms expansion and war preparations and carrying out nuclear-war blackmail, they have at the same time spread a smokescreen of "peace" and used "sugar-coated cannon balls," in an attempt to create the false impression that imperialism advocates peace. They have on the one hand resorted to ruthless suppression of revolutionary movements, and on the other, resorted to deception and bribery, in an attempt to soften and split the revolutionary movements. The imperialists have resorted to these deceptive methods for the sole purpose of concealing their predatory and aggressive nature and covering up their war preparations, in order to disintegrate the revolutionary movements in various countries, the revolutionary movements of the colonies and semicolonies, and the struggle of the people of all countries for world peace, to enslave the people of various countries and to subvert the socialist countries.

To cope with the different tactics adopted by imperialism against the people, the peoples of the world also have to use various tactics and methods of revolutionary struggle in fighting imperialism. Marxist-Leninists have always maintained that in revolutionary struggle there should be firmness in principle and flexibility in tactics. The various means of revolution and forms of struggle, including the illegal and the "legal," extraparliamentary and parliamentary, sanguinary and bloodless, economic and political, military and ideological —all these are for the purpose of unmasking imperialism to a fuller extent, showing it up for the aggressor it is, constantly raising the revolutionary consciousness of the people, achieving broader mobilization of the masses of people to oppose imperialism and reactionaries, developing the struggle for world peace, and preparing for and winning victory in the people's revolution and the national revolution.

❋   ❋   ❋

In the struggle against imperialism and its policy of aggression, it is entirely permissible and necessary and in the interests of the people of various countries that, wherever possible, the socialist countries conduct peaceful negotiations and exchange visits with the imperialist countries, strive to settle international disputes by peaceful means instead of war, and endeavour to sign agreements of peaceful coexistence or treaties of mutual nonaggression.

The Soviet Government has made great efforts to ease international tension and defend world peace. The Chinese Communist Party, the Chinese Government, and the Chinese people actively support the peace proposals put forward by the Soviet Government headed by Comrade N. S. Khrushchev for convening an East-West meeting of the heads of government, general disarmament, prohibition of nuclear weapons, and so on.

The modern revisionists have completely betrayed the revolutionary spirit of Marxism-Leninism, betrayed the interest of the people of the world, and submitted and surrendered to the bourgeoisie and imperialism. They maintain that the nature of imperialism has changed and that imperialism has abandoned the war policy of its own accord, and that therefore there is no need for anti-imperialist struggles or revolutions. They are doing their utmost to camouflage the U.S. imperialist policies of aggression and war, to prettify imperialism and Eisenhower, the chieftain of U.S. imperialism. As described by them, Eisenhower has become a "peace emissary," U.S. imperialism is no longer the enemy of peace, no longer the enemy of the national liberation movements of the colonies and semicolonies, and no longer the most vicious enemy of the people of the entire world. In a word, according to the modern revisionists, there seems to be no longer any difference between socialism and imperialism and whoever persists in fighting against imperialism and revolution is hindering peace and peaceful coexistence and is a "rigid dogmatist."

We Marxist-Leninists know very well what dogmatism is and have constantly fought against it. Our Chinese Communist Party has rich experience in combating dogmatism. The dogmatists want revolution, but they do not know how to integrate the universal truths of Marxism-Leninism with the concrete practice of the revolution in their own countries, how to exploit the concrete contradictions of the enemy, how to concentrate forces on fighting against the chief enemy, how to enter into proper alliance with the various middle forces, or how to apply flexibly the tactics and methods of struggle, thus leaving the proletariat in a position in which it fights single-handedly. We oppose such dogmatism because it is harmful to the revolution. We oppose dogmatism in order to push ahead the revolution and to overthrow the enemy. Modern revisionists are doing just the opposite. Under the pretext of opposing "dogmatism," they oppose revolution, seeking to do away with it, and distort and adulterate Marxism-Leninism. In Lenin's words, "they omit, obliterate, and distort the revolutionary side of this teaching, its revolutionary soul. They push to the foreground and extol what is or seems acceptable to the bourgeoisie." [1] Modern revisionists slander Marxism-Leninism as "dogmatism"—this is a despicable trick of these renegades to the working class to corrode the revolutionary soul of Marxism-Leninism.

Revolution is the soul of Marxism-Leninism. Marx and Engels set before the proletariat of the whole world the great historic task of wiping out the capitalist system and emancipating all mankind. Under new historical conditions Lenin aroused the world proletariat and all

[1] "The State and Revolution," August–September, 1917, *Selected Works,* Foreign Language Publishing House, Moscow, 1952, Vol. II, pt. 1, p. 202.

oppressed peoples for fiery revolutionary struggle. Marxism-Leninism was born in the proletarian revolutionary struggle, and is continuously developed in that struggle. Marxist-Leninist formulations on some individual questions may change with the passage of time and the changed situation, but the revolutionary spirit of Marxism-Leninism absolutely will not change. In the light of the historical conditions of his time, Lenin changed the formulations of Marx and Engels on individual questions, and raised questions which Marx and Engels could not have raised in their days. Far from weakening the revolutionary spirit of Marxism in the slightest, however, these changes further increased the revolutionary fighting power of Marxism. Revolution is the locomotive of history, the motive force of the progress of human society. This is so in class society and it will remain so in the future Communist society, only the revolution of that time will be different in nature and method.

We know that U.S. imperialism is the most vicious and cunning enemy of the people's revolution in various countries, of the national liberation movement, and of world peace, and that Eisenhower is now the chieftain of U.S. imperialism. Lenin pointed out long ago that U.S. imperialism is the most vicious enemy of the people of the whole world playing the role of gendarme. Now, U.S. imperialism has gone even further, appointing itself world gendarme, everywhere strangling the revolution, suppressing the national liberation movement and the revolutionary struggle of the proletariat in the capitalist countries, and sabotaging the movement of the people of the world for peace. U.S. imperialism is not only attempting every minute to subvert and wipe out the socialist countries but, under the pretext of opposing communism and socialism, is also doing its utmost to expand into the intermediate areas, in the vain hope of achieving world domination. These policies of aggression and war of U.S. imperialism have not changed to this day. No matter what deceptive tactics U.S. imperialism may adopt at any time, its aggressive and predatory nature will never change till its death. U.S. imperialism is the last pillar of international imperialism. If the proletariat in the capitalist countries is to win emancipation, if the peoples of the colonies and semicolonies are to achieve national liberation, if the people of the world are to defend world peace, they must direct the spearhead of their struggle against U.S. imperialism. Whether or not one dares to expose imperialism, and especially U.S. imperialism, whether or not one dares to struggle against it, is the touchstone of whether or not one wants to carry out the people's revolution, to win the complete emancipation of the oppressed nations, and to win a genuine world peace.

In order to oppose the aggressive policy of U.S. imperialism, it is necessary to unite all the world's revolutionary forces and peace-loving forces. World peace can be further defended and effectively defended only by linking up the struggle of the peoples of the socialist countries, the national liberation struggle of the peoples of the colonies and semi-colonies, the revolutionary struggle of the proletariat in the capitalist countries, and the struggle of all peoples for peace, forming them into a mighty anti-imperialist front and dealing firm blows at the U.S. imperialist policies of aggression and war. The socialist camp headed by the Soviet Union is the main force in defence of world peace. The national liberation struggles of the peoples of the colonies and semi-colonies, and the revolutionary struggles of the proletariat and working people in the capitalist countries are also great forces in defence of world peace. Separation from the national liberation struggles of the colonies and semicolonies and from the revolutionary struggles of the proletariat and working people in the capitalist countries will greatly weaken the forces in defense of world peace and serve the interests of imperialism.

No force on earth can hinder or restrain the peoples of the colonies and semicolonies from rising in revolution and smashing the yoke they are under. Their revolutionary struggles play the role of shaking the very foundation of the imperialist system. All revolutionary Marxist-Leninists should support these just struggles, resolutely and without the slightest reservation. Similarly, no force on earth can hinder or restrain the proletariat and working people in the capitalist countries from rising in revolution to overthrow the reactionary rule of monopoly capital. Their revolutionary struggles can tie the hands of imperialism and prevent it from unleashing aggressive war. All revolutionary Marxist-Leninists should likewise support these just revolutionary struggles, resolutely and without the slightest reservation. Firm support of these two types of struggle constitutes an effective strengthening of the struggle to defend world peace. Lenin maintained that the proletariat in the socialist countries must, with the assistance of the world proletariat and the working masses of the oppressed nations, defend the fruits of victory which the proletarian revolution has already achieved, and at the same time support the continuous advance of the cause of proletarian revolution in other countries and continuously weaken the strength of imperialism until capitalism has perished and socialism has triumphed throughout the world. As Leninists, we must always bear in mind these basic theses of Lenin.

Modern revisionism is a product of imperialist policy. The modern revisionists are panic-stricken by the imperialist policy of nuclear-war blackmail. Fear of war becomes fear of revolution, and not wanting revolution themselves becomes opposing other people's carrying out revolution. To meet the needs of imperialism, they try to obstruct the development of the national liberation movement and the proletarian revolutionary movement in various countries. Imperialism attempts to make the socialist countries degenerate into capitalist countries. And modern revisionists like Tito have adapted themselves to this need of imperialism.

It is important to oppose modern revisionism, because the modern revisionists can play a role that the bourgeoisie and the right-wing social democrats cannot play among the masses of workers and the working people. They are the agents of imperialism and the enemies of the proletariat and working people of all countries.

*　　*　　*

Modern revisionism is at present the chief danger to the international Communist movement. It is our sacred duty to bring into full play the revolutionary spirit of Lenin, and thoroughly reveal the true colors of the agent of imperialism—modern revisionism.

The Communist movement has from the very outset been an international movement. The international solidarity of the proletariat is the fundamental guarantee for the victory of the people's revolutionary cause in all the countries of the world, of the cause of the national liberation of the oppressed nations, and of the peoples' struggle for world peace. In the interests of the socialist countries, of the proletariat and working people of all countries, of the liberation of the oppressed nations, and of the defence of world peace, we must at all times strengthen the international solidarity of the proletariat. Marxist-Leninists have always guarded as the apple of their eye the unity of the socialist camp headed by the Soviet Union, the unity of the international Communist ranks, the unity of the world proletariat, and the unity of the people of the whole world. The imperialists and modern revisionists regard this great international unity as the greatest obstacle to their attempt to disintegrate the revolutionary movement of various countries. Scheming day and night in the vain hope of undermining this unity, they are carrying on the most despicably dirty work of sowing discord and spreading lies and slanders. But these base intrigues are doomed to complete bankruptcy.

Under the guidance of the revolutionary doctrines of Marxism-Leninism, the socialist cause of the proletariat certainly can and will win complete victory throughout the world. Lasting peace will certainly come to humanity.

Let us unite and advance bravely under the revolutionary banner of the great Lenin!

Long live Marxism-Leninism!

COWARDS IN THE KREMLIN

"To Be a Revolutionary, One Must Have the Revolutionary Will," comment as reprinted in *Jenmin Jihpao* (*People's Daily*), Peking, August 13, 1960, from the Shanghai magazine *Liberation*.

The U-2 incident and the subsequent collapse of the summit conference may have given the Chinese reason to believe that Khrushchev would now abandon the pursuit of his kind of peaceful coexistence. If such was the case, their hopes were soon dashed by repeated Soviet assertions that peaceful coexistence of the Khrushchev variety was the only way.

A meeting of the Communist-controlled World Federation of Trade Unions was scheduled for Peking in early June. In retrospect it appears evident that the Chinese, feeling that Khrushchev's reputation had reached a new low, attempted to rouse the assembled delegates against his policies. According to the information available, long and bitter debates ensued in which the Chinese used all their forensic ability to spark resistance to the "soft" Russian attitude, and not without some success.

Throughout the previous three years of conflict over strategy, Moscow had fairly well kept her peace. But now the attempts of Peking to turn the movement against her at this "time of troubles" called the Kremlin to action. Using the occasion of the 40th anniversary of publication of the Leninist classic Left-Wing Communism—an Infantile Disorder, the Soviet press warns against "present day leftists" who are in too much of a hurry to rush ahead. Sometimes it is necessary to halt and rest before pushing on again. Today "even Communist parties which are powerful and hardened in class struggle are running up against survivals of leftism, the erroneous views of comrades who V. I. Lenin ironically described as 'terrible revolutionaries.' "

A major Russian counteroffensive was scheduled for the soonest possible occasion, the meeting of the Rumanian party congress at Bucharest later in the same month. Khrushchev himself attended the conclave and reportedly lashed out, not only at the ideas being espoused by the Chinese Communists and at their tactics but also at the Politburo of the CCP in general and at comrade Mao in particular, whom he accused of being a poor theoretician.

Peking was probably shocked by the virulence of the Russian

counterattack, which continued during July and into August. They may have particularly been dismayed by the withdrawal of Russian technical assistance, which dates from this period. For the time being, however, the Chinese press was silent, as the party leadership took counsel. Early in August the Chinese high command convened at a mountain resort and there decided upon the next step.

By mid-August, it was apparent that the decision was in favor of continuing hostility to Russian policies. On August 13, Jenmin Jihpao reprinted the article "To Be a Revolutionary, One Must Have The Revolutionary Will," which clearly accused the Russians of cowardice. As for themselves, the Chinese say that they are bullied because they are still "poor and blank," but they shall yet conquer because they have the revolutionary will. "If we do not have this revolutionary will and do not exert ourselves, we shall then forever be pushed around and shall remain backward without being able to move even a step forward."

Regarding the Soviet withdrawal of aid, the Chinese repeatedly assert that they must "work hard and rely on our own strength." "We have, therefore, to rely on our hands to build a new world of blissful life. . . . Sole reliance on others without constantly exerting ourselves is not a revolutionary spirit." We must rid ourselves of inferiority complexes. Whatever others have done, we can do. The harnessing of nature by man is only in its infancy. This "great age where man can display his full ability is the age of socialism-communism. And this age has only just begun." Let the Russians beware.

In August, 1960, then, the Chinese call the Russians cowards, defy them, and accuse them of trying to keep the Chinese people down. And this, they make it quite clear, they will not endure.

To be a revolutionary, one must have revolutionary vigor. Under the three fluttering banners—the party's general line, the big leap forward, and the commune system—we have done our work satisfactorily and our socialist revolution and socialist construction have advanced in big strides. But we must not relax. Only by holding the banners aloft and pressing steadily forward can we prosecute our revolutionary cause to a successful finish.

Where does revolutionary vigor come from? One generally acquires it when one is forced to deal with difficult circumstances. But equally important is the fact that one must have the revolutionary will. Persons suffering oppression and bullying without complaint and too timid to attempt any change in the situation do not have anything we call revolutionary vigor and naturally cannot be revolutionaries. Revolutionary vigor comes to a person when, realizing that he is one of the oppressed and bullied, he decides that he has had enough of it, and gnashing his teeth with rage, he proceeds to change the situation thoroughly. He exerts himself and displays great heroism as a Chinese saying goes, and in this way he acquires revolutionary vigor. The degree of his revolutionary vigor matches the depth of his revolutionary character. He who lacks revolutionary vigor has no revolutionary character. There are among our comrades some who get well contented with minor achievement and lose heart in front of difficulties. The revolutionary will or revolutionary character of these comrades has declined, and there is a good chance that they will be left behind by the revolutionary rank and file. We advise these comrades to raise their revolutionary consciousness, promote their revolutionary will, and press steadily forward so that they will not be thrown behind by the revolutionary army.

Our toiling masses are fond of saying that although they are poor, they have a strong will. This strong will is the revolutionary will. They have often said that it does not matter if they are poor so long as they have a strong will. They call persons without a strong will, cowards. Landlords and the bourgeois class have money and influence. But in the eyes of the toiling masses, they are nothing. The toilers are not afraid of the landlords and bourgeoisie. They do not beg for mercy but brace themselves and start a revolution by their own efforts. We say that they have the revolutionary will. We are compelled to change our "poor and blank" conditions. But without revolutionary will, we shall not try hard to do it.

In the semicolonial and semifeudal old China, the Chinese people were bullied by the imperialists and oppressed by feudal lords and bureaucratic capitalists. While the enemies were armed to the teeth, we had to fight with our bare fists. Reactionaries at home and abroad scoffed at our helpless state and said that we could never succeed. But the Chinese people paid no attention to this derision, and worked with patience and perserverance under the leadership of the Chinese Communist Party and Chairman Mao Tse-tung. When they received setbacks, they drew lessons from them and rose again to keep up the struggle, and this was repeated until they overthrew the imperialist, feudal, and bureaucratic capitalist rule and founded the Chinese People's Republic. The "hopeless" people have succeeded. When the Chinese Communists started the revolution, they realized very well that the enemies were much stronger than they were. But was this of any decisive significance? Should they take defeat submissively on account of the superiority of the enemies? Should they permit the continued oppression and bullying of the Chinese people? No, we were revolutionaries and revolutionaries were tough people, and to be revolutionaries, we must have the will to wage a stubborn struggle. The Chinese Communists firmly believed that the broad masses of the Chinese people were not willing to be slaves and on this ground started agitation among the masses and organized them for the struggle. With the steady increase in the consciousness of the people, the number of participants in the revolution increased. The strength of the people was mustered into the struggle, and we learned the way of building up the party of the Marxist-Leninist order, fighting the war, establishing bases, and setting up a united front. Through three civil wars and the War of Resistance against Japan, the little spark kindled a great fire which has never been extinguished.

At the early stage of the founding of the Chinese People's Republic, the imperialists and the reactionaries looked down upon us, saying that the Chinese Communists, though strong in the battlefield and in political agitation, knew little about economics and less about the administration of cities and the whole country. The American imperialists imposed on us an economic blockade, and the American-Chiang clique sent planes to bomb Shanghai and many other areas of our country, and spies and secret agents to launch subversive activities. In a word, the enemies, convinced that we were doomed to failure, set about toppling the young People's Republic of China. But the Chinese people had the same revolutionary will as the Chinese Communists. We were not taken in by either the honey-coated words or the harsh intimidations of the enemies. With perseverance and patience, we kept up our struggle. We triumphed over our enemies. The young People's Republic of China not only took root but fought shoulder to shoulder with the heroic Korean people in the Aid-Korea and Anti-U.S. War, forcing the American marauders who had attempted to encroach upon Korea and invade our country to sit down at Panmunjom and sign a truce.

China has now stood up among the nations of the world as a great socialist country. Since the founding of the Chinese People's Republic, she has taken great strides in the political, economic, and military fields. But we are still being bullied. U.S. imperialists are still occupying our sacred territory of Taiwan and are constantly violating our territorial waters and sky. They have thrown a cordon of military bases around our country, and reactionaries in a number of countries are making spasmodic efforts at the beck and call of American imperialism to isolate us. In a word, American imperialists and reactionaries in the different countries hostile to the Chinese people do not permit us to advance or to become strong and prosperous. They dream of dragging the Chinese people back to the days of the old China when we were nothing but slaves or of forcing our revolution to a halt. They do not permit us to speed up the pace of our socialist construction and our preparations for transition to communism. Are we not full of rage? Rage is a very good thing. Rage is a motive power for action. Let us exert ourselves and display heroism. Let us work hard for eight or ten more years or even slightly longer. Let them see us then and they will be surprised.

The enemies dare to bully us for the simple reason that although we have become strong, we are still "poor and blank." Now let us make up our mind to change this "poor and blank" state. Under the guidance of the party's general line for building socialism with greater, faster, better, and more economical results and with the whole party and the whole people working with one heart, let us rely on our own strength and work with perseverance in building our country into a strong socialist nation complete with highly developed modern industry, modern agriculture, and modern science and culture. If we do not have this revolutionary will and do not exert ourselves, we shall then forever be pushed around and shall remain backward without being able to move even a step forward. Are we willing to remain that way? Of course not. Chairman Mao Tse-tung has said: "When one is poor, one wants a change, wants to do something and wants to start a revolution." He has also told us that, though we are late, we must strive to become superior. If we think of no change and content ourselves with the present status, we shall not think of doing anything and we shall have no vigor or not sufficient vigor. If we do not exert ourselves, we shall never have a chance to succeed. If we decide to work, we must work at a revolutionary pace and with revolutionary methods. Slow work and lukewarm effort is not what we want. We want the kind of work and effort that proceeds with full speed by dispelling superstitions and breaking through the bonds of old regulations and conventions. Also we must work practically. Unless we do this, we cannot surge ahead of others. Of course, when we say that we want to surge ahead, we do not mean that we shall allow none to catch up with us or even overtake us. If we have that idea, we are not Communists. While striving to get ahead, we want the others to surpass us, and as this takes place, we shall try to catch up with and surpass them. Under the impetus of this emulation, the socialist-communist cause develops without interruption, society advances steadily, and science and culture grow.

If we have the revolutionary will and the spirit of exerting ourselves, no difficulties can prevent our advance. There are numerous facts to prove this. One handy example is the countless number of cooperatives or areas which previously were very backward and were objects of derision and which have since the liberation, especially since the commencement of the Great Leap Forward, transformed themselves into successful cooperatives or areas through the exertion of strenuous efforts. The New Fifth People's Commune at Sungchiang *hsien* formerly was so poor that it had only three harvests in nine years and that nobody would be willing to marry off his daughter to any of its members. Intense with rage, the members of the commune decided to turn it into a prosperous organization. In the movement for building irrigation facilities, they brushed aside the suggestion of the rich peasants that they were attempting the impossible and worked day and night despite the cold weather. Fighting hard for 100 days, they dug out a river which they called the Construction River and which was 11 *li* long. In disregard of the suggestion of the rich peasants that successful planting of wheat and rice crops would be impossible unless more land was made available, they invented a wheat planting method which enabled them to make the best possible use of the land available. Life has now come back to the river banks of the commune.

On the industrial front, the large number of workers were compelled to plunge into a revolution on acount of the low technical level and the relatively backward equipment available. By ridding themselves of an inferiority complex, they made it possible for the work style of daring-to-think-and-act to grow. In the Huafeng Enamelware Factory, a number of veteran workers built an automatic kiln. At the beginning, they did not have the materials or the techniques to build the kiln. But they said: "If the foreigners can do it, there is no reason why we cannot do it as we also have a head and a pair of hands." With this vigor, they built the kiln, spending only 10 percent of the cost of an American kiln, but achieving an increase in production by 2.6 times.

The revolutionary will of exerting oneself is the spirit of struggling with perseverance and relying on one's own strength. We started the revolution and the program of construction virtually from scratch. We have, therefore, to rely on our hands to build a new world of blissful life, and in this connection, there is no alternative but to work and struggle hard. Sole reliance on others without constantly exerting ourselves is not a revolutionary spirit. At the high tide of the socialist transformation in agriculture, Chairman Mao Tse-tung said: "The Wang Kuo-fan cooperative which had 23 poor peasant households as its members and a donkey only three-fourths paid for was called the 'poor cooperative.' But the members, by exerting themselves, obtained within three years large quantities of means of production 'from the mountain.' This deed moves the visitors to tears. I see this as a symbol of the whole country." There are "Wang Kuo-fan communes" on both the agricultural and industrial front and on all other fronts. Poverty drives us to exert ourselves, to work hard, to struggle with perseverance, and to rely on our own strength. The most fundamental and reliable way of changing the scientific and technical backwardness of our country and building it into a strong and prosperous nation is to work hard and rely on our own strength. Only in this way shall we have our eyes on the broad masses and on the available material and technical conditions. Only in this way shall we bring into full play the spirit of the "poor commune" and all favorable factors, and lead the masses in creating the kind of situation we want. Matters of this nature have appeared one after another in the different areas. In the rural areas, there are cases where pig sties were built without costing practically anything, land was utilized to the fullest possible extent, and chemical fertilizer factories and farm tool plants were set up from scratch. In factories, waste materials are turned into precious things through multiple-purpose utilization, native equipment and apparatus

are made from the materials readily available, and the technical revolution is launched on a full scale with efforts being made for one thing
to do the work of several. There are too many such examples to be all
cited here. They represent the rapid approach of the country to prosperity. If everyone of our areas, our departments, our units, and even
our comrades works so hard without looking to others for help, we
shall have no difficulties which we cannot solve. In eight or ten years,
the face of our country will be fundamentally changed.

True, we shall come across a great deal of difficulties in our efforts
today to storm modern and relatively advanced scientific and technical fortresses for the sake of placing the different departments of the
national economy on a modern technical footing. But if we lack the
spirit of hard struggle and self-reliance and if, instead of imposing on
ourselves a high ideal of struggle so as to catch up with the others,
we stretch our hands and wait for help to come in the hope of finding
a short cut to success, then we shall get nowhere. If we rely on the
great strength of the party and the broad masses, we shall be able to
do either immediately or in the near future whatever mankind can do,
and there will be nothing which we cannot accomplish. Although quite
a number of scientific and technical achievements have been recorded
in the course of the development of human society, the fact remains
that man is still poorly equipped for the fight to harness nature. He
may control the earth, but he is not able to control the sky. Even the
earth which he controls is nothing but one layer of earth. Let us not
be frightened by the achievements of the Western capitalist countries.
As far as the history of the development of mankind is concerned, the
present highest modern scientific and cultural achievements are still
in their infancy. The great age where man can display his full ability
is the age of socialism-communism. And this age has only just begun.

The revolutionary will of exerting the utmost effort is, stripped to
the bone, an expression of revolutionary resoluteness. We Communists
work for the realization of communism because we understand the
objective law governing the development of history and are determined to carry out the communist ideal. The enemies may suppress
us and curse us, and some of the less enlightened people may call us
stupid fellows and charge us with attempting at something we are not
capable of. But inasmuch as we have already chosen our revolutionary
goal, we are determined to carry it out. In the course of the revolutionary struggle, we are bound to meet setbacks and suffer great
sacrifices. But we shall not lose courage, and shall stand undaunted
and fight on no matter how severe the setback is. Lenin often advised
the people to work with the revolutionary spirit. On the victorious conclusion of the October Revolution, he pointed out: "The revolution
must necessarily go through the most severe test in practice, struggle
and even bombardment. If you are exploited and oppressed, then
you want to overthrow the political regime of the exploiters. If you

are determined to prosecute the cause of overthrowing the exploiters to a successful finish, then you ought to know that you will be subjected to attacks by all exploiters in the world. If you decide to deal a counterblow, are not afraid of sacrifice and persevere in the struggle, then you are a revolutionary. Otherwise, you will be eliminated." He added: "Patience, perseverance, determination, judgment, and ability to make experiments and improvements until the goal is reached— these qualities of the proletarian class are the sure guarantee of success for the proletariat." This means that we must have revolutionary resoluteness and the revolutionary will to exert to the utmost.

Without revolutionary resoluteness, it will not be possible to work up fervor for exerting to the utmost. Some people are content with their backward status, without feeling the agony of backward life. They have therefore no rage or complaint, and it is not possible to work up the fervor in them for changing the backward status. There are also some who, though realizing that they are backward, feel that somehow they can get along and are not disposed to change the status early. All this is a manifestation of the lack of the necessary consciousness and a decline in the revolutionary will.

The present international situation in general is good. The East wind continues to prevail over the West wind. The domestic situation is also good. The leap forward is being well kept up. But at present, imperialism still exists and the threat of the imperialists starting a war of aggression still exists. If we do not exert ourselves to push our program of construction forward at the fullest possible speed, and catch up with the capitalist countries economically within the shortest possible period, we shall not be able to consider our security fully guaranteed. In order to accelerate the change, we must build up, within a relatively short period of time, a modern industry, modern agriculture, and modern science and culture to raise the material and cultural level of our people; and unless we do that, the material foundation of our socialist system will not be very strong. The steadily growing socialist camp headed by the Soviet Union is the reliable guarantee of success in checking imperialist aggression and defending world peace. China is a socialist country and is a big country. We exert ourselves primarily for the purpose of strengthening the socialist camp and checking imperialist aggression and defending world peace. At the present stage, revolutionary resoluteness is reflected in the common animosity against the imperialists, in the determination to prosecute the socialist revolution to a successful finish and in the boundless fervor for socialist construction.

It takes man to get things done on earth. With the necessary objective conditions available, man's subjective initiative is the key to success or failure. Man's subjective initiative does not mean an effort without a goal or without any plan. It means that we must analyze the situation in a practical way, painstakingly search for the objective law, take practical measures, and work in a practical work. With the brilliant leadership of the CCP Central Committee and Chairman Mao Tse-tung, we shall be able to push forward our socialist construction in the different fields at great pace despite the host of difficulties with which we shall have to grapple as long as our party members and the broad masses treat all revolutionary and construction problems with the revolutionary spirit of exerting our utmost efforts, with revolutionary determination, and with the revolutionary attitude, stand up against imperialist aggression, be not contented with poverty and backwardness, be full of rage and ambition, and work in a practical way.

PAPERING OVER

"A Great Anti-Imperialist Call," editorial in *Hung-Ch'i* (*Red Flag*), Peking, December 16, 1960.

In November, 1960, the 81 Communist parties of the world responded to a summons to Moscow to attempt to reconcile the differences that were threatening to demolish even the semblance of international Communist solidarity. In the preceding six months the exchange of bitter accusations between the Soviet and the Chinese, and the taking of recriminatory actions, the latter mostly on the part of the Russians, had multiplied, to the extent that a complete rupture of Russo-Chinese relations did not appear entirely beyond possibility.

The leaders of world communism assembled on November 10 and held sessions for the next three weeks in what was to prove to be one of the most hard-fought and memorable meetings that the movement has ever had. For the first time since Stalin's ascendancy there was what approximated freedom of expression in an international Communist conclave. The meetings demonstrated that communism was beyond the point where the Russian comrade could give orders which the international comrades would automatically and unquestioningly obey. Even the myth of Communist monolithism would find it difficult to survive the November, 1960, experiences.

The subject matter of the arguments that raged back and forth consisted of the differences over military and political strategy which had occupied the Russians and the Chinese since the November, 1957, conclaves: the inevitability of war, the spread of the revolution, the commune, in all their ramifications.

As the forum proceeded it became apparent that the Russians and Chinese would not appreciably alter their position. Yet, it seemed impossible to the delegates to adjourn the sessions without a statement of agreement and renewed pledges of unity. Such was the tradition and, it was felt, the strength of communism. There appeared little inclination at this point to emphasize the intensity of Sino-Soviet differences by permitting the meeting to disintegrate.

In consequence, a preliminary draft, which had originally been submitted by the Russians in September and had been kicked around by the various parties for over two months, was transformed into a cloud of ambiguity that satisfied everybody and satisfied nobody, yet could serve as a vehicle for suspiciously overrepeated protests of international Communist solidarity.

In "The Declaration of the Eighty-one Communist Parties,"* an occasional point is won by the Russians. For example, China apparently concedes that there is the possibility of removing world wars from the "life of society" before the complete elimination of imperialism. In return, Russia is willing to allow it to be stated that such a development can transpire only after she has achieved the status of the world's mightiest industrial power and China has become a "mighty" one. Thus the Russian hypothesis is adopted, but its effectiveness is vitiated by what amounts to the indefinite postponement of its possible implementation.

In general, the Russians seem to gain more than the Chinese. But in most instances the document makes no attempt to reconcile the Sino-Soviet differences but places both positions alongside one another. Thus, in signing the Declaration the Russians and Chinese commit themselves to nothing, but remain free to go their own ways. Within weeks, if not days, it is apparent that this is exactly what both intend to do.

On December 16, 1960, the foremost Chinese journal on Marxist theory, Red Flag, published an editorial on "A Great Anti-Imperialist Call." This alleged "commentary" on the 81-party declaration is not an expostulation of the document itself, but a reiteration of earlier Chinese positions. Even the quotations used in "A Great Anti-Imperialist Call" are not primarily from the Declaration, but are preconference statements of Mao, Liu, and Chou setting forth preconference positions. Whatever statements the Declaration included that were unacceptable to the Chinese, they disregard (for example, the terrible destructiveness of nuclear war to all participants). On the other hand, the parts of it that they find acceptable, especially those having to do with the continuing menace of imperialism and its role as the instigator of war, they dwell on at length.

Thus, the great assemblage of November, 1960, settled nothing in the Sino-Soviet dispute.

The documents issued by the Moscow meeting of representatives of 81 Communist and Workers' Parties are warmly welcomed by the broad masses of the people in all countries.

The main document of the meeting, "The Statement of the Meeting of Representatives of the Communist and Workers' Parties," is a program document, heir of the 1957 Moscow declaration. The statement gives a penetrating analysis of the developments in the balance of international class forces in the past three years; elucidates the many important and pressing questions confronting the international communist movement and all progressive mankind; and indicates to the Communist parties, the working class, and all progressive forces in all

* See, D. N. Jacobs, The New Communist Manifesto, 2nd., Harper & Row, New York, 1962.

countries the line and the road to victory in their common struggle. The publication of the statement has given rise to panic-stricken outbursts in the imperialist camp. This document, adopted unanimously by the 81 Communist and workers' parties, is bound to advance greatly the struggle against imperialism and for world peace, for national liberation, democracy, and socialism on a worldwide scale.

Although the specific conditions of the 81 independent Communist and workers' parties in various countries of the world are different, they all take Marxism-Leninism as their guiding ideology and are responsible not only to the working class and laboring people of their respective countries but also to the entire international workers' and Communist movement. This is why they are able to reach common conclusions on many important questions through consultations. This fact itself shows the great vitality of Marxism-Leninism and the great united strength of the international Communist movement.

The Chinese Communist Party was represented by its delegation at the Moscow meeting. The delegates of the Chinese Communist Party, together with the delegates of the Communist Party of the Soviet Union and the other fraternal parties, worked jointly in drawing up the documents of the meeting. The Chinese Communist Party and the Chinese people rejoice in the achievements of this meeting and will, as in the past, faithfully abide in practice by the documents unanimously adopted by the Chinese Communist Party and the other fraternal parties. To carry out resolutely the proposals and demands on various important questions contained in the statement of the meeting, is in complete accord with the line and principles consistently pursued by the Chinese Communist Party.

The statement of the meeting points out in clearcut terms that imperialism is the enemy of all progressive causes of human society in our time and is also the enemy of world peace. Imperialism has created grave dangers for all mankind through its plans for launching a nuclear war. The imperialist group headed by the United States calls the world under its rule a "free world" and attempts to use empty talks about peace to hoodwink the peoples of all countries. According to the apologists of imperialism, whoever wants freedom must submit to the system of imperialist domination and whoever wants peace must give up the anti-imperialist struggle. To smash this reactionary propaganda of the imperialists before the broad masses of the people in all countries of the world is, undoubtedly, of great importance.

On the basis of irrefutable facts, the statement thoroughly exposes the true colors of imperialism. The statement says, "International developments in recent years have furnished many new proofs of the fact that U.S. imperialism is the chief bulwark of world reaction and an international gendarme, that it has become an enemy of the peoples of the whole world." The statement points out that the source of modern war is the capitalist system and the imperialist system. So long as imperialism exists there will be soil for wars of aggression. U.S. imperialism is the main force of aggression and war. The danger of a new world war still persists; on the contrary, the peoples must now be more vigilant than ever.

It is an irrepressible objective law that the people of different countries who are oppressed and menaced by imperialism rise up against it. It is impossible for the imperialists to try to quell this struggle. As the statement says, "The peoples are rising with growing determination to fight imperialism. A great struggle is getting underway between the forces of labor and capital, of democracy and reaction, of freedom and colonialism." It stresses, "The broadest possible united front of peace supporters, fighters against the imperialist policy of aggression and war inspired by U.S. imperialism, is essential to preserve world peace. Concerted and vigorous actions of all the forces of peace can safeguard the peace and prevent a new war."

To safeguard the peace, it is necessary to wage an active struggle against imperialism, the creator of war. This is the fundamental stand of Marxists-Leninists on the question of peace. Now, in addition to the Marxists-Leninists, more and more people in the world are becoming aware of this truth. On this point, the statement of the meeting sums up the valuable experience gained by the people the world over from practice.

For a long time in the past, the Chinese people had suffered from bullying and oppression by imperialism as well as its armed occupation and large-scale military aggression. It was only after their victory in the hard-fought revolutionary struggles against imperialism and its lackeys, that they were able to build their own country in a peaceful international environment. Soon after the founding of the People's Republic of China, it laid down in its program for the building of the state that the principle of China's foreign policy "is protection of the independence, freedom, territorial integrity, and sovereignty of the country, upholding lasting international peace and friendly cooperation among the peoples of all countries, and opposition to the imperialist policy of aggression and war" (the Common Program of the Chinese People's Political Consultative Conference). It is also provided in the Constitution of the Chinese People's Republic that "in international affairs our firm and consistent policy is to strive for the noble cause of world peace and the progress of humanity." This basic principle of China's foreign relations has always been carried out consistently.

Shortly after the founding of the Chinese People's Republic, U.S. imperialism unscrupulously launched an armed aggression which forced the Chinese people to wage the war to resist U.S. aggression and aid Korea. But we carried on this war precisely in order to realize peace. Comrade Mao Tse-tung declared in October, 1951, "The great struggle to resist U.S. aggression and aid Korea is now continuing. It must be carried on until the U.S. government is willing to settle the question peacefully. We do not desire to encroach upon any country. We are simply opposing imperialist aggression against our country. Everyone knows that if American forces had not occupied our Taiwan, had not invaded the Korean Democratic People's Republic and pushed their attacks to our northeastern borders, the Chinese people would not be fighting against American troops" (Chairman Mao Tse-tung's opening speech at the 3rd session of the 1st National Committee of the Chinese People's Political Consultative Conference). The joint struggle of the Korean and Chinese peoples finally forced the U.S. government to accept an armistice. As is generally known, the Chinese side had made prolonged, unremitting efforts to bring about an armistice in Korea.

In the first half of 1954, after the armistice, the Chinese government took part in the Geneva Conference to bring about an armistice in Indo-China and further restore the peaceful situation in the Far East on the one hand, and, on the other, proposed jointly with the Indian and Burmese governments the five principles of peaceful coexistence. At that time, the Chinese government declared, "All our efforts are directed toward building our country into a prosperous and happy socialist industrial state. We are going ahead with our peaceful work and we want a peaceful environment and a peaceful world. This basic fact determines the peaceful policy of our country in foreign affairs." It also stated that the five principles of peaceful coexistence which apply to relations between China and India and between China and Burma should apply likewise to relations between China and other Asian countries, as well as to international relations in general (Premier Chou En-lai's Report on the Work of the Government, made at the first session of the First National People's Congress of China in September, 1954).

Peaceful coexistence and peaceful competition among nations with differing social systems is a principle all socialist countries commonly abided by. The imperialists and the revisionists are of the opinion that the prerequisite for putting this principle into effect is the renunciation of struggle against imperialism in the political, economic, and ideological fields. This is, of course, preposterous. The statement of the Meeting of Representatives of the Communist and Workers' Parties says: "Peaceful coexistence of states does not imply renunciation of the class struggle as the revisionists claim. The coexistence of states with different social systems is a form of class struggle between socialism and capitalism. In conditions of peaceful coexistence, favorable opportunities are provided for the development of the class struggle in the capitalist countries and the national liberation movement of the peoples of the colonial and dependent countries. In their turn, the successes of the revolutionary class struggle and the national liberation struggle promote the consolidation of peaceful coexistence."

In past years, the Chinese government has, in accordance with the five principles of peaceful coexistence, established and developed relations of friendship and cooperation with a series of Asian, African, and Latin American countries and neutral states in Europe. It has also established and developed normal diplomatic relations with many other capitalist countries. As early as July, 1955, the Chinese government has on many occasions put forward the proposal that countries in Asia and around the Pacific, including the United States, sign a peace pact of mutual nonaggression and make the entire region a nuclear weapons-free area, a peace area.

In his report to the first session of the 8th National Congress of the Communist Party of China, Comrade Liu Shao-ch'i declared: "In our foreign relations, we consistently follow a firm policy of peace and advocate peaceful coexistence and friendly cooperation among all nations. We believe in the superiority of the socialist system and we are not afraid to engage in peaceful competition with capitalist countries. Our policy accords with the interests of all the peoples of the world."

It is the imperialist forces of aggression headed by the United States that obstruct peaceful coexistence of nations with differing social systems. Therefore, as the statement of the meeting says, it is essential to weaken and press back steadily the positions of imperialism by the active struggle of the people for peace, democracy, and national liberation. Only then it is possible to force the imperialists into accepting peaceful coexistence.

While persisting in the policy of peaceful coexistence, China, together with the other socialist countries, has all along insisted on combating the imperialist policy of aggression and war and giving support to the struggles waged by all anti-imperialist forces throughout the world. Our faith in the policy of peaceful coexistence is founded on the triumphant progress of the anti-imperialist struggles. Speaking at the 5th session of the First National People's Congress in February, 1958, Comrade Chou En-lai said: "The world forces for peace are stronger today than ever before and the conditions for securing a lasting world peace are unprecedentedly favorable. So long as all the peace-loving countries and peoples maintain their solidarity and persevere in the struggle as they have up till now, they will be able to cause the international situation to continue to develop in a direction favorable to peace and compel the imperialist aggressive forces to accept peaceful coexistence."

China has always given firm support to the disarmament proposals put forward by the Soviet Union. For imperialism, disarmament is a grave question. The imperialists would not concede easily to the carrying out of even partial disarmament. The statement of the meeting notes that the program for general disarmament has encountered the stubborn resistance of the imperialists. Hence, it is essential to wage an active and determined struggle against the aggressive imperialist forces with the aim of carrying this program into practice. This is entirely correct.

All this proves that the forming of the broadest united front against the imperialist policies of aggression and war and the successful unfolding of the struggle against imperialism, which pursues the policies of aggression and war, constitute the most important guarantees for realizing a lasting world peace. The Communists of all countries are fighters who are in the van of the struggle against imperialism and, at the same time, are also the most active fighters for peace. To say that Communists do not want peace because they advocate a struggle against imperialism is nothing but imperialist slander against us.

The statement adopted at the Meeting of Representatives of the Communist and Workers' Parties of all countries convincingly proves that, in the current world arena, the forces of socialism have more markedly surpassed those of imperialism and the forces of peace have more markedly surpassed those of war. The world socialist system is vigorously on the upgrade and is becoming a decisive factor in the development of human society. The peoples who are building socialism and communism in the socialist countries, the revolutionary movement of the working class in the capitalist countries, the national liberation struggle of the oppressed peoples, and the general democratic movement—these great forces of our time, are merging into one powerful current that undermines and destroys the world imperialist system. The world imperialist system is going through an intense process of decay and disintegration. The instability of the capitalist economy is growing, the contradictions among the imperialist countries are becoming ever more acute and a new stage has begun in the development of the general crisis of capitalism. The statement correctly points out: "The development of international relations in our day is determined by the struggle of the two social systems—the struggle of the forces of socialism, peace, and democracy against the forces of imperialism, reaction, and aggression—a struggle in which the superiority of forces of socialism, peace, and democracy is becoming increasingly obvious." Proceeding precisely from this situation, it can be seen that, although imperialism is stubbornly carrying out its policies of aggression and war, a new world war can be prevented by relying on the concerted efforts of the world socialist camp, the international working class, the national liberation movement, all countries which oppose war, and all peace-loving forces.

This world situation in favor of peace and socialism represents the inevitable result of the development of the situation in the past 15 years after the second world war.

In June, 1950, the year after the founding of the People's Republic of China, Comrade Mao Tse-tung said: "The war threat from the imperialist camp still exists. The possibility of a third world war still exists. However, the forces fighting to check the danger of war, to prevent the outbreak of a third world war, are growing very rapidly. The degree of consciousness of the great majority of the people in the world is rising. So long as the Communist Parties of the whole world are able to continue to unite all the possible forces for peace and democracy, and enable them to grow still further, a new world war can be thwarted." (Report at the Third Plenary Session of the 7th Central Committee of the Communist Party of China.)

In November, 1957, Comrade Mao Tse-tung pointed out: The international situation has now reached a new turning point. He said: "The characteristic of the situation today is that the East wind prevails over the West wind. That is to say, the socialist forces are overwhelmingly superior to the imperialist forces." Comrade Mao Tse-tung elucidated the possibility of preventing a new war in the light of the new change in the balance of world class forces.

The Chinese communists always proceed from this evaluation in their observation of the question of war and peace and other important international questions.

The possibility of averting world war does not arise because the nature of imperialism has changed, or that it may change. The statement of the Moscow meeting points out: "The aggressive nature of imperialism has not changed." That a world war can be averted is due to the real forces that have come into being capable of smashing the aggressive plans of imperialism—and these forces are growing daily.

To prevent a world war remains a serious task. The statement calls upon the people not to underestimate the possibility of preventing a world war or to underestimate the danger of war. All those who struggle for peace should maintain the greatest vigilance, indefatigably lay bare the policy of the imperialists, and keep a watchful eye on the intrigues and maneuvres of the warmongers. While pursuing unswervingly the policy of peaceful coexistence between countries with different social systems, the Communist parties of the socialist countries at the same time display the greatest vigilance against imperialism, exert to their utmost to consolidate the might of the socialist camp and the strength of national defense, and adopt every necessary measure to safeguard the security of the people of all countries and to defend peace.

Marxists-Leninists observe questions strictly from objective reality instead of from subjective desire. For things about to happen, all the practical possibilities should always be taken into consideration. It is only thus that the people can always retain the initiative in practice. Alongside the possibility that the people can tie the imperialists hand and foot and prevent war, the possibility that the most aggressive forces of imperialism would impose war on the people come-what-may, should also be taken into account. In the light of the practical situation with regard to the balance of class forces, the statement points out: "Should the imperialist maniacs start war, the peoples will sweep capitalism out of existence and bury it."

No Communist believes in the need for wars between states in order to overthrow the capitalist system and establish the socialist system. All socialist countries stand firmly for peaceful coexistence and peaceful competition between states with different social systems, believing that revolution is the affair of the people themselves of each country concerned. Only imperialists could slander the socialist countries as being in need of a world war to "push forward a world revolution." The Communists are firmly convinced that in the absence of a world war, all capitalist states will eventually go through a socialist revolution and embark on the road of socialism through the efforts of the people of these countries. To safeguard the life and security of all peoples and to spare the world the catastrophes of a nuclear war, we have to redouble our efforts to hold the imperialists in check in their attempts to resort to war gambles in a desperate struggle.

The statement points out that the peoples of the colonies win their independence through armed struggle or by nonmilitary methods, depending on the specific conditions in the country concerned. It also points out that in the transition from capitalism to socialism, there is the possibility that it is achieved in different countries without a civil war, and the possibility that the people are forced to resort to non-peaceful transition in the event of the exploiting classes resorting to violence against them. The meeting of the Communist and Workers' Parties expresses sympathy and support for the armed struggles waged by the oppressed peoples for their own liberation.

The statement of the Meeting of Representatives of the Communist and Workers' Parties has fully estimated the importance of the present-day national liberation movement, which is a basic force in smashing the world imperialist system, and also in blocking an imperialist war and in the struggle for world peace.

The statement has concisely summed up the essential experiences of the national liberation movement gained in the past years. It lays bare the efforts now being made by the imperialists headed by the United States for the maintenance of their colonial rule by new methods. It states that in countries which have shaken off the colonial yoke, it is both necessary and possible, under the conditions of waging a determined struggle against imperialism and the remnants of feudalism, to form a national-democratic united front. In addition, it puts forward tasks for the working class, under the condition of establishing a firm alliance with the peasantry, to carry the national-democratic revolution to the end and to strive for a future noncapitalist development. The dual nature of the national bourgeoisie and the correct policy to be adopted towards it in the national liberation movement are scientifically analyzed in the statement. All this is of particular importance. The statement declared that it is the duty of all the socialist countries, the international working class movement, and the Communist movement to render the fullest moral and material assistance to the peoples fighting to free themselves from imperialist and colonial tyranny.

The Chinese Communist Party and the Chinese people have always attached great importance to the national liberation movement of the peoples of Asia, Africa and Latin America. Comrade Liu Shao-ch'i, in his report at the first session of the Party's 8th National Congress, pointed out that the national independence movement had become a formidable world force. He held that after the second world war, the extensive victories gained in the national independence movement were a new development of great historic significance, following the emergence of the world socialist system. The Chinese Communist Party has always held that the support extended by the socialist countries to the national independence movement accords fully with the interests of world peace. Comrade Liu Shao-ch'i said in his report: "There can be no doubt that the existence of the socialist countries and their sympathy and support for the national independence movement have greatly facilitated the development and victory of this movement. At the same time, the upsurge of the national independence movement has likewise weakened the imperialist forces of aggression. This is favorable to the cause of world peace, and therefore favorable to the peaceful construction of the socialist countries. That is why the friendship and cooperation between the socialist countries and the nationally independent countries conform not only to their common interests but to the interests of world peace.

The statement of this meeting has also elucidated the problems of the workers' movement and the struggle for socialism in the capitalist countries.

The Meeting of Representatives of Communist and Workers' Parties has made a correct evaluation of the present state of the balance of world class forces and has correctly put forward the policy of struggle. Hence, the statement of the meeting has opened prospects for the broad masses of the people to win brilliant victories through struggles. The statement points out with full confidence that "whatever efforts imperialism makes, it cannot stop the advance of history. A reliable basis has been provided for further decisive victories for socialism. The complete triumph of socialism is inevitable."

The definition of the present epoch formulated by the statement has a scientific basis and is of enormous significance. The statement says: Ours is a time of struggle between the two opposing social systems, a time of socialist revolutions and national-liberation revolutions, a time of the breakdown of imperialism and of the abolition of the colonial system, a time of the transition of more and more peoples to the socialist path, of the triumph of socialism and communism on a worldwide scale.

Just as the statement has pointed out, the central factors of our time are the international working class and its chief creation, the world socialist system. Therefore, the constant developing of construction in the socialist countries, the constant strengthening of the unity of the socialist camp and of the unity of the vanguard of the working class of all countries—the Communist parties—are the guarantee of the victory of the struggle for peace, democracy, national liberation, socialism, and human progress.

The more the socialist countries develop their construction, the greater will be their role in the current political life in the world. The great Soviet people are now rapidly building the material and technical basis of communism and all other fraternal countries have also continuously scored new achievements in building socialism. We the Chinese people, under the leadership of the Chinese Communist Party, must also push forward our work of construction even more efficiently to turn our country swiftly into a really powerful socialist country. This is demanded by the interests of the Chinese people themselves and it is also our contribution to the people the world over.

This Moscow meeting has once again demonstrated the great unity of the countries of the socialist camp and of the Communist parties of all countries and the documents adopted by it will surely promote this unity still further. The Chinese Communist Party has always regarded as its important international duty supporting the unity of the two countries, China and the Soviet Union, and their two parties, of the unity of the entire socialist camp, and of the unity of the entire international Communist movement. This unity is based on the common foundation of Marxism-Leninism, a unity forged in the struggle against the common enemies, a unity formed for the purpose of winning victory in the common cause. Therefore, this unity can withstand all tests, will develop continuously, and no enemy can wreck it by any means.

With the unity of the socialist camp and the unity of the international Communist movement, it is certainly possible to rally the broadest forces of the peoples throughout the world and to surmount the obstacles on the road of advance of the peoples of all countries.

The statement of the Meeting of Representatives of Communist and Workers' Parties has issued a great anti-imperialist call to the people the world over. The struggle of the people throughout the world against imperialism, in defense of world peace, for national independence and socialism will certainly register a new upsurge and score fresh great victories!

PEKING AND TIRANA

"Glorious Albanian Party of Labor," by Ho Tsung, in *Peking Review*, November 17, 1961.

The Soviets and the Chinese have avoided levelling their public attacks directly at one another. Thus, Yugoslavia became the Chinese bête noir, and Albania served the same purpose for the Russians.

Though Albania's chief function in the dispute has been as the creature of the CCP, the Albanian Communist leadership has its own reasons for opposing Soviet policies and Khrushchev, in particular. Indeed, it is on record that Albania had taken an anti-Soviet position even before that stance was assumed by the Chinese.

The Albanian Party of Labor was founded under the auspices of the Yugoslav Communist Party in 1941 and it continued under Yugoslav domination until Tito and his followers were read out of the Cominform in 1948. In the eyes of the Albanian Communists, therefore, their independence began with and was dependent upon the isolation of Yugloslavia from the rest of the Communist world.

It is little wonder then that the Albanians viewed Khrushchev's visit to Belgrade in June, 1955, with alarm and feared the consequences of the Soviet-Yugoslav rapprochement that seemed to be developing prior to November, 1957. Albanian apprehension was further increased by Khrushchev's "Secret Speech"* before Party Congress XX in February, 1956, in which he took dead aim at Stalin and much of what he stood for. Hoxha, the Albanian dictator, ran his country according to strict Stalinist principles and probably felt that only the continuation of these would keep him in power. Moreover, it was Stalin who had engineered Albanian independence and it was Khrushchev whom the Albanians saw as murdering it. Even while Peking still favored Yugoslavia, Albania—already long experienced in the struggle against Yugoslav revisionism—had embarked upon the defense of Stalin and Stalinism.

Beginning in early 1958, common cause threw the Yugoslavs and Chinese together. Though their reasons for opposing the Yugoslavs, Khrushchev, and the Russian policies may have differed, the tenor

* See, D. N. Jacobs, The New Communist Manifesto, 2nd ed., Harper & Row, New York, 1962.

of the arguments they offered, especially those naming revisionism as the "greatest enemy" of contemporary communism, was roughly the same.

One of the bitterest Soviet-Albanian exchanges took place at the Moscow meetings in November, 1960, when, in a direct confrontation, Hoxha reportedly called Khrushchev "a traitor to the Communist idea, a weakling, and a revisionist," in return for which the Soviet First Secretary warned Hoxha that he would "pay" for his insults.

The already strained Soviet-Albanian relations thereafter deteriorated even further. Soviet submarines based in Albanian waters were withdrawn and Soviet technical assistance ended. But, as Russia pulled up stakes, Peking moved in. The Chinese felt that they must support their only ally in the socialist camp. Even in the midst of their own economic difficulties, they granted considerable material aid to the Albanians.

It is under these circumstances that Khrushchev's violent outburst against the Albanians occurred at Party Congress XXII. Khrushchev reported that "people who today advocate friendship with the Soviet Union, with the C.P.S.U., are regarded by the Albanian leaders as enemies." He accused Hoxha and Shehu, the Albanian leaders, of "hypocrisy and deception" and urged the Albanian Communists and the Albanian people to unseat them.

In the face of such an attack, the Chinese could not remain silent and continue to maintain their prestige. The counterattack was begun by Chou En-lai in Moscow, and it rapidly spread through the Chinese press. Peking heaped praise upon Hoxha, the "long-tested" leader of the Albanians and Khrushchev's particular target. The Albanian Party of Labor was credited for its role in preserving the spirit of Marxism-Leninism, and the cause of Sino-Albanian friendship was hailed.

The November 17, 1961, article by Ho Tsung in Peking Review is representative of the support given to the Albanians by the CCP following Khrushchev's attack. The Albanians are presented as "faithfully" applying the principles of Marxism-Leninism: they have long been admired by the Chinese people "for their firm adherence to proletarian principles and revolutionary militancy in the struggle against imperialism and modern revisionism," and "no force on earth [could] shake this comradeship-in-arms between the Chinese and Albanian peoples."

Russians take notice!

On November 8, the 20th anniversary of the founding of the Albanian Party of Labor was warmly observed by the Chinese people. Press and radio, exhibitions, meetings, and rallies marked the occasion.

Peking's citizens celebrated the day with a mass rally jointly sponsored by the Commission for Cultural Relations with Foreign Countries and the China-Albania Friendship Association. Chiang Nan-hsiang, president of the association, and the Albanian Ambassador to China, Reis Malile, were the main speakers. Ch'en Yi and Li Hsien-nien, Members of the Political Bureau of the Central Committee of the Chinese Communist Party and Vice-President of the State Council; Lu Ting-yi, Alternate Member of the Political Bureau of the Central Committee and Vice-Premier; and leaders of various people's organizations were in attendance. Albanian embassy officials, Albanian visitors, and students in Peking were among the guests.

Other activities included the opening of pictorial exhibitions simultaneously in Peking and Shanghai. These show the Albanian people's successes achieved under the leadership of the Albanian Party of Labor, both during the struggle for liberation and in socialist construction today. Members of the China-Albania Friendship People's Commune on the outskirts of Peking invited Albanian guests to the commune for a happy get-together. The Albanian play, *A Fisherman's Family*, is playing in the capital. News about these events has been given wide coverage over the radio, and *Jenmin Jihbao* gave the anniversary two and a half pages, including an editorial and an article by Comrade Mehmet Shehu, Member of the Political Bureau of the Central Committee of the Albanian Party of Labor.

A Heroic Path

On November 8, 1941, when Albania lay bleeding at the feet of the Italian fascist invaders, representatives of three Marxist-Lenist groups met secretly in a small house in occupied Tirana. There the Albanian Party of Labor, vanguard of the proletariat, was born and the strategy of the revolution mapped out. Thus in the country's darkest hour the beacon light of hope and struggle was lit. Overcoming tremendous difficulties, the newly formed party organized the Albanian people's own armed forces, rallied its patriots into a national-liberation front, and waged a bitter armed struggle against the fascist invaders. Finally in November, 1944, with the support of the Soviet Army's powerful thrust in the Balkans, the aggressors were driven out. Albania was free.

Following liberation, the Albanian Party of Labor led the people in the tasks of reconstruction. Quickly healing the wounds of war it went on to complete democratic reforms and then to carry out socialist revolution. Feudal and foreign rule had left Albania with no industry to speak of, a backward agriculture, and a population that was 80 percent illiterate. Albania, separated by Yugoslavia, has no common border with other countries of the socialist camp. In spite of all these unfavorable conditions, the Albanian people, led by the Albanian Party of Labor, and relying mainly on their own efforts, have achieved great successes in the building of socialism. In the 17 years since liberation, People's Albania has changed from an agricultural country with a low level of production into an agricultural-industrial one. A solid socialist economic base has been established and the country is set for full-scale socialist construction.

Albania in Construction

The Second (1956–1960) Five-Year Plan's targets were fulfilled ahead of time. The total value of industrial production in 1960 was 2.18 times that of 1955, or 25 times that of 1938. During this period, labor productivity in industry rose annually by an average of 9.4 percent, which is higher than in the neighboring capitalist countries— Italy, Greece, and Yugoslavia.

Collectivization of agriculture, the basis of socialist economy in the countryside, was also completed ahead of time. By 1960, socialist farming had extended over 86 percent of the country's cultivated land. Today, Albania's mechanized collective farms show a sharp rise in productivity.

Great advances have been made in science, education, and culture. The national income in 1960 was 48 percent higher than in 1955. The people's living standards, both material and cultural, have appreciably improved.

Albania not only is successfully working to build socialism but is also carrying on an unremitting struggle against imperialism and its stooges, the Yugoslav modern revisionists. True to its revolutionary tradition, the Albanian Party of Labor displays a fearless militancy in the face of continuous provocations and other disruptive activities of these enemies. By steadfastly pursuing a peaceful foreign policy and resolutely struggling for world peace; by working for the realization of peaceful coexistence among countries with different social systems and opposing U.S. imperialist policies of war and aggression; and by actively supporting the Asian, African, and Latin American peoples' struggle for national independence, Albania is making outstanding contributions to the cause of world peace and human progress.

Loyal to Marxism-Leninism

These brilliant successes achieved by the Albanian people in their home and foreign policies are inseparable from the correct leadership of the Albanian Party of Labor, which in its 20 years of existence has faithfully applied the general principles of Marxism-Leninism to the concrete conditions of Albania. As *Jenmin Jihpao* states in its editorial of November 8: "The Albanian Party of Labor, headed by

Comrade Enver Hoxha, the long-tested leader of the Albanian people, is a party which takes Marxism-Leninism as its guide to action, a party long steeled in the flames of revolutionary struggle, and one that maintains close ties with the masses. It has always been loyal to Marxism-Leninism, to the principles of proletarian internationalism and to the 1957 Declaration and 1960 Statement of the Moscow Meetings. It has resolutely safeguarded unity with the Soviet people and the people of the other socialist countries and the unity of the international Communist movement. With its high Marxist-Leninist sense of principle, the Albanian Party of Labor has carried on an uncompromising struggle against the modern revisionists represented by the Tito clique of Yugoslavia and resolutely defended the purity of Marxism-Leninism, playing an important role in safeguarding and strengthening the unity of the socialist camp and of the international communist movement."

Unshakable Friendship

The Chinese people have long admired the Albanian people and the Albanian Party of Labor for their firm adherence to proletarian principles and revolutionary militancy in the struggle against imperialism and modern revisionism. They have rejoiced at the Albanian people's brilliant successes in socialist construction. At the same time they have always felt the fraternal Albanian people's sincere support for their own socialist construction and in their struggles in the international arena. Marxism-Leninism and proletarian internationalism have bound the two peoples together in a militant friendship which transcends the vast geographical distance that separates them. As the celebrations of the 20th anniversary of the founding of the Albanian Party of Labor demonstrate, no force on earth can shake this comradeship-in-arms between the Chinese and Albanian peoples.

PEKING AND BELGRADE

"Our Age and Edward Kardelj's 'Dialectics'" by Wu Chiang, in *Hung-Ch'i (Red Flag)*, Peking, March, 1962.

Yugoslavia has been a bone lodged in the Chinese craw ever since the Chinese turn to the left in late 1957. During the preceding year of turmoil in the Communist bloc, Peking had given more than cautious approval to some of the internal changes effected by the Yugoslav Communists. But as the concern with bloc unity grew, the Chinese became increasingly aware that Yugoslavia had been the first Communist country to split that unity and remained the greatest threat to it.

Beginning in June, 1955, Tito and Khrushchev engaged in a game of diplomatic "footsie." Both wanted Yugoslavia back in the arms of the fraternal Communist nations, but neither was willing to pay the other's price. In November, 1957, all hopes for immediate reconciliation vanished, as Chinese pressure for strict bloc unity forced Nikita Sergeyevich to turn away from Belgrade. The failure of the almost Soviet-Yugoslav embrace to take place was followed by a Soviet propaganda offensive against the Yugoslavs. In the spring of 1958 the Chinese spiritedly entered the lists and took over the leading role from the Russians, using far tougher language than Moscow had ever employed. They referred to Tito as a "traitor" and in September, 1958, broke off diplomatic ties with Belgrade.

From time to time from 1958 through 1961 Moscow sought improved Soviet-Yugoslav relations, but always the Soviets were inhibited by the knowledge that such overtures would only deepen the split with China and raise doubts as to Moscow's Marxist orthodoxy. And so, in large part to placate China, Moscow attacked "revisionism," and the Yugoslav League of Communists replied in sometimes hurt, sometimes belligerent tones. However, as Sino-Soviet tensions built up in mid-1961, the Soviet Union no longer felt bound by Chinese demands. And a steady improvement in Russo-Yugoslav relations ensued.

In the spring of 1962, it appeared that the Russian and Yugoslav comrades were moving closer together. The Soviet foreign minister was scheduled to make a state visit to Belgrade. There were reports that Tito would soon be officially received in the Kremlin. At the same time there were also reports of Chinese initiatives for the stabilization of the dispute with Russia. Even so, Peking felt it necessary to warn the Russians, once again, of the danger represented by Tito and his revisionists.

The vehicle used by Peking to extend its caveat was a "review" of Socialism and War,* a series of articles that the leading Yugoslav theoretician, Edward Kardelj, had published in August, 1960. Kardelj had written that, if the Chinese believed in the inevitability of war, sooner or later they would precipitate a conflict that would have catastrophic repercussions for the entire world, Communist and capitalist. Kardelj insisted that "a great number of anti-imperialist factors which in Lenin's time were still extremely undeveloped now constitute a tremendous force, both material and political." Under these changed conditions, which make peace imperative, the struggle for socialism will not be abandoned, but on the contrary, it "will develop more intensively than in the circumstances of the cold war and fear of a new world war." And he adds, "ultra-radicalism in words and sectarian phraseology is no sort of proof of a revolutionary quality, and still less [is it] the path to any real revolutionary results."

The belated Chinese answer to Kardelj's roughly Soviet-paralleling hypothesis is not so personally vindictive as some anti-Yugoslav diatribes that have emanated from Peking—though Kardelj is accused inter alia of being a highly paid lackey of imperialism—but it does quite clearly reveal the Chinese position. The Yugoslavs (read the Russians) are opposed to the class struggle, to revolution. They are opposed to any action that involves force. "Any small struggle in any place—even a demonstration against imperialist atrocities in a place far removed from imperialism . . . will scare them out of their wits, for they are afraid of offending the imperialist lord." They are not true revolutionaries, but skilled sophists. They are not disciples of Lenin, but modern revisionist servants of the bourgeoisie and of imperialism.

Lenin once said that revisionists talked about dialectics merely because they wanted to "emasculate the revolutionary spirit of Marxism with sophistry" ("The Proletarian Revolution and Renegade Kautsky," Complete Works of Lenin, People's Publishing House, 1956, Vol. 28, p. 211), and to "please the bourgeoisie by shamelessly distorting dialectics" ("Bankruptcy of the Second International," Complete Works of Lenin, People's Publishing House, 1959, Vol. 21, p. 195). That was what the old revisionists did in the past and that is exactly what the modern revisionists of Yugoslavia are doing.

We may take as an example Socialism and War, a pamphlet published in August, 1960, by Edvard Kardelj, chief propagandist of the Yugoslav modern revisionists. The object of Kardelj's booklet was to meet further the needs of imperialist organization at the time of

* See D. N. Jacobs, The New Communist Manifesto, 2nd ed., Harper & Row, New York, 1962.

a world-wide anti-Chinese, anti-Communist, anti-people movement and a movement to split the international Communist movement, and also to lend a certain theoretical form by all possible means to the turncoat utterances and writings of modern revisionism. Kardelj talks brazenly about dialectics in this booklet. He tries to prove that as a result of their "contravention" of Lenin's dialectics, those who take a stand opposed to that of modern revisionism cannot but sink into "subjectivism and stagnant dogmatism," [1] whereas Kardelj and Co. are completely "faithful" to Marx's "epochal scientific method," particularly to "the thought of Lenin as a whole," and are opposed only to those "who like Stalin take an antidialectical stand." Pompously regarding himself as the defender of the philosophy of Marx and Lenin, Kardelj declares that he objects to dragging Marxist philosophy into "dirty political attacks," and that therefore he thinks it "necessary to discuss the philosophical aspect."

In this way, Kardelj's pamphlet gives us an opportunity to see how the modern revisionists of Yugoslavia serve the bourgeoisie and imperialism by distorting dialectics.

* * *

The Moscow Declaration of 1960 points out that the principal content of our age is "the transition from capitalism to socialism begun by the great October Socialist Revolution." The principal summing up of the Declaration of these several years is this: "The power of the world socialist system and its international influence are rapidly growing; the colonial system is rapidly falling apart under the blows of national liberation movements; class struggle in the capitalist world is daily increasing; and the world capitalist system is ever declining and rotting. On the world stage, the forces of socialism are obviously surpassing those of imperialism with each passing day, and forces of peace are obviously and increasingly surpassing those of war." That is to say, the East wind is increasingly prevailing over the West wind. Imperialism rots with each passing day, while we become better and better. The days of imperialism are numbered. However, the Declaration points out that "the aggressive character of imperialism has not changed." Imperialism is still imperialism. Imperialists headed by the United States are still carrying out a policy of aggression and war, trying their utmost to preserve the old colonies, and promoting colonialism in a new form. Internally, they are intensifying their exploitation [of the working class] and promoting Fascism. Imperialism will certainly not be willing to retire from the stage of history of its own accord. "Therefore, practical life urgently demands that the socialist countries, the international working class, anti-imperialist national movements, all peace-loving countries, and all peace fighters join

[1] Unless otherwise indicated, all quotations attributed to Kardelj in this article are taken from his book, *Socialism and War*.

forces more and more closely and take resolute action to forestall war
and safeguard the peaceful life of the people. Practical life urgently
demands that all revolutionary forces unite themselves further and
wage a struggle against imperialism and for national independence
and socialism."

In this way Marxist-Leninists observe the present times and estimate
the condition and fate of imperialism. What do modern revisionists
do in this respect? In the eyes of Kardelj and Co., things are entirely
different. They hold that as a result of the change in the relative
strength of social forces today, a qualitative change is taking place
in two respects in the world: "Capitalism is changing in many respects, and socialism is also changing in many respects." The changes
in many respects of socialism mentioned by them we shall discuss
later on. Here we shall deal with capitalism first. Concerning the
changes in capitalism, the "Program of the Communist League of
Yugoslavia" (of which Kardelj was the reporter) points out that as
a result of new victories won by forces of socialism in many countries
and the disintegration of the colonial system and as a result of the
daily increasing influence and role of the working class, "a great
change has been induced in capitalist society" and the "changing of
the capitalist system" is being promoted. Imperialism seems to have
become meek, conciliatory, sensible, and "easily susceptible to the
pressure exerted by the working people and democratic masses and
to social influence," unceasingly "compromising with and making
concessions to the working class." According to Kardelj's argument, all
this is forced [on capitalism or imperialism], "but whether 'forced' or
'not forced,' the historical effect is the same. It is exactly this type of
'being forced' that is the law of history."

*   *   *

Concerning the "forms and methods of struggle," the "Program"
of Yugoslav modern revisionism writes:

"At present, in addition to the direct everyday struggle waged by
the working masses to solve their problems of everyday economic interests and democratic rights, the following questions are raised: nationalization and other forms of socializing the means of production
and the economic functions, various forms of management and autonomy of enterprises, the struggle against bureaucracy, the development of democracy, the position of the working people in production
and society, the participation of the working people and consumers in
the economic administrative machinery, and their supervision over
such machinery. All these questions as forms of struggle for strengthening the social influence of the working class, for unifying the
working class, and for raising the socialist awakening of the working class and as the form of struggle for winning the state power, are
of momentous significance to the workers' movement as a whole."

Here, all the "attractive" targets within the capitalist limit are set forth: Demand "nationalization"! "Participate in the management and autonomy of enterprises"! Wage "a struggle against bureaucracy"! "Develop the bourgeois democracy"! "Participate in the economic administrative machinery and in its supervision"! In his report on the "Program" Kardelj calls all this *"unity of revolution and evolution"* or *"leap taken through a comparatively peaceful process."* That is to say, within the limit of the capitalist social and economic systems, "the working class and the leading socialist forces will take a series of measures to strive for and acquire the leading role in state power and social life and will effect socialist transformation of the society step by step." What a "peaceful and gradual leap"! But of all things he does not mention the most important thing in the proletarian revolution and does not mention the thing that distinguishes the proletarian revolution from the bourgeois reform, namely, to smash the bourgeois state machinery, overthrow the reactionary rule of the bourgeoisie, conduct a revolutionary struggle with this as the *target*, and train, and educate the proletarian masses in this spirit.

*   *   *

Kardelj and his like point to us that with the help of the bourgeois "states" the society seems to have steadily entered into a period of transition from capitalism to socialism. Naturally these are nothing but false words. In philosophy Kardelj fears mention of the absolute of struggle and talks only about the absolute of movement; moreover, he talks about peaceful, gradual "leap." Politically, he evades the question of really revolutionary struggle and indulges in extravagant talk about so-called "transition." Obviously, the so-called "transition" Kardelj has in mind actually means *no transition* and *opposition to transition*.

*   *   *

While, on the one hand, depicting modern capitalist imperialism in a way as if it has deeply entered socialism or simply as socialism, Kardelj and his like have, on the other hand, described socialism as capitalism or as something even worse. This is what is referred to as the "changes of qualitative correlation" in Kardelj's philosophy.

Kardelj and his like are opposed to any assertion that capitalism or socialism is "overabsolute." As they see it, the two sides of a contradiction, antagonistic as they are to each other, have their own peculiar characteristics, there being no intrinsic differences between them; thus capitalism is not necessarily bad, while socialism is not necessarily good. Nothing is absolute. In the thirties of this century, Kautsky in an article entitled "The Blind Alley of Bolsheviki" had attacked Bolsheviki in these words: "Basing itself on Marx's conclusions, it, however, does not in the least understand Marx's methods. According to Marx's viewpoint, nothing is absolute. So, neither the superiority of socialism over capitalism nor the superiority of the large farms over the small farms is absolute." These words were used to attack the then First Five-Year Plan of the Soviet Union and the agricultural collectivization movement going on at the time. As always, the revisionists often use their "opposition to absolutism" in philosophy as a pretext to peddle their sophistry of relativism, and often grasp only the certain phenomena of things and ignore their essence. The aim is to confuse right with wrong and black with white, and to obliterate all demarcations of principle and the intrinsic differences of things.

In the view of Kardelj and his like, although capitalism is different from socialism, yet the present development of capitalism "has already *subordinated* itself to the pressure of factors outside itself." That is to say, its development has already *subordinated* itself to the "new socialist factors" provided by the State-monopoly capitalism which are being gradually accumulated within the capitalism system; on the contrary, the development of socialism is subordinated to the "old capitalist factors" embodied in it. How do they explain such a fallacious idea? The modern revisionists, as a rule, start with State power. Look, the countries of bourgeois dictatorship have become things safeguarding the interests of all classes and the whole body of citizenship; they have a huge capacity of "reforming the capitalist structure," and such a capacity in turn gives rise to the huge possibility of "peaceful transition" toward socialism. How nice capitalism is! And precisely opposite is the case with socialism. According to the revisionists, countries of proletarian dictatorship are the source of all evils. The "State" itself is a capitalist factor, and as long as countries of proletarian dictatorship exist, then such things as "State paternalistic relations," "State totalitarianism," "bureaucratic nationalism," "hegemonism," "the cult of the personality," etc., will always exist as concomitants.

*   *   *

The October Revolution created a "brutal," "bureaucratic ruling system," under which the Soviet socialism was founded. This is the common language we can hear from the revisionists, both old and new, ever since the October Revolution.

This time, Kardelj has applied the same methods described in his book in his attack of socialism, primarily concentrating on the question of war (which is naturally connected with State power). Viciously he denounces the socialist countries for their "bellicosity." In order to carry out such vilification, he has raked his brain to distort the source of modern war.

Concerning the source of war, the "Moscow Statement" has pointed out: "War is a constant companion of capitalism. The system of exploitation of man by man and the system of extermination of man by man are two aspects of the capitalist system." And as Lenin said: "The basic principle of application of dialectics on the issue of war is this: 'war is none other than a continuation of policy in another form (namely, violence) ("The Bankruptcy of the Second-International," *Complete Works of Lenin*, People's Publishing House, 1959 ed., Vol. 21, p. 195). Modern war is a continuation of the imperialist policy. Owing to the changes of the balance of the international class forces, a combined struggle by the powerful forces which are defending peace can be relied on in preventing a new world war, and it cannot be said that world war is totally inevitable under any conditions. Nevertheless, as long as imperialism exists, there will be soil for wars of aggression; hence likewise it can be said that the danger of a new world war is not over. In point of fact, imperialism is still "obstinately preparing for a world war." Here, therefore, are two possibilities, not one. This is the basic thesis of Marxist-Leninists on the problem of war.

What is the basis Kardelj has advanced to counterpose these correct assertions? Here vociferously he opposes the so-called "overabsolute" idea, and he describes things in such a way as if Lenin had never specifically mentioned that one must look for the source of modern war within the capitalist system. He says: "When Lenin points out that as imperialist factors 'give rise' to war and consequently when war becomes inevitable under imperialist conditions, what he refers to is precisely such a balance of forces in which these imperialist factors without restriction occupy the ruling position or at least hold the upper hand." By this, Kardelj tries to prove that when the "balance of forces" changes, the source of war can no longer be sought from imperialism.

That Kardelj is determined to confuse the issue of the origin of war is not something usual, for by so doing he tries, in one respect, namely, the imperialist respect, to cover up the genuine origin of war and, in another respect, namely, the respect of socialist countries, to look for the "source of war."

How, then, does Kardelj search for the "source of war" within socialism?

Kardelj openly obliterates the peaceful character of the socialist system and of the foreign policy of the socialist countries. He pretends to be totally ignorant of the fact that Marxist-Leninists will never give up, and will never permit themselves to give up, their own internationalist obligations to give support to the people's revolutions in various countries. At the same time, they will never impose, and will not permit themselves to impose, socialism on the people of other countries. For any revolution is always the outcome of the internal development of the various countries concerned, and revolution is always carried out by the people of various countries independently.

Kardelj tries to make people believe that the socialist countries attempt to "impose socialism from without on the people of other countries through the means of war." "A socialist country," he says, "can be responsible for a reactionary war." Not only does he make such a hideous slander, but he "theoretically" reaches the following conclusion: Modern aggressive war can no longer be simply depicted as the continuation of imperialist policy, for it at the same time also represents a continuation of the "policy of conquering the world by socialism through the means of war" on the part of the socialist countries. This is especially so when the "socialist system has become a world force." Here Kardelj again focuses the problem on the "balance of power." He presents the problem in this way: In the past, owing to the fact that "imperialism occupies the ruling position without restriction or at least holds the upper hand," it has the possibility of unleashing war; but now, as the socialist forces are daily surpassing the imperialist forces, imperialism is no longer "unrestricted," and therefore the *possibility* of it unleashing war has ceased to exist, for it now has only one aim, namely, "self-defense." And what about the socialist countries? Because their strength is becoming increasingly superior day after day and they feel their powerful might, they therefore always want to "promote world revolution through war." Thus, as far as the present is concerned, "war is no longer determined solely by the laws of internal development of capitalism; it is also determined by the laws of internal development of socialism," and so on.

After making such striking and fabulous fabrications, this Kardelj then devotes a whole chapter to condemning the policy of the socialist countries, saying that it is "Trotskyism," and the "modern form of Bonapartism." In this way, he thinks that he has accomplished the task of creating an immortal "theory." Proceeding from a new balance of power, he has created a "new" theory on the "source of war"!

However, this self-worshipped Kardelj does not sense that his fabrications which involve painstaking efforts are actually not "creation." The bourgeois politicians and journalists fabricated this lie way back 40 years and more ago. Ever since the emergence of the first socialist country, the bourgeoisie has never for one day stopped propagating such fallacious ideas as "the socialist countries attempt to export revolution by force of arms," and "communist parties in the various nonsocialist countries are the agents of foreign countries." Here we can cite an example at will. In 1958, after a visit to the Soviet Union, the U.S. bourgeois political commentator Walter Lippmann wrote a small book called *The Communist World and Ours* in which he argued that "the Communist state power in East Germany, Poland, Czechoslovakia, and Hungary" was imposed by military conquest on these countries" by the Soviet Union "during the war against Nazi

Germany," and, moreover, was maintained by the "military occupation of the Soviet Union." If we contrast Kardelj's book with Lippmann's, then we can easily find that Kardelj's attack on the socialist countries can only be regarded as a part of the rotten view of the bourgeois political commentators such as Walter Lippmann, and is only slightly "theorized."

*   *   *

Kardelj is, after all, an old hand at serving imperialism. Stating his viewpoint in the pamphlet, he asserts with affected frankness on several occasions: "In this way, you will perhaps think that 'I am again beautifying capitalism and imperialism,' won't you?" Then, all of a sudden he affectedly expresses his surprise, as if he were completely unable to understand people's criticism of the traitorous policy (especially the so-called "positive coexistence" policy) of Yugoslavia's modern revisionism:

*   *   *

Over the point at issue, Kardelj brings up the subject in the following words: "The fact that we call ours the policy of positive coexistence is the 'haphazard' condition for the distinction between 'revisionist' coexistence and 'nonrevisionist' coexistence by China's theorists. The term 'positive' has actually become the subject of all kinds of babbling to the effect that the revisionist nature of Yugoslavia's conception of coexistence differs from certain other 'genuine' or 'correct' policies of coexistence." What he deeply deplores is that even "certain critics of Yugoslavia's foreign policy of other socialist countries have also joined such distortion by China." The fact, in his opinion, is that the difference "lies not in the 'qualitative' interpretation of coexistence," but in that in Yugoslavia, the policy of coexistence is "the lasting and fundamental factor in the socialist international policy," whereas in China, coexistence is only "transitional and temporary."

All wrong, Mr. Kardelj! The truth is just the opposite. To the Marxist-Leninist, as long as there are nations with different social systems in the world, the policy of peaceful coexistence will be necessary and will be an important component part of socialist countries' foreign policy, no matter how the relation of forces may be in the world. Marxists-Leninists have said, and facts have also proved, on more than one occasion, that over the issue of peaceful coexistence, obstacles will never come from the side of the socialist countries but will always come from the side of imperialism. Hence, the difference does not at all lie in the temporary or the nontemporary nature or in the tactical or nontactical nature, but lies precisely in "the 'qualitative' interpretation of coexistence" which Kardelj tries his utmost to evade.

*   *   *

The revisionist nature of Yugoslavia's conception of coexistence, which Kardelj did his utmost to conceal, lies exactly in the exclusion of class struggle and of revolution and the placing of coexistence in *absolute opposition* to class struggle and revolution. Two things, the relations between which are essentially ones of unity between opposites, have been separated from each other, and each has been made absolute without regard for the other, in such way that each side excludes the other and each principle excludes the other. Such is a typical method of sophistry.

*   *   *

Among revisionists, opposition to Marxism in this way has no lack of precedents in history. People like Bernstein and Kautsky placed democracy in absolute opposition to dictatorship and proposed so-called "pure democracy" in exclusion of class struggle and dictatorship. In doing so, their purpose was to deny the dictatorial substance of bourgeois democracy (which is reactionary dictatorship to the broad masses of the laboring people who form the majority of the population) and, at the same time, to obliterate the democratic nature of proletarian dictatorship (which is the true and the most extensive democracy to the broad masses of the laboring people who form the majority of the population). By a similar method, Yugoslavia's modern revisionists have proposed so-called "positive coexistence" to the exclusion of class struggle and revolution. Among them, "positive coexistence" is the absolute, supreme category of contemporary international politics, which is above and beyond struggle and all revolutions and to which the interests of all revolutions must be subordinated. Such coexistence means *complete, unconditional* international class cooperation and cooperation among nations. There is neither any international class struggle (or, if there is such a struggle, it consists in ideological struggle only and not in any political struggle), nor any struggle for national liberation against imperialist enslavement. Also, when they talk about struggle, they distort the conception till it is beyond recognition and till it seems that every mention of revolutionary struggle is "an intention to settle the question of the world revolution by force." Such absolutism even forcibly (and therefore absurdly) regards all struggles as capable of destroying peaceful coexistence. Any small struggle in any place—even a demonstration against imperialist atrocities in a place far removed from imperialism, such as the demonstration held by the workers of Belgrade in protest of the chiefly U.S.-inspired murder of the Congo's national leader Lumumba—will scare them out of their wits, for they are afraid of offending their imperialist lord. So they will charge it with "causing damage to coexistence." Such absolutism in practice will inevitably place them on a stand opposed to revolution (and therefore to dialectics).

RETREAT

"Be Realistic and Practical" by Kuan Ch'ing, in *Nanfang Jihpao*, Canton, February 14, 1962.

* * *

"One Must Concretely Analyze Views which Differ from One's Own" by Chang Yu-min, in *Jenmin Jihpao*, Peking, February 23, 1962.

* * *

Press Communique on the National Peoples' Congress, April 16, 1962.

During November and December, 1961, and into January, 1962, the Chinese continued their angrily independent course. They reiterated their position on peace and war, as at the December sessions of the Communist-sponsored World Peace Council in Stockholm. New agreements with Albania were negotiated and there were additional exchanges of delegations and expressions of mutual admiration.

But in February, a new note began to be sounded in the Chinese press. It was one of slackening and moderation, leading in the direction of retreat.

The Chinese retreat* in the winter and spring of 1962 became evident in different areas. There was a renewed attempt, first seen in the campaign against youthful marriages, to limit the still rapid population growth. Articles such as "Early Marriage Hinders My Study" appeared in the press. No man should become a father before he is 26, it was stated, nor a girl a mother before she is 23.

There were also increasing reports of the large-scale return to the countryside of those who had gone to the city during the heyday of the Great Leap Forward in 1958. There were evidences of a rethinking of the role of the great man, specifically Stalin, in history. Jenmin Jihpao acknowledged that some historical figures received too much praise, that it sometimes happens that "the figure of history is overextolled with the result that his merit is exaggerated."

Editorials appeared in the press, urging "prudence" and "realism," the necessity of conducting "an overall and penetrating investigation and analysis of concrete things, and on the basis of a full understanding of the situation, reach [ing] judgements and decisions." Attacks, albeit not overly violent, were made upon those who tend to "look at

* Or at least the decision to moderate their approach in some areas and to still their hostility in others.

things in an oversimplified way, thinking as they always do that things are easy and simple. . . . They always proceed from the assumption of the best possibilities without considering the worst possibilities, and consequently they make preparations for the best and not the worst."

A particularly significant landmark in the "retreat" appeared in the Canton daily Nanfang Jihpao, of February 14, 1962. The article "Be Realistic and Practical" accused comrades of having drifted away from "realism." The matter of waging revolution is a "practical business," it said, and admits of not the "slightest pretense." Some hope to overcome obstacles by "sheer luck," by "fancy kicking and fisting." But "no hope should be entertained for a 'short cut' to the sky in one jump." It is necessary to advance one step at a time, to eat one mouthful of rice after another. Some people prefer to "handle big problems," to "do big things," and refuse to pay attention to what they consider trivial matters. But, "big things" depend on smaller ones being done first. Consequently, "unwillingness to solve concrete problems one by one leads to the accumulation of big problems."

Derision of the Great-Leap-Forward psychology is paralleled by an appeal in the press for greater discussion of diverging opinions. This is essential to "fostering the democratic work style," read one article, and it pointed out that no one person (or country) has a hammerlock on the truth. The February 23, 1962, article in Jenmin Jihpao carrying the title, "One Must Concretely Analyze Views Which Differ From One's Own," it seems, was particularly clearly aimed beyond China's frontiers. It argued that if one is correct, one must uphold one's opinions, but it must be done "in the spirit of submitting to truth" and while paying "attention to the maintenance of unity with one's comrades. Even when one's own view is quite correct and very well founded, one must convince others of this peaceably."

"However," continued the Jenmin Jihpao article, "truth and error usually cannot be distinguished from each other at a glance." Arriving at the "truth" in any situation requires careful "analysis." "If we honestly analyze all opinions, we shall usually discover that there are similarities among different opinions and that there are some not quite correct points in every correct opinion . . . and some good points in every erroneous opinion." This does not mean, said the Chinese, that we want to "settle the struggle between right and wrong through compromise." Yet, it must be concluded, that this is exactly what they were proposing to the Kremlin.

The "retreat" of February and March, 1962, led into the convening of the plenary sessions of the People's Congress in April. The press communique of that Congress made the "retreat" official and sought to give a reason for it: "the serious natural calamities" which have struck China for three years in a row. The Congress gave the order to emphasize agriculture production "first and foremost," to "shorten the front of capital construction" and to concentrate on consumer industries.

Jenmin Jihpao revealed that these decisions, which would be considered by Communists only in extremis, were reached after "heated" discussions. Certainly the retreat was a bitter pill for the CCP in general—and the Chinese left in particular—to swallow. To the left it may well have seemed more like surrender than retreat.

The role that the Russians played in forcing retreat upon the Chinese under conditions of near, if not actual, famine and economic disintegration did not bode well for future Sino-Soviet relations, even if, for the time being, a complete break was avoided.

"BE REALISTIC AND PRACTICAL"

Fancy kicking and fisting [in shadow boxing] is pleasing to the eye at an exhibition but is no match for hard blows and firm footwork in an actual fight. A silvery spearhead made of wax looks good but is of no practical use. Walls of plastered bamboo matting are beautiful to look at but cannot stand the blasts of wind or the beatings of rain. Their common weaknesses are showiness instead of utility, superficiality instead of depth, and fragility instead of sturdiness. In a word, they are impractical.

To wage a revolution or to undertake construction is practical business. It permits not the slightest pretense. Fancy kicking and fisting is useless, however much of it may be done. Results can only be achieved with hard blows and firm footwork. Revolutionaries are honest people and know full well that without a realistic attitude it is basically impossible to accomplish anything in this world. That is why we always despise fancy kicking and fisting and favor hard blows and firm footwork in tackling actual work realistically. In other words, we call on every comrade to have a realistic style of work to be able to develop every kind of work realistically and achieve practical results.

This realistic style of work is the Marxist-Leninist style of work. It is also a fine tradition of our party. It stands in opposition to the style of work of those accustomed to fancy kicking and fisting and to the style of work of empty talkers who "make resolutions only in speech, formulate plans only on paper, and take action only at meetings." It is different in principle from the style of work of routinists who bury themselves only in trifles for lack of ambition, foresight, and perspicacity. It is a manifestation of the combination of a revolutionary's lofty ambition with his spirit of seeking truth from facts and of the combination of his revolutionary fervor with his scientific attitude. The reason is that only people with ambition, foresight, and perspicacity will not lose their sense of direction while marching forward and will realize the truth of "heading for big targets but starting with small ones" (in Lenin's words). Thus, by integrating foresight with current practical struggle, they will do practical work realistically, solve practical problems effectively, and push their work forward toward distant, big goals with hard blows and firm footwork. Also, only people with the scientific attitude of seeking truth from facts will probe objective laws realistically, plant the roots of ambition into the foundation of reality and, realistically according to objective laws, adopt methods and measures to bring their ambition to fruition.

This realistic style of work of combining lofty ambition with the spirit of seeking truth from facts is most valuable at all times. At present, while implementing the policy of "adjustment, consolidation, reinforcement, and improvement," we must, like eating one mouthful of rice at a time, swallow difficulties one by one and, like ascending a flight of stairs, push the national economy forward to a new upsurge step by step. This makes it all the more necessary to popularize the realistic style of work. However, some comrades, confronted by difficulties, talk vainly of ambition in hopes of winning by sheer luck. They are unwilling to work realistically as if difficulties could be blown away more easily than ash. There are also other comrades who, having done some work realistically, achieved relatively good results, and brought about a highly satisfactory situation in their localities, are drifting apart from reality as a result of their initial success. In the course of work, they are fond of empty talk without going for practical results. They are in hot pursuit of only figures to the neglect of quality in their work. Their enthusiasm is for size, for show and not for skill or refinement. They are content with issuing general calls without paying attention to solving concrete problems individually. They look upon any complex problem as one of extreme simplicity which can be successfully solved by holding a meeting, issuing a call, and setting a target. All these styles of work should be regarded as "fancy kicking and fisting" and not as hard blows and firm footwork. They run counter to the realistic style of work. In this context, the four words "be realistic and practical" need further explanation.

To be realistic and practical, the basic requirement is to be honest people, to do practical work, to speak realistically, and to seek practical results. Concretely speaking, it means standing on solid ground, penetrating into reality, going deep among the masses, and doing practical work assiduously with reality as the starting point. Under any condition, work, whatever it may be, should be pursued realistically and in proper order. No attempt should be made to win by luck and no hope should be entertained for a "short cut" to the sky in one jump. Emphasis should be laid on practical work and not on empty talk. The object should be to seek practical results and not names of vanity. Only actual conditions, without falsification, coloring, or exaggeration, should ever be reflected.

In order to be realistic and practical, we must do thorough and careful work among the masses in an honest and earnest manner. The masses can be likened to land. Without land we shall have no place to plant the roots of reality. If no account is taken of the masses, we shall be like duckweed, drifting hither and thither with no roots firmly planted in the ground. Basically there is no reality to speak of. When performing a task, we must rely closely on the masses and consult with them. We must rely on them to think of methods of performing it and must organize them to put the methods into operation. That is to say, we must realistically tread the mass line, pass on the party's guidelines, policies and tasks to the masses, do careful ideological work among them, raise their consciousness, and turn the intentions and plans of the leadership into their conscious action. Only when this stage is reached can roots be planted on the fertile soil of the masses and can we develop our work realistically and achieve practical results. Is there any necessity for reiterating the truth of the mass line and for adding the words "realistic and practical" to the manner of treading the line? The answer is that some people know only one phase and not both phases of the problem. They know only the spectacular phase and not the practical phase and even stand the two in opposition to each other. They are unwilling to penetrate earnestly into the masses to do careful work, much less to use the method of opening a lock with its special key to do the hard work of ideological mobilization among persons and households individually. They are content with issuing general calls, holding meetings to do a little mobilization, and announcing a few policies. Their reason is that when there are policies, targets, plans, and measures for implementation, everything will be ready. But they do not realize that although everything is ready, nothing can be called complete without the "East wind" which is the finishing touch. A realistic style of work is precisely the indispensable "East wind." As a result of their failure to do thorough, careful mass work in a realistic manner, correct guidelines and policies cannot take root or can take root only among a small number of progressive elements and not among the broad masses. The roots of the best plans are seen only at suddenly called meetings and do not find their way into each family and each household. The roots of effective methods and measures do not extend into the consciousness action of the masses. In this way, with the roots lacking in length and failing to penetrate deeply, extensively, and firmly, how can we start talking about developing work realistically? Where can the practical results in work come from?

To be realistic and practical calls for seeking truth from facts and for concretely analyzing concrete conditions and concrete problems. The reason is that in a situation in which socialist construction undertakings are expanding at lightening speed, new conditions and new problems keep cropping up from time to time. If we make decisions by relying on subjective imagination and limited experience or on subjective guesswork on the strength of one-sided and superficial data instead of by conducting thorough investigation and research and making a concrete analysis of the things around us, the roots of work will inevitably be planted in the hollow mist of subjectivism. It is only by having a detailed knowledge of the conditions in various fields and at various periods and by making concrete scientific analyses to find the objective laws of things and grasp the particularity of the contradictions among various things that we can, from the concrete conditions of different historical factors in different localities as the starting point, set current tasks for certain localities to find methods of solving the concrete contradictions. It is only then that we can find effective, feasible concrete measures, methods, and plans to implement party policies and fulfill party tasks. It is only then that we can become adept in doing work in the order of importance and urgency, by stages, in batches, and in a planned and systematic manner. It is only then that we can adapt our subjective knowledge to objective conditions and thereby push our work forward realistically.

To be realistic and practical also calls for effectively solving concrete problems one by one. A task of any kind includes many small links and a large number of problems. The process of work is a process of solving these problems one by one. This is a general law on work. The fulfillment of a task or the solution of a major problem is invariably the result of the effective solution of many concrete problems. Is there any exception to this law? Rice must be eaten one mouthful by one mouthful; several dishes of meat and vegetables and several bowls of rice cannot be swallowed at one gulp. A peasant has to plow his fields piecemeal. If the problem of a chain is to be solved, the first thing to do is to solve the problem of its links. The solution of the first link creates conditions for the solution of the next link and ultimately for the solution of the whole chain. Actually this truth is quite obvious, but it is not so easy to apply it to revolutionary work. The reason is that the effective solution of concrete problems one by one looks trifling and troublesome on the surface but requires tenacity and pliability. People without the qualities of tenacity and pliability and people who are showy and not practical, rough and not refined, and superficial and not solid are naturally unwilling to act in this way. They look at many concrete problems without paying attention to them or dealing with them. They often attempt, in violation of the general law on work, to solve concrete problems by doing a little fancy kicking and fisting and by employing the method of chopping with a big axe instead of carving with a small chisel. They are unwilling to proceed step by step; they want to reach the sky in one stride. As to people who are content with issuing general calls to the neglect of giving concrete guidance and who are content with exercising so-called "leadership in principle" without willingness to do practical, thoroughgoing work and to pay attention to solving concrete problems, they often disdain tackling one by one concrete problems which they regard as trifles on the pretext that they are out to "handle big problems" and "do big things." As a result, small problems are left alone but big problems are beyond their ability; small things are left undone but confidence is lacking in doing big things. Their unwillingness to solve concrete problems one by one leads to the accumulation of big problems. Thus, work cannot be developed realistically nor can practical results be achieved.

"ONE MUST CONCRETELY ANALYZE VIEWS WHICH DIFFER FROM ONE'S OWN"

It is true and only right that both similar views and different opinions will arise when a question is discussed, a piece of work is studied, or some experience is summed up. The presence of different opinions which can be compared with one another for the purpose of mutual enlightenment, supplementation, and correction can help all concerned to make their minds more active and their understanding more correct and deeper. It is therefore not a bad thing but a good thing.

Before one can correctly deal with views which differ from one's own, one must analyze them concretely. One must distinguish among all such views and find out which are correct and which are erroneous, and distinguish among all the parts of each such view and find out which are correct and which are erroneous. One must do so before one can decide which attitude one should take toward each such view.

If an opinion which differs from one's own is correct, then one must listen to it humbly and accept it boldly, whether it has proceeded from one's superior or from one's subordinate, whether it is held by the majority or by the minority. Only such an attitude is the attitude of submitting to truth. Whenever one finds that one's understanding is incorrect or partly incorrect, one must boldly admit this fact and make up one's mind firmly to discard the incorrect view or the incorrect part of one's view. Only such an attitude is the serious attitude of Marxism. Marx himself was "a man who knew only how to worship truth, a man who, when he had been convinced that some facts were incorrect, would immediately discard them no matter what trouble he might have gone to in acquiring them and no matter how much he might have treasured them." (*Recollections of Marx*, People's Publishing House, 1954 ed., pp. 38–39.) We should learn this great scientific spirit of Marx's.

If an opinion which differs from one's own is incorrect, one must, in the spirit of submitting to truth, uphold one's own correct opinion boldly and disagree with the incorrect view, irrespective of the number or the position of its advocates. To be sure, though, while upholding one's own correct opinion, one must pay attention to the maintenance of unity with one's comrades. Even when one's own view is quite correct and very well founded, one must convince others of this peaceably by means of patient reasoning and persuasion, and must help those comrades who hold different (and incorrect) opinions to analyze the causes of their mistakes and rouse them to conscious action in correcting their mistakes and improving their understanding. In *A Letter to Yuan-chiu,* Pai Chu-yi, a poet of the T'ang dynasty, proposed that criticism should be "sharp in opinion and mild in language." He was right. If one expresses shallow views but uses strong language, if one does not have much truth on one's side but acts as though one were teaching another a lesson, if one forcibly imposes one's shallow or even incorrect opinion on another, one will hardly be able to attain the aim of upholding truth, distinguishing right from wrong, and yet maintaining unity with one's comrades.

Upholding truth and correcting error are harmonious. If one does not uphold truth, one will not be able to correct error. In other words, if one wants to correct error, one must uphold truth. Upholding truth and correcting error are complicated matters. Take man's understanding for instance. On the one hand, man's subjective understanding is a reflection of objective reality. On the other hand, limited by social conditions and his power of understanding, man's subjective understanding does not agree fully with objective reality. To put it more concretely, the understanding of every one of our comrades is comparatively correct at certain times and incorrect at other times. It is rarely completely correct. Because of this, one must be prepared to make criticism and self-criticism in order to distinguish between correct understanding and incorrect understanding. One must give help to others and receive help from them, must be able to convince others and to be convinced by them, and must be prepared at all times to uphold truth and correct error.

However, truth and error usually cannot be distinguished from each other at a glance. Sometimes, a correct opinion is not immediately accepted by people because it has not yet been proved by abundant facts or because it is not explained clearly. Sometimes, an erroneous opinion is not immediately discerned as such because it is presented so cunningly that it appears to be correct. Besides, a correct opinion is usually not 100 percent correct but contains some not quite correct parts, and, similarly, an erroneous opinion is usually not 100 percent erroneous but contains some correct parts. That is why we usually say that an opinion is "basically correct" or "basically erroneous." Things are really quite complicated. Hence the need for the analysis of facts.

Only analysis can distinguish right from wrong and truth from error. This is specially so in the case of opinions which contain both correct and erroneous parts. Such opinions must be   analyzed repeatedly, penetratingly, and concretely before one can gradually see the truth and the error in them in their true perspectives. Concerning this, Lenin once said, "Without considerable independent effort, the truth over no grave issue whatsoever can be found; whoever is afraid of hard work cannot find truth" (*Complete Works of Lenin*, People's Publishing House, 1959 ed., Vol. XIX, p. 136).

By analysis is meant looking at every problem honestly and dialectically, establishing facts and finding truth from them, and conducting investigation and research, doing some thinking, and thus arriving at conclusions which agree with objective reality. For instance, when we are summing up some experience or discussing a problem, if we honestly analyze all opinions, we shall usually discover that there are similarities among different opinions and differences among similar opinions, and that there are some not quite correct points in every correct opinion and some good points in every erroneous opinion. In other words, we shall discover that there are differences in similarities and similarities in differences, that truth and error are mixed, and that some opinions are basically correct and some basically wrong. The fact that we admit such a state of affairs does not mean at all that we do not want to distinguish between right and wrong but want to make everything smudged and settle the struggle between right and wrong through compromise. It only means that we should proceed from such a state of affairs and adopt an attitude of scientific analysis. We should not allow ourselves to be bound and restricted by the metaphysical method of thinking which leads to the conclusion "Yes is yes, no is no, and everything else is nonsense" (Engels: *Anti-Duhring*, People's Publishing House, 1956 ed., p. 20). Comrade Mao Tse-tung always tells us to keep our heads cool, to learn to use the method of scientific analysis, and to form a habit of analyzing problems scientifically. Objective practice is the only criterion of truth. We must not separate ourselves from objective practice and not look at any problem with subjective whims. We must not think that because a thing is good, it must be absolutely good and good in all respects, or that because a thing is bad, it must be absolutely bad and bad in all respects. To think so is to cultivate the bad habit of "being unwilling to analyze and study complicated things repeatedly and penetratingly and eager to draw simple conclusions of absolute affirmation or absolute negation" (*Selected Works of Mao Tse-tung*, Vol. III: "Study and the Current Situation"). If one does not concretely analyze views which differ from one's own but eagerly draws "simple conclusions of absolute affirmation or absolute negation," the conclusions drawn will not conform with reality or dialectics, and, instead of being helped to understand objective truth or correctly learning lessons from experience, one will only be prevented from doing so. As we know, before any rich experience of work has been subjected to highly scientific generalization, it is reflected through different kinds of understanding and different views from different sides and different angles. That there is a great deal of controversy over a thing or a problem means only that the substance of this thing has been adequately revealed, or that this problem has drawn general attention. At such a stage, one is not far off from the time when "the whole picture will become clear" and scientific conclusions will be drawn. If one does not analyze views which differ from one's own but simply declares such views to be correct or incorrect, absolutely affirming or negating them, or even regards all such views as "opposite" views and attacks them, one will wittingly or unwittingly place a barrier of stone between oneself and others, obstructing the speech of others and one's own thinking, and seriously hindering any improvement of understanding. Conversely, if one carefully analyzes views which differ from one's own, observes them closely, goes deep into them, subjects them to a process of elimination of falsehood and selection of truth, and critically absorbs them, one will find it easier to increase and improve one's knowledge continuously and to learn lessons from experience correctly.

In short, one must concretely analyze all views which differ from one's own. One must find out which of them are correct and should be upheld, which of them are erroneous and should be corrected, which parts of each such view are correct and should be absorbed, and which parts are erroneous and should be discarded. While upholding correct views, one must, in the spirit of finding flaws in jade, observe them closely and try to make them more correct still; one must not be careless and preserve the error along with the truth in them. While correcting incorrect views, one must, in the spirit of finding gold in sand, observe them closely and absorb their good points, no matter how few or how small; one must not indiscriminately cast the whole of them away, discarding their good parts along with the bad ones. This is very important. When truth is in the bud, it is always imperfect and defective. If we nip truth in the bud merely because at this stage it has some defects, how can it develop? In other words, we must uphold a thing to the exact extent to which it is true. We must fully affirm what we should affirm and yet must not uphold any error as truth. Similarly, we must correct a thing to the exact extent to which it is erroneous. We must unreservedly negate what we should negate and yet must not treat correct things as erroneous things. These are required of us by the practical spirit of scientific analysis.

*　*　*

PRESS COMMUNIQUE ON THE NATIONAL PEOPLE'S CONGRESS

The Second National People's Congress of the People's Republic of China held its third session in Peking between March 27 and April 16. Before this, a preparatory meeting was held on March 22.

At the beginning, the session heard a report on the work of the Government made by Chou En-lai, Premier of the State Council.

Premier Chou En-lai's report fell into two parts. The first dealt with the international situation and China's foreign policy, and the second part discussed the domestic situation and the tasks of the Chinese people.

The Main Trend in the World Situation

Analyzing the international situation, Premier Chou En-lai first expounded that the fact that the East wind prevails over the West wind was the main trend in the development of the international situation. He emphatically pointed out that the formation and growing strength of the world socialist system and the upsurge of the national-liberation movement together with the emergence of a series of newly independent countries on the basis of this movement were two great tides of historic significance since World War II. They supported and inspired each other, pushing history forward and changing the face of the world. The world capitalist system was going through a process of further decline and disintegration. The imperialist camp was riddled with contradictions and was splitting up at an accelerated rate. Whatever the twists and turns, the tide of history was irresistible; the struggle for peace, national liberation, democracy, and socialism of the people of the world would surely continue to forge ahead; and the revolutionary cause of the world's people would surely triumph all over the world.

U.S. Policies of Aggression and War v. World Peace

Premier Chou En-lai then dealt with the question of opposing the policies of aggression and war of U.S. imperialism and defending world peace. He pointed out that since its inauguration the Kennedy Administration had been playing various "peace" tricks while still further intensifying its arms expansion, war preparations, and aggressive activities. Premier Chou En-lai stressed that in opposition to the

U.S. imperialist policies of aggression and war, we should strengthen the unity and might of the socialist camp, support the struggle of the masses of the various countries against U.S. imperialism and its followers, unite all forces that can be united with, isolate U.S. imperialism to the maximum extent, and strive for lasting world peace.

China's Foreign Policy

Premier Chou En-lai explained in detail China's foreign policy. He said that China had consistently pursued a foreign policy of peace. It firmly and unswervingly developed its relations of friendship, mutual assistance, and cooperation with the Soviet Union and the other fraternal socialist countries; strove for peaceful coexistence on the basis of the Five Principles with countries having different social systems; opposed the imperialist policies of aggression and war; and supported the revolutionary struggles of the oppressed peoples and the oppressed nations against imperialism and colonialism. This was the general line of China's foreign policy. China had always advocated the settlement of international disputes through negotiations; firmly stood for the banning of nuclear weapons and supported the struggle of the peace-loving countries and peoples of the world against the arms expansion and war preparations by imperialism, and for the realization of disarmament. China firmly opposed the forcible occupation of Taiwan by U.S. imperialism and its schemes of creating "two Chinas." Premier Chou En-lai said that China's foreign policy had won widespread praise and support from the people of the world. China had friends all over the world. U.S. imperialism and its followers had vainly used every means to isolate China and venomously slandered it. But all their efforts had ended in ignominious defeat.

The Domestic Situation

Premier Chou En-lai then reviewed the situation at home and the tasks of the Chinese people. In an analysis of the current domestic situation, he pointed out, first of all, that under the leadership of the Chinese Communist Party and Chairman Mao Tse-tung and on the basis of the successful completion of the First Five-Year Plan, the people of various nationalities of the country had embarked in 1958 on the Second Five-Year Plan for national economic construction. In the past few years, the general line of going all out; aiming high; and achieving greater, faster, better, and more economical results in building socialism had demonstrated its great power and had been still further developed. People's communes, which were of great historic significance, had been set up in China's vast rural areas and had gradually embarked on the road of sound development. A big leap forward had taken place in the economic and cultural construction of the country; this had brought tremendous achievements and laid the preliminary foundation for the building of a system of national economy which is independent, complete, and modern. At the same time, China had suffered from serious natural calamities for three consecutive years from 1959 to 1961, and considerable difficulties had occurred in the national economy. The people of various nationalities throughout the country had made tremendous efforts and achieved outstanding results in overcoming the natural calamities and economic difficulties. Many new problems which had emerged during the great development of the socialist cause had been tackled step by step. At the present time, the economic situation of the country had already begun to take a turn for the better.

In his report, Premier Chou En-lai described in detail the successes and shortcomings in the past few years in socialist construction and summed up the experience gained in the work. He stressed that the tasks confronting the Chinese people were to continue to hold aloft the three red banners of the general line, the big leap forward and the people's commune, unite still better the people of various nationalities of the country, conscientiously and effectively do the work of adjusting the national economy, consolidate the successes already won, do more in overcoming the present difficulties, and strive for new victories.

Ten Tasks in Adjusting the National Economy

Referring to the work of adjusting the national economy and the current tasks, Premier Chou En-lai stated that the policy of adjusting, consolidating, filling out, and raising standards centered on adjustment must continue to be carried out in the work of the national economy. He put forward ten tasks in the adjustment of the national economy in 1962:

1. to strive to increase agricultural production, first and foremost, the production of grain, cotton, and oil-bearing crops;
2. to make a rational arrangement of the production of light and heavy industry and increase the output of articles of daily use as much as possible;
3. to further shorten the front of capital construction and use material, equipment, and manpower where they are most urgently needed;
4. to reduce the urban population and the number of workers and staff members to an appropriate extent by persuading, first of all, those workers and staff members who have come from the rural areas to

return to rural productive work and strengthen the agricultural front;

5. to take stock inventories and to examine and fix the amount of funds for each enterprise so that the material and funds lying idle can be used where they are most needed during the present work of adjustment;

6. to insure that the purchase and supply of commodities are well done and market supply conditions improved;

7. to work energetically to fulfill tasks in foreign trade;

8. to adjust cultural, educational, scientific research, and public health undertakings and improve the quality of their work;

9. to carry out, firmly and thoroughly, the policy of building the country with diligence and thrift and to economize on expenditures and increase revenue;

10. to improve the work of planning further and insure an all-round balance between the branches of the national economy: agriculture, light industry and heavy industry.

Political Life of the State

Premier Chou En-lai touched upon the question of the political life of the state. He said that in the course of China's great socialist construction, the people of various nationalities throughout the country under the leadership of the Chinese Communist Party and Chairman Mao Tse-tung had become still more united and organized, and their political consciousness had been further enhanced. The workers, peasants, intellectuals, and other working people of various nationalities; the democratic parties and nonparty democrats; patriotic elements of the national bourgeoisie and patriotic overseas Chinese had all taken part in and supported the construction of the country with enthusiasm. The great unity of the people of various nationalities of China which had been forged in protracted struggles was the basic guarantee for the victory of China's socialist cause.

Premier Chou stressed that in the political life of the state, it was essential to develop democracy still further and carry out democratic centralism thoroughly, making efforts to create a vigorous and lively political situation in which there was both centralism and democracy, both discipline and freedom, and both unity of will and personal ease of mind. It was necessary to strengthen ceaselessly the people's democratic united front under the leadership of the working class and on the basis of the worker-peasant alliance, to continue to carry out the policy enunciated by the Chinese Communist Party of "long-term coexistence and mutual supervision" with the democratic parties, and to unite all forces that could be united to serve socialism. It was necessary to unite further all patriotic intellectuals, the overwhelming majority of whom were already intellectuals of the working people, to enable them to play a greater role in socialist construction, and to continue to carry out thoroughly the party's policy of "letting a hundred flowers blossom and a hundred schools of thought contend" in the fields of scientific research, literature, and art. It was necessary to continue to unite the patriotic elements of the national bourgeoisie and help them further in educating and remoulding themselves and to prolong the period of paying a fixed rate of interest to them for three years beginning with 1963. Further consideration would be given this question at the end of the extended period. It was necessary to continue to carry out thoroughly the party's national policy and strengthen the unity among the various nationalities in the country. It was necessary to continue to do the work in the matter of overseas Chinese affairs well, and further unite all patriotic overseas compatriots and relatives of overseas Chinese in the country. It was necessary to continue to carry out thoroughly the policy of freedom of religious belief and further unite all patriotic religious believers. As regards functionaries in state organs, cooperation between Communist Party members and non-Communists should be further strengthened. Government functionaries should constantly make on-the-spot investigations, develop a working style characterized by seeking truth from facts and adhering to the mass line, and they should be good servants of the people.

Premier Chou also pointed out the necessity of strengthening the dictatorship against the enemies of the people. He said that it was necessary to continue to strengthen the national defences and the People's Liberation Army as well, so as to safeguard the socialist construction of the country and the peaceful life of the people. He pointed out that the Chiang Kai-shek clique entrenched in Taiwan was still carrying out sabotage activities with the support of U.S. imperialism. U.S. imperialism was still using the many military bases around China to carry out military provocations and war threats against the country. We must sharpen our vigilance, he said.

In conclusion, Premier Chou En-lai declared: We are deeply convinced that under the guidance of Mao Tse-tung's thinking and the radiance of the brilliant red banners of the general line, the big leap forward and the people's commune; the workers, peasants, intellectuals, and other working people of various nationalities of the country; the democratic parties and nonparty democrats; the patriotic elements of the national bourgeoisie and patriotic overseas Chinese will certainly unite still closer around the standard of the Chinese Communist Party and the People's Government with one heart and one mind, working energetically for the prosperity of the country, and making persistent and untiring efforts to overcome all the difficulties on the road ahead, to fulfil the tasks of adjusting the national economy and finally get rid of economic poverty and cultural backwardness, so as to turn China into an advanced, prosperous, and powerful socialist country.

Premier Chou En-lai's report was discussed at the session from March 29. Deputies carried out group discussions from March 29 to April 9. Plenary sessions were held from April 10 to 16, at which a total of 164 deputies spoke.

Group Discussion and Plenary Sessions

Both the group discussion and the plenary sessions were held in a warm, democratic, and cooperative atmosphere of unity. Deputies in their speeches thoroughly voiced their views. They discussed in detail the present international and domestic situation, and carefully studied the foreign policy and domestic policy and tasks set out in the report on the work of the Government.

The deputies unanimously held that the general line and the specific policies carried out by the Government in foreign relations were in accordance with the interests of the people of China and the people throughout the world.

The deputies cited a great number of facts which showed vividly that the great achievements made during the past few years in the fields of industry, agriculture, science and technique, culture, and education had proved the complete correctness of the general line for building socialism, the great leap forward, and the people's commune. The deputies expressed their deep conviction that the three red banners would show their great significance more and more clearly throughout this historical period. The deputies put forward many useful proposals and raised practical criticisms about the work of the Government. The deputies unanimously held that the principles, policies, and tasks put forward in the report on the work of the Government concerning adjusting the national economy and the political life of the state were entirely necessary and feasible. They expressed full confidence that difficulties would be overcome and new victories won in socialist construction in China.

At the plenary meeting on the afternoon of April 16, Premier Chou En-lai made a speech in which he replied to questions raised by deputies during the discussion on the report of the work of the Government.

Premier Chou's Report Unanimously Approved

The session unanimously adopted a resolution on this report.

The session also approved the report on the work of the Standing Committee of the National People's Congress, the report of the Budget Committee, the views of the Motions Examination Committee, and the report of the Credentials Committee on the examination of the credentials of deputies elected in by-elections.

During the session, the Foreign Ministry of the People's Republic of China distributed to the Congress 22 notes exchanged between the Chinese and Indian Governments from December, 1961 to March, 1962 and a report of Chinese and Indian officials on the boundary question submitted in December, 1960.

At 5:30 p.m. on April 16, Chu Teh, Chairman of the Standing Committee of the National People's Congress, declared that the Third Session of the Second National People's Congress of the People's Republic of China had completed its work successfully.

Among the party and state leaders who attended the session were Chairman Mao Tse-tung; Liu Shao-ch'i, Chairman of the People's Republic of China; Soong Ching Ling and Tung Pi-wu, Vice-Chairmen of the People's Republic of China; Chu Teh, Chairman of the Standing Committee of the National People's Congress; Premier Chou En-lai; Lo Jung-huan, Shen Chun-ju, Kuo Mo-jo, Huang Yen-pei, Peng Chen, Li Wei-han, Chen Shu-tung, Saifudin, Cheng Chien, Panchen Erdeni, Ho Hsiang-ning, Liu Po-cheng and Lin Feng, Vice-Chairmen of the Standing Committee of the National People's Congress; Teng Hsiao-ping, Ho Lung, Ch'en Yi, Li Fu-chun, Li Hsien-nien, Nieh Jung-chen, Lo Jui-ching and Hsi Chung-hsun, Vice-Premiers; Hsieh Chueh-tsai, President of the Supreme People's Court; and Chang Ting-cheng, Chief Procurator of the Supreme People's Procuratorate.

Among those who attended the session as observers were leading members of various departments of the State Council; Vice-Presidents of the Supreme People's Court; the Deputy Chief Procurator of the Supreme People's Procuratorate; high-ranking officers of the Chinese People's Liberation Army; all members of the National Committee of the Chinese People's Political Consultative Conference attending the current Third Session of the Third CPPCC National Committee; and the more than eight hundred observers from different walks of life invited to attend the current CPPCC session.

INDEX

233

harper ⚜ torchbooks

[Selected Titles]

American Studies

JOHN R. ALDEN: The American Revolution, 1775-1783. *Illus.*   TB/3011

RAY A. BILLINGTON: The Far Western Frontier, 1830-1860. *Illus.*   TB/3012

JOSEPH CHARLES: The Origins of the American Party System   TB/1049

T. C. COCHRAN & WILLIAM MILLER: The Age of Enterprise: *A Social History of Industrial America*   TB/1054

FOSTER RHEA DULLES: America's Rise to World Power, 1898-1954. *Illus.*   TB/3021

W. A. DUNNING: Reconstruction, Political and Economic, 1865-1877   TB/1073

HAROLD U. FAULKNER: Politics, Reform and Expansion, 1890-1900. *Illus.*   TB/3020

LOUIS FILLER: The Crusade against Slavery, 1830-1860. *Illus.*   TB/3029

EDITORS OF FORTUNE: America in the Sixties: *the Economy and the Society. Two-color charts*   TB/1015

LAWRENCE HENRY GIPSON: The Coming of the Revolution, 1763-1775. *Illus.*   TB/3007

FRANCIS J. GRUND: Aristocracy in America: *Jacksonian Democracy*   TB/1001

MARCUS LEE HANSEN: The Atlantic Migration: 1607-1860. *Edited by Arthur M. Schlesinger; Introduction by Oscar Handlin*   TB/1052

JOHN HIGHAM, Ed.: The Reconstruction of American History   TB/1068

WILLIAM LEUCHTENBURG: Franklin D. Roosevelt and the New Deal, 1932-1940. *Illus.*   TB/3025

ARTHUR S. LINK: Woodrow Wilson and the Progressive Era, 1910-1917. *Illus.*   TB/3023

JOHN C. MILLER: The Federalist Era, 1789-1801. *Illus.*   TB/3027

PERRY MILLER & T. H. JOHNSON, Editors: The Puritans: *A Sourcebook of Their Writings*
Volume I   TB/1093
Volume II   TB/1094

GEORGE E. MOWRY: The Era of Theodore Roosevelt and the Birth of Modern America, 1900-1912. *Illus.*   TB/3022

WALLACE NOTESTEIN: The English People on the Eve of Colonization, 1603-1630. *Illus.*   TB/3006

RUSSEL BLAINE NYE: The Cultural Life of the New Nation, 1776-1801. *Illus.*   TB/3026

GEORGE E. PROBST, Ed.: The Happy Republic: *A Reader in Tocqueville's America*   TB/1060

TWELVE SOUTHERNERS: I'll Take My Stand: *The South and the Agrarian Tradition. Introduction by Louis D. Rubin, Jr.; Biographical Essays by Virginia Rock*   TB/1072

A. F. TYLER: Freedom's Ferment: *Phases of American Social History from the Revolution to the Outbreak of the Civil War. Illus.*   TB/1074

GLYNDON G. VAN DEUSEN: The Jacksonian Era, 1828-1848. *Illus.*   TB/3028

LOUIS B. WRIGHT: The Cultural Life of the American Colonies, 1607-1763. *Illus.*   TB/3005

LOUIS B. WRIGHT: Culture on the Moving Frontier   TB/1053

Business, Economics & Economic History

REINHARD BENDIX: Work and Authority in Industry: *Ideologies of Management in the Course of Industrialization*   TB/3035

THOMAS C. COCHRAN: The American Business System: *A Historical Perspective, 1900-1955*   TB/1080

PETER F. DRUCKER: The New Society: *The Anatomy of Industrial Order*   TB/1082

ROBERT L. HEILBRONER: The Great Ascent: *The Struggle for Economic Development in Our Time*   TB/3030

PAUL MANTOUX: The Industrial Revolution in the Eighteenth Century: *The Beginnings of the Modern Factory System in England*   TB/1079

WILLIAM MILLER, Ed.: Men in Business: *Essays on the Historical Role of the Entrepreneur*   TB/1081

PERRIN STRYKER: The Character of the Executive: *Eleven Studies in Managerial Qualities*   TB/1041

History: General

L. CARRINGTON GOODRICH: A Short History of the Chinese People. *Illus.*   TB/3015

DAN N. JACOBS & HANS BAERWALD: Chinese Communism: *Selected Documents*   TB/3031

BERNARD LEWIS: The Arabs in History   TB/1029

SIR PERCY SYKES: A History of Exploration. *Introduction by John K. Wright*   TB/1046

History: Ancient and Medieval

A. ANDREWES: The Greek Tyrants   TB/1103

HELEN CAM: England before Elizabeth   TB/1026

NORMAN COHN: The Pursuit of the Millennium: *Revolutionary Messianism in medieval and Reformation Europe and its bearing on modern totalitarian movements*   TB/1037

G. G. COULTON: Medieval Village, Manor, and Monastery   TB/1022

F. L. GANSHOF: Feudalism   TB/1058

J. M. HUSSEY: The Byzantine World   TB/1057

SAMUEL NOAH KRAMER: Sumerian Mythology   TB/1055

FERDINAND LOT: The End of the Ancient World and the Beginnings of the Middle Ages. *Introduction by Glanville Downey*   TB/1044

J. M. WALLACE-HADRILL: The Barbarian West: *The Early Middle Ages, A.D. 400-1000*   TB/1061

History: Renaissance & Reformation

JACOB BURCKHARDT: The Civilization of the Renaissance in Italy. *Introduction by Benjamin Nelson and Charles Trinkaus. Illus.*
Volume I   TB/40
Volume II   TB/41

27